# Grace

## MATTERS

OTHER BOOKS BY CHRIS P. RICE

More Than Equals: Racial Healing for the Sake of the Gospel
*(with Spencer Perkins)*

# Grace
# MATTERS

A True Story of Race,
Friendship, and Faith in
the Heart of the South

# CHRIS P. RICE

JOSSEY-BASS
A Wiley Company
www.josseybass.com

Published by Jossey-Bass
A Wiley Imprint
989 Market Street, San Francisco, CA 94103-1741   www.josseybass.com

Cover of *World Vision* magazine used courtesy of *World Vision*. Cover photo used
by permission of Patrick House, copyright © 1999.

Photo of Chris and Spencer at "Healing the Heart of America" conference used by
permission of Robert Lancaster.

Lyrics from "The Potter's House" used courtesy of V. Michael McKay.

"Lift Every Voice and Sing"—James Weldon Johnson, J. Rosamond Johnson.
Used by permission of EDWARD B. MARKS MUSIC COMPANY.

Jossey-Bass books and products are available through most bookstores. To contact
Jossey-Bass directly call our Customer Care Department within the U.S. at 800-956-7739,
outside the U.S. at 317-572-3986 or fax 317-572-4002.

Jossey-Bass also publishes its books in a variety of electronic formats. Some content
that appears in print may not be available in electronic books.

Library of Congress Cataloging-in-Publication Data
Rice, Chris P., date.
   Grace matters : a true story of race, friendship, and faith in the
heart of the South / Chris P. Rice.
      p.  cm.
   ISBN 0-7879-5704-6 (alk. paper)
   1. Rice, Chris P., date. 2. Antioch (Religious community : Jackson,
Miss.)—History. 3. Voice of Calvary Ministries (U.S.)—History—20th
century. 4. Race relations—Mississippi—Jackson—History—20th
century 5. Race relations—Religious aspects—Christianity—History—
20th century.  I. Title.
BX9999.J3 R53 2002
277.62'510828—dc21                                    2002006835

FIRST EDITION
*HB Printing*        10  9  8  7  6  5  4  3  2

*To the African American members
of Voice of Calvary Church,
for hanging on,
and never letting go*

## AUTHOR'S NOTE

*Grace Matters* is a personal story, one person's experience of a life that I shared with many other people. Descriptions of people at any one time are, at best, only snapshots from one perspective. I am a pack rat when it comes to paper. Using letters, memos, meeting minutes, date books, publications, interviews, and other research, I have attempted to reconstruct events and conversations as accurately as possible, and to the best of my memory. Many people involved in the story helped me with that process. Any mistakes, however, were my own and are unintentional. In some cases, names and identities have been changed.

# Contents

## PART THREE
### YOKEFELLOWS

## PART FOUR
### DEMONS RISING

## PART FIVE
### BREAKTHROUGH TO GRACE

## PART SIX
## SEPARATION

*"An act of God was defined as something which no reasonable man could have expected."*

—A. P. HERBERT, *Uncommon Law*

# PROLOGUE

I ARRIVED IN JACKSON, MISSISSIPPI, at the tail end of the Afro hairdo age, in 1981, and left long after bald became cool. And after seventeen years of living, working, and worshipping as a white man among African Americans, I still couldn't sing, sway, and clap at the same time.

But inside a zip-code-sized terrain in Jackson, Mississippi, inside an intimate, often turbulent, life that whites and African Americans and others shared across America's most divided lines, I did come to imagine the possibility of a different world. We shared geography, friendship, family life, work, and worship, with the treacherous fault line of race always lurking beneath. All of us, I came to see, were addicts, a few to crack cocaine and burglary, others to ego and envy. Our journey to become a people of common dreams, desires, and destinies—a community of friends—is the true story of this book, the story as I experienced it. It is a story about what sought to break us apart, what kept us together, and unexpected gifts that sustained us along the way.

My central African American companion across the racial chasm, Spencer Perkins, carried the scars of his and his family's frontline duty in the civil rights movement. As we were drawn together into a national work of justice and reconciliation, we became so close that countless times people called him "Chris," and me "Spencer"—and, believe me, it was hard to confuse us visually. But the odds were stacked against our coming together, and our staying together, and that is part of this story, too. The first words I ever heard out of Spencer's mouth were "What are all you white people doin' here?" From then on, until death did us part, until the moment I walked toward his body in a hospital room hoping desperately that he was still alive, we and our families shared a rich, tumultuous journey of joy and pain, victory and disappointment. I don't know if either of us would have signed up for such a story, had we known what lay ahead. But I do know that without that entire story, I would not have learned of the hope of redemption and the power of grace.

My years in Mississippi, and with Spencer, were the most wondrous gift I ever received. I came to Jackson to help others. But I discovered, eventually, that I was there to be transformed.

## PART ONE

# Converted

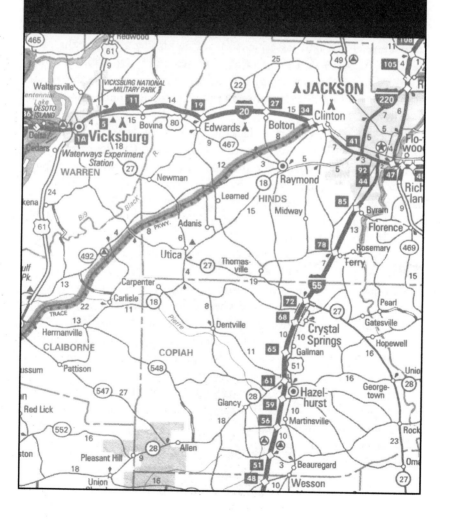

# "WHAT ARE ALL YOU WHITE PEOPLE DOIN' HERE?"

*I* was about to be blindsided by a burly, big-shouldered black man named Spencer Perkins.

It was December 1981. A skinny freshman named Michael Jordan was starting his first college basketball season. One year of a Ronald Reagan White House had Jesse Jackson contemplating a run for the presidency. *African American* was a good ten years from the national vocabulary. And I was finishing up another fulfilling day after three exhilarating months in the heart of one of America's most daring and enduring interracial projects.

The warm winter evening in Jackson, Mississippi, was just turning dark as I turned my rusty white Peugeot sedan onto St. Charles Street. I was headed to a hastily organized gripe session, with people who had inspired as much scribbling in my new copy of *The Autobiography of Malcolm X* as there was in my trusty old Bible.

Meetings here never started on time. I'd gotten over being irritated, but my stubborn internal clock still had me right on schedule as I turned into the parking lot past the lit-up sign in the grass that said "Voice of Calvary Ministries."

Across the street I noticed a dozen or so adults and children milling in front of the notorious gray house where a drug-dealing, anything-stealing family lived. Having traded America's whitest state for its blackest and a rural village for a five-month volunteer commitment in the urban "'hood," I found west Jackson a world apart, a planet apart, from my student life at Middlebury College in Vermont.

Here neighborhood kids called my old Peugeot a hoopty, definitely not a cool epithet. Here Voice of Calvary people casually referred to convenience stores as Stop 'n' Robs. Discussing the latest break-in to someone's house seemed as normal to them as dissecting the previous Sunday's big football game.

My action that night was instinctive as I stepped out of my car: *Better lock up. Even a hoopty with a hole in the floor might be fair game tonight.*

Dean Cousar was climbing out of his old but well-preserved brown van. I greeted him with a "What's up?" While the standard stay for white transplants like us was only a few months, Dean was a *long-termer,* which meant he'd been here for a few years and didn't plan to leave.

Bearded and thickly built, an Illinois native and musician, Dean was wearing one of his way-out-of-style loud polyester shirts with a wide collar. He had worn one just like it in September during my first Sunday in Jackson, when he sat at a piano during the worship service and pounded out his song "I Really Care," blasting religious hypocrites who ignored the world's poor. "I really care, but I'm not called to go and feed the poor," crooned Dean, who always got right to the point.

I really care, don't you know I'll give, if they come to my front door?
I really care, but I'm not called to forsake all like *you* folks do.
I really care, I'll do my share, I'll pray for you.

*These Voice of Calvary folks are intense,* I had thought to myself.

Dean and I walked toward the Fellowship House, a sprawling, two-story brick residence with wraparound porch. It was headquarters for community development projects that ranged from a health center to housing renovation, from business enterprises to youth development. Much more than a hub, the Fellowship House was an icon, Voice of Calvary's Plymouth Rock, its Alamo, its Wittenberg door. This was where Voice of Calvary was founded in 1973, where black and white staff broke bread over lunch every day, and where we gathered—as we were tonight—for tribal meetings.

To our right, behind the Fellowship House, was another piece of Voice of Calvary's urban beachhead, a small, former barn converted into offices. I noticed the light was off in the second-story office of Lem Tucker, only twenty-nine years old, the energetic new president of Voice of Calvary Ministries who had taken over in June. *Lem's probably working at home,* I thought. *He just doesn't quit.*

From the rumblings I'd heard in this tight-knit world, most of tonight's meeting would focus on Lem's leadership.

It wasn't that anybody questioned Lem's commitment. From his black middle-class upbringing in Norfolk, Virginia, to his degree from prestigious William and Mary College, to his nomination as an Outstanding Young Man in America, and from his seminary training in Philadelphia to his sudden plunge into west Jackson in 1977, Lem had come a mighty long way in downward mobility. I had seen that a few days after I arrived.

My first night at Voice of Calvary had been spent a few blocks from the Fellowship House, in what they called the Study Center, a huge, two-story, rambling building. There, alone and terrified, I listened all night long to the din on the street. Big-engine cars with broken mufflers zoomed past, music pounding through open windows with the ba-boom, ba-boom of the bass cranked up. *Why,* I wondered, *were people shooting off firecrackers?* Then I thought, *those aren't firecrackers; they're gunshots.* I'd never heard them before. My body lurched at each unfamiliar noise, and I kept jumping to my bedroom window, sure that my car would be gone.

Later during that first scary week, Lem had stopped by to get a book from the Study Center library. Underneath his small, neat Afro and thin mustache, he had cracked a wide and gentle grin. "Did you know I almost got killed in this building?" he said nonchalantly as he browsed a shelf.

"Noooooooooo," I said, not exactly eager for more information.

"A guy broke in and attacked a girl, a volunteer, in there," he said, pointing toward the next room. "Just then I was walking into the Study Center. I heard screams, and I rushed down the hallway into the room. The guy fired a gun straight at me from four feet away and ran out. He fired twice. But there's only one bullet hole." I looked where Lem pointed. Yup, there it was, above the door. *Oh. Great.* "I have no idea where that other bullet went, or how it missed me. A guardian angel, I think." Lem said good-bye and left.

Lem's visit had left me shaken but inspired. I was quickly enraptured by Voice of Calvary's peculiar breed of die-hard activists who accepted both danger and divine presence as everyday and normal.

Now, on the night of the meeting, Dean and I strode into the Fellowship House's large meeting room. I stopped to talk with my friend Tressa Knutson, who was also making a brisk adjustment to this unfamiliar world.

Tressa pronounced her native state's name "Woos-*gone*-son," as though her fingers were pinching her nose. Her sturdy build, dogged determination, and last name had ice-and-snow surviving Norwegian written all over them. I could picture Tressa helmeted, standing at the front of a Viking boat with spear in hand, her sandy blonde hair blowing in the wind.

Waiting for the meeting to start Tressa and I laughed about the day before, when we'd driven house to house near the Study Center, rounding up a group of neighborhood kids for our weekly group, the Good News Club. It amazed me how the children flocked to us, though I wasn't sure what drew them. Our two hours of undivided attention? The Bible stories we told? Or the Kool-Aid and cookies? The kids were wiggling into my heart.

I told Tressa how three of them—Shamika, Tawanda, and Dwan—had waved me down on my way to tonight's meeting. I had stopped and rolled down the window.

"Mistah Chris," Shamika had said, "is we fittin' ta go ta Gu Noo Cluh?"

I did a double take, still slow on my translations of local talk. *Fittin' ta*, I realized, meant "fixing to," and that meant "about to." In this slower-paced Mississippi culture, people actually said things like "I'm fixin' to start to get ready to go now."

I had smiled. "Good News Club was yesterday, Shamika—remember? Me and Miss Tressa will come pick you up next week."

After our laugh I left Tressa to find a seat and saw Derek Perkins walk in. Derek was what the neighborhood called a *bruthah*, a black male, as in "bruthah-man," "hangin' with the bruthahs," or "my bruthah!" followed by a palm slap (female counterparts were sistahs). I was twenty-one, Derek was twenty-two, but he was more hero to me than peer.

During my newcomers' tour a staff member had opened my eyes to class differences in the neighborhood, taking me to Derek's old outpost. It was in one of the roughest parts of town, about a mile from the Fellowship House and a stone's throw from Jackson State University, Mississippi's largest historically black university.

"You see, there's poor," she had said with a chuckle as we had driven into an alley lined with crumbling shacks, "and then there's what we black folks call po'." *Po'*, I saw, was trampled front yards littered with trash, toys, and jacked-up, wheel-less cars, constant loud music, and parent-to-child screams like "Git in dis house fo' I tear yo' butt up, boy!"

"That's the house Derek moved into," she had said, pointing. A thick wooden cross stood in the tiny yard. She told me how Derek and a white comrade had brazenly entered a hangout down the street called Velma's Purple Pantry. Inside was a drug-running crowd of teenagers hustling pool, including thirteen-year-old JJ. Disarmed by Derek's boldness, JJ accepted an invitation to dinner. Soon, as the story went, JJ started coming to Voice of Calvary and then surrendered his life to God and pledged to give up gangsterhood for good.

Voice of Calvary wasn't out just to "get folk saved." They were after *disciples*: committed, believing followers. As Kenyan boys were formed into Masai warriors by their tribe, here disciples of Jesus were made, in community. Becoming a Christian meant becoming apprenticed to fellow disciples and being initiated into a new culture. And nobody did all that initiating better than Derek. A few blocks from headquarters, he had started up Harambee House (*harambee* was a Swahili word that meant "let's get together and push"), where JJ and several other boys lived with him around-the-clock.

And now here came Derek with JJ, as always, trailing along behind: grinning, slapping backs, loudly chatting with everybody. I avoided eye contact. Derek was warm and friendly to me, but JJ—only fifteen—was already my nemesis.

JJ was the poster boy for what Lem memorably dubbed "Harvard minds with ghetto opportunities." He grew up, he'd tell you, "on the screets." JJ got to eighth grade without learning to read or write, aided and abetted by absentee parents, teachers' low expectations, high intelligence, and his tall, lean, and very cool charisma.

JJ soaked up Derek's full-time attention and a steady stream of Voice of Calvary tutors, odd jobs, and second chances. He was a hard and tireless worker, often making himself indispensable and amusing everyone with his verbal antics. "Derek," he'd say, "that's *un*impossible, man! You know I can't do that!"

But JJ knew exactly how to get under anybody's skin, and white volunteers like me were his favorite targets. We'd had several run-ins at Voice of Calvary's Thriftco clothing store, where I worked in the warehouse every afternoon sorting clothes. *Mr. Unimpossible,* I thought, *is gonna be a royal pain over my last two months in Mississippi.*

I finally took a seat near Donna Wheeler, in her customary clogs and jeans. Another white transplant to Voice of Calvary, Donna was Lem's assistant. A few minutes after my arrival in Jackson she had routed me like a boot camp recruit. "Do this. Go there. Next." A week later she barked orders to me and other volunteers to set up chairs before a city-wide fundraising banquet. I don't know whether it was a latent bias against take-charge women or being handled like an army private, but Donna kicked my highly competitive nature into overdrive. *How is Miss Runnin' Things going to react,* I wondered, *if Lem gets raked over the coals tonight?*

Thirty-odd people filled the room now, evenly split between whites and blacks, all of us in our twenties. We were descended from Protestant and Catholic, from "frozen-chosen" just-war Presbyterian to pacifist Mennonite legacies, from stiff Lutherans to choir-rocking Missionary Baptists, from the suburbs and "the screets." Most of us worked at the Ministries, and all of us were members of Voice of Calvary Church. Sorting out the ties between those two entities of Ministries and church wasn't easy, but it was crucial for understanding almost anything that happened around here.

Voice of Calvary Ministries was a million-dollar community development corporation with paid staff, while Voice of Calvary Church was a
separate voluntary association of about 275 weekly worshippers. But the
Ministries and the church were like two siblings in one family, with
the church affirmed as the family's soul through its fellowship, worship,
and relationships. Structural and personal requirements solidified the family tie: Ministries staff, for example, were required to attend the church,
whose pastor was Phil Reed.

Phil was also conspicuously absent tonight. Like Lem, he wasn't invited
by the upstarts who organized this gathering.

An Indiana native, Phil Reed had arrived in 1975 as a recovering alcoholic and know-it-all seminarian. He was shocked to find Christians
who embraced both racial justice and a resurrected Jesus, and who
brashly confronted his skepticism about the latter. "Phil, you just need to
know Jee-zus," said a black church member one evening, as if his personal
friend—God in the flesh—was waiting outside the door. That night, said
Phil, he let Jesus in. A few months later, in 1976, the church asked the
seminary dropout to become its first official pastor. Choosing a white pastor in a black neighborhood was part of an unusual racial logic I was still
trying to unravel.

What was clear to me was that any conflict here had huge ripple effects
in the overlapping spheres of work, play, and fellowship. The people you
worked with, you worshipped with. If people were ticked off at the Ministries, they vented at home and at church to fellow employees and church
members with major responsibilities. If the Ministries got the flu, the
church got sick too, and vice versa.

Even church members who didn't work at the Ministries saw themselves as its stakeholders. Case in point: Derek's older brother Spencer,
who worked at a local fast-food restaurant. I noticed him as the meeting
was about to start.

Spencer sat where he did in every setting, it seemed, toward the back
of the room, next to one of his bruthah housemates from Valley Street
two blocks away. Spencer's linebacker build made me look like a skinny
placekicker. He sat stone-faced, with body language I read as "Handle
with Care." Spencer was the polar bear next to Derek's teddy bear, a militant enigma to me, unfriendly and unapproachable. *What's his interest
in this meeting?* I wondered.

One of the white volunteers who pulled the meeting together stood up
and kicked things off. "There's been a lot of talk about problems around
here," she said. "We called this meeting so we can air stuff out, get it on
the table."

You never had trouble getting people to talk at Voice of Calvary, and someone spoke up immediately.

"Lem is making things too corporate around here."

I thought of the charts and graphs filling Lem's office. Of his thick annual plans, crisp white shirts with three different-colored pens neatly arrayed in the pocket, and references at weekly staff meetings to "managing the vision."

Other voices chimed in.

"I agree. Lem ain't relational enough."

"Yeah, we're losing touch with our neighbors," said another. "Lem is making Voice of Calvary into just another impersonal *agency*." Heads nodded.

The Lem I knew had turned down twice the salary from a respected black church in Philadelphia to work at Voice of Calvary. He was a patient nuts-and-bolts builder who was imposing businesslike discipline upon the Ministries.

But the people speaking up didn't want to work at a streamlined institution. Corporate. Management. Agency. Those were like four-letter words at Voice of Calvary. I felt a little twinge. What was this peculiar vision that seemed to be at stake tonight, this culture that had sucked my passions into its idealistic orbit?

"Let's face it, y'all," griped another person in the room. "Lem ain't no JP."

*Whoa,* I thought, *nobody is JP—Reverend John Perkins,* the founder of Voice of Calvary, our apostle to the poor with an international reputation. What St. Francis was to Franciscans and Mother Teresa was to the Missionaries of Charity, JP was for Voice of Calvary. He was Lem's beloved predecessor, and he was Derek and Spencer's daddy.

At age fifty-one John Perkins was a veteran of the Mississippi civil rights movement, a survivor of its brutal violence, and a high-octane community organizer. The third-grade dropout and self-described son of "sharecroppers, bootleggers, and gamblers" had advanced justice for the poor and racial reconciliation through three books, a broad speaking platform, and Jackson's living laboratory. The "beloved community" that Dr. Martin Luther King Jr. had preached, some said, JP had turned into grassroots flesh and blood. And most of us were in this room because of him, because of being hypnotized at some point by JP's spellbinding talk at a far-off college and deciding to come to Jackson to volunteer. A few days or months might turn into longer stays as volunteers got pulled into some glamorous-sounding project, endured routine break-ins, poor living conditions, and puny salaries, and soon were happily over their heads doing a job they had never, ever done before. Such was the power of JP that many of the long-termers had ended up ditching their graduate school, two-car-garage-in-the-suburbs plans.

But JP's great gift was creating, not maintaining—and he knew it. After eight years in Jackson, having launched the Voice of Calvary Church and the multitude of Ministries projects, having wed the two into a close confederation, having developed a highly committed layer of leaders throughout, having inspired dozens to move into the neighborhood and dozens more inside to see success as staying put or coming back, JP handpicked Lem to succeed him and was starting all over again in an inner-city neighborhood in an unlikely place—Pasadena, California, just a couple miles from the Rose Bowl.

Tonight's meeting signaled something about this turbulent post-JP era, but I wasn't sure what. I knew somehow that more was stirring than criticism of Lem. The meeting was turning into a free-for-all, with people standing up, one after another, voicing concerns. All kinds of concerns.

A tall, white, dark-haired woman named Nancy Horst spoke up. "What does it take," she asked, "to get a guy to ask you on a date around here?"

I was impressed by Nancy's passion and confidence. She wasn't raising this important matter for herself, but for all the singles in the room.

Nancy had grown up wearing a white-laced head covering which—outside of her Pennsylvania Mennonite upbringing—made her look like she'd dropped in from a time warp. It was long gone, put to rest during a volunteer stint in Nicaragua. When Nancy first arrived in west Jackson, she had said she heard black girls talking about putting "steak sauce" in their hair. After a couple of weeks Nancy realized the girls were referring to Stay Soft, a black hair care product. I was sympathetic. White folks had expected a different culture, but not a new language.

Nancy's question tonight pushed my thoughts toward romances inside the Voice of Calvary tribe. While tonight's meeting had drawn the singles crowd, many of Voice of Calvary's married couples had met here. Even some in the room tonight were likely to match up.

Oddly though, there wasn't a single interracial marriage. There was even a curious public silence about it. A brief unsympathetic paragraph in the Ministries' policy manual basically amounted to "We neither confirm nor deny interracial marriage. Enter at your own risk." Given all the racial intimacy, this cryptic opposition seemed strange.

People wanted to release tensions tonight, not resolve anything, and nobody responded to Nancy's question. There were other gripes to make.

An earnest white volunteer from Illinois named Tom Brown stood up. "I think those of us who work in less glamorous roles get slighted around here," said Tom. He worked at People's Development, Inc., the housing renovation crew.

Tom turned to my hero. "Derek, I especially feel slighted by you. You act like our work is less important than yours."

A load of Voice of Calvary idealism was packed into Tom's challenge: the expectation that blacks and whites would push each other and that no position, education, economic status—or even being a Perkins child—made you better than somebody else. Still, Tom's in-your-face comment made me uncomfortable. But it wasn't unusual at Voice of Calvary. They called it "holding each other accountable." It was what they were doing with Lem tonight.

Derek stood, faced Tom, and answered calmly. "Listen, brother, I don't feel that way at all. Each part of our body here is just as important as any other."

Body. Folks here loved that word. They saw themselves as a local expression of what the apostle Paul called the body of Christ, as people with a claim on each other. We were bound in sickness and health; the well-being of the whole depended upon the gift and growth of each part, and no one could say to another member, "I have no need of you."

"Look, Tom, I'm committed to working this out with you. Let's get together after the meeting, OK?"

Tom agreed. I admired how Derek was trying to understand, not write off, this white volunteer.

I admired Tom too. He was one of the many white college graduates who scorned their middle-class options for a simple lifestyle. So was his roommate, Phil Eide, with his endless pairs of dusty Hush Puppies. Tom, Phil Eide, and I were giving ourselves up for something, and the camaraderie energized us and, I guess, others. I spent mornings as an assistant at the Study Center, the Ministries' training arm, where hundreds of students and grassroots leaders streamed in from across the country and world each year to glean inspiration from Voice of Calvary.

None of tonight's honesty or the disagreements it pointed to made me question interrupting my Middlebury education to spend five months here.

As I saw it, people in meetings like this one tonight dispensed with politeness because so much was at stake. The disgruntlement with Lem had nothing to do with being worked too hard or paid too little. Nobody was calling for Lem's resignation. The argument was about how, not who, about the best way to accomplish our mission. The feuds here were family feuds. I found this profoundly energizing, like having coal shoveled into the furnaces of my purpose.

❖

Then Spencer Perkins rose from his seat at the back of the room.

Until now I had only seen him on the fringes of Voice of Calvary life, streaking around the neighborhood on his jet-black Suzuki 1000 motorcycle and being fairly subdued during the lively upbeat worship services. At age twenty-seven his aloof disposition seemed strange, considering he was the founder JP's oldest child. In three months I'd never heard Spencer utter a word in public. Finally, I was going to hear something that would put flesh on his cryptic public persona.

Spencer's eyes narrowed. His voice was gruff, defiant, and confident. "What I want to know," he said, "is, what are all you white people doin' here?"

That's all he said. And then he sat back down. He gave no diplomatic smile to temper his bluntness. He offered no explanations.

All lessons about how to win friends and influence people went right out the window. With one quick sentence, Spencer Perkins iced over the sunny land of my racial idealism.

On the one hand, the answer to Spencer's question was so simple. *Why am I here, Spencer? Duh. To do racial reconciliation. To help the poor. To be the hands and feet of Jesus among "the least of these." Isn't that why all of us are here?*

But Spencer asked his question so matter-of-factly, I was sure I was missing the point.

Who was the accused *you* of "all you white people"? I couldn't imagine which whites in the room he was talking about. *What,* I wondered, *did white long-termers have to prove?* Dean's music wasn't exactly easy listening, and people like Miss Runnin' Things and Phil Reed, the pastor, had endured all kinds of trials. Was he talking about them? Or was he talking about white short-termers like me, who weren't staying beyond a few months to a year? Was Spencer insinuating that Tressa, Phil Eide, and I weren't welcome, that we couldn't be trusted until we signed up for the long haul? Every week some long-termer asked me, "How long are you here for?" or more bluntly, "So when are you leaving?" *Leaving* seemed to be like another four-letter word, better translated as "desertion." The attitude was "We're fighting a war here. Are you in or out? Can we count on you?"

I wasn't prepared to make a commitment like that. I was headed back to Middlebury with a notch for racial progress in my belt.

The meeting quickly moved on from Spencer's question. But I didn't.

Why did this militant's words matter so much to me? I found Spencer decidedly unlikable. Not all blacks here had his rough manner or spoke with that edge.

Yet there was something about Spencer that made me want to please him, to win his respect, to be granted absolution. Partly it was his commanding presence. Mostly it was that he was a Perkins. As the oldest of JP's eight children, Spencer had an almost mythic standing in my eyes, a larger-than-life stature that grew out of the story that Voice of Calvary lived by.

I knew Spencer grew up on the all-black side of small-town Mendenhall, Mississippi, thirty-five miles southeast of Jackson, where JP spent a tireless decade organizing among rural blacks. I knew Spencer carried the scars and authority that came with frontline duty during those years growing up in the civil rights movement. For two horrible years he and his sister, Joanie, were soldiers of integration in Mendenhall's all-white high school, enduring countless humiliations.

I knew about Spencer's strong black consciousness. He and Derek returned from a 1980 Kenya trip with JP armed with the Harambee self-determination concept, and soon Spencer had launched a blacks-only group of church peers, both male and female, who had mostly grown up together in Mendenhall. They called themselves *Jamaa* (meaning "cooperation" in Swahili). With only volunteers and a shoestring budget, Jamaa had done an end run around Lem and the Ministries, launching a weekly after-school program called the Harambee Christian School of Business.

I knew by heart the bold and brash Harambee Creed that Spencer wrote and forty-plus neighborhood youth shouted in unison every Wednesday afternoon, a pledge of allegiance to a "completeness in Christ" strong enough to "stand against the social and economic injustices of our time." "We are what we make of ourselves," the kids proclaimed. "We will no longer fit into the mold that has been prepared for us." Spencer had peppered the creed with *we*s and *our*s that meant "us blacks." It ended with fists punching the air, "Harambee! Harambee! Let's get together and push!" The no-nonsense message was blacks helping blacks, without a hint of a call to racial harmony.

Being black gave you legitimacy at Voice of Calvary, but being indigenous like Spencer and Jamaa gave you more. Here *indigenous* meant "I grew up among the black poor, if not poor myself; they see me as one of them, and I can identify." Many in Jamaa, armed with college educations, were on their way to becoming doctors and lawyers, business owners and professionals. Yet Spencer and his peers rejected the trappings of success. They lived in the neighborhood among youth like JJ, who saw them and believed "I can be like you."

I knew all this about Spencer. Yet there was something that Spencer did not know about me.

He didn't know what declared me racially innocent.

He didn't know about my bloodline. He didn't know about my father's perilous trip to Mississippi seventeen years before mine as a civil rights movement volunteer. He didn't know about my twelve years growing up in a third-world country as a missionary kid or my parents' work for social justice and for "the least of these." Surely if he knew, he would see that my parents were on the side of good. This was the legacy I claimed, that made my blood pulsate with righteousness. It brought me onto shared turf with Spencer, and it surely declared me innocent.

Black folks here talked about "good white people" and "whi'folks," pronounced not as two words—*white folks*—but one, as if it were one idea, a single force and foe, a form of shorthand because it was used so much. *Whi'folks* were the mass of white people who were not "on our side." For Voice of Calvary, *them* and *us* was "us" who lived in the neighborhood versus just about "all them whi'folks" outside it. I was "good white people." At least I thought so.

When the gripe session ended after two hours, I climbed back into my hoopty and headed back to my apartment at the Study Center, consumed by new thoughts and questions.

Voice of Calvary's whites and blacks had shared eight years in Jackson. Whites weren't just on the sidelines passing out towels and cups to black leaders, and black transplants like Lem had major roles. Lem was black and in power. But he was not one of the highly venerated "indigenous." And only Spencer was the apostle's oldest child, with the birthright of heir. When JP had been here, everybody knew who was in charge. What about now?

Spencer's Jamaa was the one group of blacks I was most uncomfortable with. Their years of interaction with white outsiders had honed bloodhound instincts that sniffed out shallow motives and sent flighty do-gooders running up trees. Whatever Spencer's meaning was, his terse words and icy body language left a distinct impression: Don't do us black folks no favors by being here.

Only a few blocks separated his house from mine. I felt as if it might as well be the Great Wall now. Life in this black neighborhood, where I had begun to feel at home, had suddenly become confusing. One minute I was on the right side, the next I felt accused of being a mole for the other side.

"What are all you white people doin' here?" Was it possible to establish a kind of trust that made such a question unnecessary? I was too shy and intimidated to ask Spencer.

But it was all academic. I was out of here in two months.

# 2

# LETTING THE SPIRIT LEAD

For weeks after we left the Fellowship House gripe session the concerns and complaints that had been voiced there seemed to float into the air we breathed, lurking and unresolved. Spencer slipped off my radar screen again. I was so busy that I had little time or reason for racial navel-gazing. I was spending long hours at Thriftco and the Study Center.

My cross-cultural education, however, continued. In this neighborhood you "carried" someone in your car to "the sto'" to "make groceries," "mashed" a button, and "cut on" a light. *Hardheaded* meant stubborn, and a common parental warning was "Little girl, don't you know a hard head makes a soft behind?" At least conjugating "to be" was easier: I be, she be, you be, they be, we be.

I duked it out with cockroaches, from the peewee honey-tinted house variety to jumbo molasses-toned waterbugs. The women hated those molasses monsters. "They fly," I heard Donna Wheeler claim over staff lunch, "and they always go right for your face." It never happened to me. *Maybe,* I smirked, *it went back to the Fall or something, back to revenge on the daughters of Eve.*

My nemesis, JJ, continued to hound me regularly. Mr. Unimpossible had a sixth sense about when I was trying to steer clear of him. "Hey, Chris Rice," he'd yell across the Ministries parking lot. "Wha'chu avoidin' me for, man?" *How does he know this?* I ducked into the Fellowship House. "Hey, Chris Rice! It's your world, man! I'm just livin' in it!"

JJ kept me on my toes, and Voice of Calvary's activist life was too invigorating and made faith too meaningful to return to Middlebury's demanding academics so soon. In January I decided to extend my stay to a full year, signing on for seven more months with an August return to Vermont.

In February I had my first encounter with Black History Month. In a staff meeting, when Lem explained why it was a major Voice of Calvary event, he nailed me to the wall. "Most people's idea of black folks starts on a slave boat, moves to getting freed by good ol' Abe Lincoln, and ends with Dr. King's 'I Have a Dream' speech. It's time we honored black roots before America and all our contributions here in spite of oppression."

Every Sunday that February the church sang "Lift Every Voice and Sing," always introduced as "the Negro national anthem." The song's poetic magnificence became fondly fixed within me, becoming a distinct story within the American story, speaking truth to it:

> Stony the road we trod,
> Bitter the chastening rod
> Felt in the days when hope unborn had died.
> Yet with a steady beat,
> Have not our weary feet
> Come to the place
> For which our fathers sighed?

The song's final words were

> Shadowed beneath Thy hand,
> May we forever stand.
> True to our God,
> True to our native land.

I wondered what land the black writer James Weldon Johnson was calling his people to be true to: whether to America, Africa, or to the black church, source of true strength and identity, safe refuge, the womb for resistance, a constant voice reminding a persevering people of God's ultimate victory.

In a special black history program, we depicted scenes of sorrow and triumph. I was asked to don a white hood and cloak to play a Ku Klux Klan grand dragon. My lines had me ranting and raving against interracial marriage and the "ungodly mongrelization of the races." Acting was one of my latent talents, and I played my role with vigor, thrusting my arm dramatically forward as I screamed, "Mongrelization!" But it was awkward afterward when black church members slapped me on the back, congratulating me on how well I played a rabid racist. "Hey, say 'Mongrelization' one more time!" said Derek, laughing raucously. "I loved the way you said that!" "Heh, heh," I answered timidly. "Mongrelization! Heh, heh."

Where in America did black and white people share everyday life like this? It was, I felt, a redemption of the neighborhood's recent history, when race displayed its ugly idolatry.

Although west Jackson was now a striking mix of black middle-class, blue collar, poor, and po', it had been a flourishing web of white home-owners from the 1930s through the 1960s. But when federally mandated desegregation hit, racial integration followed, the kind famously described as the time between the first black coming in and the last white moving out. Whites fled, turning hundreds of houses into rentals. Property values declined, and lower-income households and bank redlining moved in. Massive all-white churches became well-defended compounds attended by people who now commuted from the suburbs.

But along with the white flight, a group of people had swept in who kept alive the hope of an interracial social life. I saw Voice of Calvary's Sunday morning worship as the climax of that hope.

There, where I had finally mastered clapping on beats two and four instead of one and three, we defied what Dr. King had called "America's most segregated hour"—though the hour here stretched to two or three. Amidst the rhythm of welcoming visitors, Scripture reading, the offering, prayer, and preaching, two peculiar practices became weekly grace notes for me. They formed a liturgy of bonding at the heart of this family, no matter what happened during the week.

One of those grace notes was the gospel choir, and Arthur Phillips, the church pianist and choir director, was its mediator.

Arthur was a bruthah from Mendenhall, one of Jamaa's gentler members, a top-notch plumber during the week and a former Jackson State running back who had briefly made the pros. It didn't matter that Arthur couldn't read a lick of music. He played and improvised by ear with majestic skill and eloquence. From soprano to baritone, he could perform every choir part. But Arthur's gift to Voice of Calvary wasn't merely musical—it was his character: patiently teaching new white choir members how to sing, rock, and clap at the same time, blending bicultural styles into congregational songs and traditional hymns, barking encouragement to song leaders while they sang—"All right, son! Sing it now!"—as his large, nimble hands ripped across the keyboard. Under Arthur, music was declared, not sung; proclaimed, not pronounced; shouted, not enunciated. When Arthur was leading, you knew when the choir and congregational songs would begin, but not when they would end. He called it "letting the Spirit lead." You did not organize the Spirit. The Spirit organized *you*.

Most of the choir's lead singers were in Spencer's Jamaa group. They had no idea how their music touched me, from Lawrence Hayes's "God Is a Mighty God," to Arthur's sister Lynn's "He Must Have Loving Eyes," to "Lord, You Been So Good to Me." As the choir sang, I felt more bold, comforted, and hopeful, more bound to those around me, and I felt I could understood why music like this carried the civil rights movement. Music as shaped by Arthur was, it seemed, a great unsung hero in holding black and white together here—reshaping hearts, reordering thoughts, and pointing souls toward God. It did that for me every week.

The music revealed a transparency about heartache, weakness, and tension that was a cultural transgression in my heritage. Black folks slowed down "Amazing Grace" into their own fifteen-minute version, making one word a line in itself: "Uh-uh-ahhhhhh-maaaay . . . zeeee-uh-inggggggg gra-uh-aaaaace." When they sang "that saved a wretch like me," they let "wretch" and "me" linger, like they felt it from a history of trials, from the agony of being crushed and having no greater power to depend on, no triumph to look to, except God's.

White folks in my Waspy upbringing sang the same words with the confidence of those who tasted victory here and now, speeding them up to a happier triumphant pace. Singing "a wretch like me" was more stating an idea, a theological concept. It wasn't like I really *was* a wretch. And in my lineage, if you ever experienced being wretched—in addiction, abuse, being cheated on, or betrayed—you didn't let on. Personal pain was left outside church, stuffed in the closet at home, perfumed with public confidence, hidden by a thick veneer of niceness. When asked, "How are you?" there was one correct answer: "Fine." In other words, "I am self-sufficient."

If the music opened up my heart and soul, Voice of Calvary's other notably grace-filled worship practice, sharing time, had an equally dramatic effect on my proud perfectionist self, a self that stood more and more exposed on this turf.

For anywhere from fifteen to thirty minutes in the middle of the service, the floor was open to anyone to stand and offer thanksgiving or request prayers. What followed was not announcements, not just mentions of sickness, but raw public confession, usually from black members.

Expressions of gratefulness had a profound simplicity. Every single week an elderly blue-collar man stood up. "I thank God," he said simply, "for wakin' me up this mornin' and puttin' me in my right mind." Someone else might stand and start a spontaneous solo, and Arthur would slide over to his piano and pick up the melody. One Sunday a husband said he had an argument with his wife that morning. "Baby, I'm sorry," he said, turning toward her. I nodded my head with concern as my eyes filled with disbelief. *This is being said, like, in public?* Sometimes there was a confession about an ongoing struggle with alcohol or drugs. Often those who stood to make their confessions were the least of the least in our midst. They seemed to have no fear, nothing to lose. Worship was like a three-hour scream for help. Their confessions boiled down to "I'm screwed up! I need God! I need y'all!" At these moments people left their seats, surrounded those hurting or confessing, put hands upon them, and prayed, proclaiming forgiveness and begging for deliverance. The spirit they all had, I needed more of.

In the spring I was invited to move into a house with four other white guys from the church. It wasn't unusual for households of single men to be all white or all black. It didn't occur to me to analyze this or to wonder how much it limited my racial education. Spencer's all-bruthahs household on Valley Street was only a block away.

I woke up many mornings to my roommate Bill Tanner's fervent, whispered prayers. Dean Cousar taught piano lessons out of his room, and sometimes I heard him teaching "I Really Care" to neighborhood youth. Over dinner Bill Refroe, the genius medical student, told about the day's cadaver dissection as if he was explaining how to carve a turkey. We were fortunate that our other roommate, Tim Ralston, a Stanford graduate, didn't push his cooking too far. Once when a truckload of noodles had been rejected for overseas shipment, Voice of Calvary accepted it, and Tim and Phil Eide had grabbed up fifty-pound bags. They were undeterred by the bugs they found inside. "Listen," Tim had said, "when we boil the noodles, the bugs'll die and rise to the top. We'll just skim 'em off. So what if we miss a few? It's good protein."

One night my roommates and I all got into an intense debate about the meaning of the word *black* in the slogan on the Ministries' letterhead: "Pioneering in Black Christian Community Development Through the Church."

Did *black* mean *any* black people or black *neighborhood* people? And if the Ministries was supposed to be an operation of, by, and for blacks or neighborhood people, what did that mean for relocated whites like us?

Were whites like temporary workers, meant to depart once a black indigenous structure was in place? Or were we a permanent supporting cast, meant to perpetually serve under black leaders, learning humility and submission? Or were whites intended to be fellow citizens living and working side by side with blacks in a structure built as one, with equal visibility and voice, together being a witness of the goal of racial reconciliation?

The five of us couldn't agree.

For me, the night's debate echoed Spencer's hounding question of last December. It still haunted me. Spencer didn't seem to leave room for fellow citizenship. And maybe he just wanted us to go away. I was confused and still felt like I was missing something.

In June, with my departure just over two months away, JP came to town from Pasadena to lead a workshop. The founder's visits always energized the community. At the sight of his familiar goatee and mustache, and his angular body's energetic gait across the Fellowship House parking lot, people dropped their tasks and flocked around him.

When JP spoke at the workshop I saw why Voice of Calvary often provoked more hisses than applause in Jackson. JP decried both the whites who had fled west Jackson and the black middle class who had abandoned the neighborhood.

He preached at church that Sunday, his voice rising higher and higher. "Individualism, selfishness, and greed! Individualism, selfishness, and greed! Don't think Voice of Calvary ain't immune to it!" he cried, hands flying through the air, torso leaning over the podium, left foot spread in front of the right like he was about to launch into the front row.

"Everybody lookin' after their own needs! No time for these boys dyin' on the streets or strugglin' young mothers hooked on drugs! No, we got no time 'cause we got our *own* children to take care of now!"

At least this time JP hadn't named names. But I left church inspired. To me JP was driving his disciples out of complacency. He wasn't afraid to crunch toes and feelings to remind us that radical movements always drifted toward less commitment, not more.

Hearing his sermon made my decision about returning to Vermont even harder. My life in Jackson had such a powerful hold on me that I was contemplating leaving Middlebury behind, this time forever. The thing was, I couldn't bear the thought of staying. Or leaving.

# 3

# MIDDLEBURY VERSUS
# MISSISSIPPI

*I* chose a Saturday morning in July for the final showdown between Middlebury and Mississippi. I settled into a room in the empty Study Center and began to list on a big blackboard the pros and cons of staying and leaving.

The intensity of the internal battle in that little office over the next several hours took me completely by surprise. I was a novice in trench warfare waged in unseen dimensions, where legitimate and illegitimate voices contended for territory, one sometimes disguised as the other. I struggled to distinguish between friend and foe, and I was stunned by the power and pull of each force upon me.

It was very important to me that Middlebury was one of America's top liberal-arts colleges. Should I continue the journey I had envisioned for myself there, toward a public career in government, or keep plugging away in the boondocks with this struggling little tribe of Christian renegades? Was the next step the glamour of law school or stacking boxes in the muggy Thriftco warehouse? The glory of a national stage or an obscure witness of interracial life inside a single congregation and zip code? What would help humanity more, influencing policies that affected millions or reshaping a few dozen JJs and Shamikas in the neighborhood into faithful disciples of Jesus? Somehow the latter seemed just as difficult and important to me now.

At twenty-two I had never faced a decision where such starkly different courses of life seemed to hang in the balance. It didn't even occur to me that maybe I should stop taking myself so seriously, have some fun, and go backpacking in Europe in hopes, say, of a fling with a gorgeous French girl.

Even in childhood my causes were serious and my ideals high. By age eight I knew far more about Abraham Lincoln and Gettysburg than the Flintstones and Bedrock. I spent countless hours entranced by Civil War picture books filled with intricate maps and rousing battle scenes. Jeez, I even donned a homemade stovepipe hat to be Honest Abe for Halloween.

No, this decision was about deciding the purpose of my life and giving myself to that completely—whatever it was. Always a reformer at heart, I saw my faith-driven life's quest as nothing less than attaining justice for all. But which pathway should I take to get there?

The recent advice of my Study Center boss echoed in my head. "Think back on your past," Warren Godfrey had told me. Warren, a white seminary graduate from California, had become a mentor. "Reflect on the steps that brought you to this point. Maybe the next step will become clear."

On the one hand, Mississippi seemed like just a brief interruption adding some healthy do-goodism to my résumé. But so much of life's mystery was about interruptions and deciding what to make of them. Already, three major interruptions of normality had profoundly shaped me and, I felt, brought me to this point.

The first one was my father's trip to Mississippi, seventeen years before mine.

Mom and Dad had each made a decisive break from their prosperous country club upbringings near Niagara Falls, New York. Neither one fit the mold prepared for them. My dad, Randy, didn't care for the office work at his father's real estate business, and my mother, Sue, was restless for adventure. A road less traveled took them to an inner-city apartment in Pittsburgh where Dad went to seminary and where I was born in 1960. From there they went on to serve churches in Ohio and Connecticut.

Then in 1964 my father went to Mississippi, answering Dr. King's call for volunteers to join Freedom Summer. Dad wanted to go, but he was terrified. Earlier in the summer three young civil rights workers had disappeared.

For two weeks my father slept on a concrete floor in Hattiesburg, Mississippi, and went into black homes to register voters, receiving their cold, sweet tea and seeing the photos of their presidential trinity: Lincoln, Roosevelt, and Kennedy. One night he darted into a rabbi's darkened house, where he heard sordid stories of segregation and violence. Another night he traveled out to a country church. Under the moonlight he joined hands in a circle of white and black volunteers who swayed to "We Shall Overcome." Headed back north his car passed an exit sign that said "Mendenhall." A detour would have landed him on JP's doorstep in minutes. Freedom Summer volunteers were in Mendenhall that summer too, working with the Perkins kids and other children.

⟡

Two years after Dad's time in Mississippi came the second major interruption that shaped me: my twelve precious years in South Korea as part
of my parents' missionary efforts there. Beloved grandparents and rela-
tives couldn't quite understand why Randy and Sue were taking their little boys, Rick, Chris, and Mark, and nine-month-old daughter, Elizabeth,
to a poor strange place like that. On my first day of first grade at Seoul
Foreign School in 1966 I showed up in a worn flannel shirt, buttoned all
the way to the top, that was the trademark hand-me-down of an MK—
missionary kid.

The gloomy rain on the day we arrived in Seoul made a city only thirteen years recovered from the end of the Korean War seem dark and dirty,
unlike the prosperous metropolis Seoul would become a mere two decades
later. When I think of that city and time, I see the dirt roads with bottomless potholes, beautiful proportions of the rice paddies, Seoul's exploding
neon signs, deep bows, shoes lined up outside the front door, the unfamiliar smell of diesel exhaust pouring from buses that hurtled across the
city of six million, the elegance of women in traditional dress, and the ex-
treme hospitality of a homemade Korean meal. "Sorry there's so little, but
please eat well," they would say, as we looked at a mountain of barbecued *pulkogi* "fire meat" and over a dozen side dishes. The daily curfew,
the routine air raid drills, and the ever-present heavily armed soldiers were
regular reminders of Korea's greatest pain: the 1950s civil war that split
the country into North and South, left two hostile governments on military alert, with both countries' citizens feeling in constant danger. Every
family we knew had northern kin they would likely never see again.

Growing up in Korea made tragedy and oppression personal for me.
Throughout its difficult history Korea was a determined minnow surrounded by sharks—Japan, China, Russia. I heard such sadness in the voice
of Mrs. Cho, who worked for our family. She was an earthy, country-bred
woman. "There are no evil spirits in your house because Reverend Rice
lives here," she once declared. As Mrs. Cho worked in our kitchen, she
sang ancient Korean songs that stirred me deeply, even as a child. These
sorrowful melodies have been compared to the blues of black people, and
the resemblance is striking. I didn't understand the words, but I felt the
stirrings of a long-suffering people.

My parents insisted that we live in Korean neighborhoods and not in the
usual missionary compounds. Although it could feel like an intrusion, the
boundaries between family and ministry were often blurred in our house.

On many evenings Korean college students packed a large upstairs room, and I heard the echoes of my father teaching the Bible in Korean and their hearty singing, laughter, and prayers. My mother worked as a social worker with young unwed mothers, women who often suffered social discrimination. One Christmas I saw Mom choke back the tears as she watched the girls mesmerized by the story of Mary, another teenage mother and refugee.

❖

But looking back, nothing had bonded fervent faith and an acute social conscience together for me more than my parents' plunge into Korea's tumultuous human rights movement.

Throughout the 1960s, as industrialization heated up, President Park Chung Hee had stifled the press, jailed and tortured protestors, and squelched labor unions. In 1972 student demonstrators took to Seoul's streets. In response President Park declared martial law. I was only twelve, but I grew accustomed to seeing tanks parked at university gates and to dodging the tear gas that had become all too familiar.

Mom and Dad joined the Monday night meetings, an underground network of support for the Korean protest movement. Missionaries once seen as harmless Bible-thumpers became dangerous subversives in the Park government's all-seeing gaze.

Every week, often at our house, an eclectic crowd of Peace Corps workers, visiting scholars, and Protestant and Catholic missionaries gathered. When they learned of the horrendous conditions at a textile factory supplying a U.S. business, they raised funds to have the workers' eyesight tested and confronted an American company representative with the findings. Three student activists went into hiding in our basement for two months, duplicating thousands of leaflets titled "Return to Democracy" while our family life buzzed on above them. Mom and Dad just didn't make a big deal of it all.

By the time I turned fifteen in 1975, the gentle woman we children called the sewing lady was one of the regular visitors in our home. She was a gifted seamstress, and the Monday night group helped her keep her sewing business going when her husband and seven other laborers were arrested on false charges of being North Korean spies. Later in 1975, when the Korean Supreme Court decided their fate, my parents braved a pounding rain to help pack the downtown courtroom.

As a sentence of death by hanging was pronounced the sewing lady and the other wives began to pound benches with their umbrellas. One umbrella shattered, and pieces flew across the room. "This can't happen!

You can't do this to our husbands!" shouted one woman as police dragged her out of the building.

The next morning brought chilling news. A newspaper headline said: "Eight Hanged." The wives had not been notified before the executions, and only one was allowed to view her husband's body. Many believed they had been tortured before being killed.

A few days later my father and six other missionaries responded. They slipped black hoods over their heads and nooses around their necks, stood near one of Seoul's busiest intersections, and held two signs up before the oncoming traffic and a *Newsweek* magazine photographer. One said "Is This Nothing to You?"; the other, "Must the U.S. Support Oppression of Human Rights?"

Within hours Korean immigration officials had come to our house and escorted my father away in an entourage of dark cars. Mom was gone on a visit to the United States. My siblings and I were hustled over to other missionary homes for refuge. It was the only time I was really afraid.

Downtown they interrogated Dad and told him to sign a statement admitting involvement in a political demonstration.

"No," he insisted. "What we did was a religious act. A biblical witness to truth."

After a long debate the interrogator gave in. "OK, how about we call it a prayer meeting?"

My father could admit to that. He was released after a tongue-lashing.

My parents stayed on in Korea for seven more years. A few days before they left, on a cold winter night, the sewing lady came to their house to say good-bye. She had traveled by bus from far across town.

She bowed and handed my father a package. "Reverend Rice, you know I don't have much. But I want you to have this. In memory of me." My father opened the package to find a sweater that the sewing lady had knit for him.

They spoke for a few minutes. Then the sewing lady said she had a final question for my father. "When my husband was killed, a lot of my Christian friends said that he or I had done something wrong. They said God was angry with us and that I should repent. Reverend Rice, what do you think of that?"

"I don't think God is like that," said Dad.

She quietly nodded her head. "Well, I don't think God is like that either." They bowed deeply, said farewell, and the sewing lady walked back into the cold night for the long trip home.

Now as I pondered the decision of whether to return to Middlebury, I knew my experiences in Korea were part of the reason I was drawn to

Voice of Calvary and why I was having a hard time leaving. Korea had taught me how to be comfortable being a minority, how to look at the whole world as the terrain of my possibilities and my loyalties. There I had learned how to set down roots in places where I stood out like a fly in milk, and there I received a grounding in truth and justice that I knew was my foundation.

Strange, but I felt more at home now as a white boy in west Jackson than I had among Middlebury College's preppies.

Although I had followed three generations of Rices to Middlebury, I had had a miserable first semester in the fall of 1979. Plagued by a combination of culture shock and natural shyness, I struggled to fit in. I was bewildered by small-town isolation and the drinking binges of so many guys in my residence hall. I felt like a hidden immigrant—inside I felt like an international student, but outside I didn't look or speak the part. In a small poetry and writing class with ten other students, I was too shy to say a single word the entire semester, even though my writing got me an A.

I loved Vermont's beauty and found solace there, but I eventually found human camaraderie in the rigors of Chinese language classes, in a Christian fellowship group, and in political organizing. While the nation was transfixed watching the underdog U.S. men's hockey team defeat the Soviet Union in the 1980 Winter Olympics, I trudged through snowbound streets campaigning for an obscure presidential candidate named John Anderson. When he won a sizable Vermont vote, I was completely energized. I could envision myself groomed by the Middlebury milieu, being launched from there into government and politics to better the world.

Little did I realize how that trajectory would be interrupted during February of my sophomore year, when John Perkins was invited to speak on campus.

I had never seen a face like his, the ebony skin deeply etched by experience and perseverance, his dark eyes sparkling with urgency and hope. I was mesmerized by this Mississippi man, with his battery of *ain't*s and double negatives, who said God loved everybody "ekally" and maintained that the key economic issue was who controls "the asses" ("assets," I realized, after a couple seconds). To some, I'm sure he was butchering the English language. To me his lack of sophistication only magnified the persuasive powers that captivated me in his story, full of sorrow, faith, and redemption.

His mother dying of a malnutrition-related disease when he was seven months old.

Hauling hay all day for a white man as a teenager, only to be paid "a dime and a buffalo nickel."

His older brother, Clyde, a decorated World War II veteran, dying in his arms, murdered by a racist policeman.

Heading to California a year later, in 1947, leaving Mississippi's poverty and racism behind, moving up into the blue-collar middle class, finding faith in Christ, and returning to Mississippi to, as he put it, "preach good news to the poor."

He told of being nearly beaten to death ten years later, in 1970, for his civil rights work. Of struggling to forgive his persecutors and from that forgiveness forging a vision to see "justice roll down like mighty waters," and oppressed and oppressors being healed.

In hearing JP I experienced something profoundly new: for the first time in my life a black man was schooling me, leading me, reshaping me with his words and his witness. When JP invited the audience to come to Mississippi to volunteer, he didn't pull any punches. "You might get robbed if you come to our neighborhood! Your car might get stolen! Everybody ain't cut out for this!"

Early the next morning I drove JP and his staff member to the airport. It was bitter cold, and my Peugeot had no heat and a growing, raggedy, rusty hole in the floor. Barely awake, I drove with my coat and gloves on. But this man was undeterred. He slapped open a Bible in the front seat and did a spontaneous, high-spirited teaching to the two of us. When he was gone, I couldn't shake him or the place he described.

A year later, in early 1981, I became weary of studies and decided to take a year off from Middlebury. Voice of Calvary accepted me as a five-month volunteer. After seven months in Korea studying Korean, I headed to Jackson.

As I drove into Mississippi's suffocating September heat, over the gently sloping "hills and molehills" that Dr. King once described, I marveled at the many shades of green, at the thick forests blanketed by emerald acres of leafy kudzu vines and fields exploding in a blizzard of cotton blossoms. The gleaming golden dome of Jackson's capital building became visible from the highway. The eagle on top stubbornly looked south, not toward Washington, D.C.

Then I plunged into the Voice of Calvary culture, where the 'hood was their parish, where everybody lived within a fifteen-minute walk of each other, where job descriptions ended with a famous "etc.," where eight to five often stretched to nine or ten without complaint, and where everybody from the Sheetrock crew to the CEO got nearly the same modest paycheck.

And now, after nearly a year living in the world that JP had described on that snowy Vermont night, I sat alone at the Study Center with my dilemma.

Would it be Middlebury or Mississippi?

In a way it was a no-brainer. As one of the nation's most selective and prestigious small colleges, Middlebury looked so much better on paper. Did I want to be known as a Middlebury graduate or a Middlebury dropout? I couldn't bear the thought of giving up the glory of a Middlebury diploma. I wanted to walk in the halls of power where the headlines of real social change were made.

Speaking to me counterintuitively, and more quietly, were "sharing time" lessons from humble spiritual masters called "the least of these." A life with others who patiently planted, tended, and witnessed inside one little corner on earth. Exuberant moments of the choir, the "Gu Noo Cluh" kids and their hugs and hopes, the mysteries of grace at work, and the joy of people who allowed me to share in their lives, all of us coming together as community.

My instincts told me that growth was somehow ending in Vermont and just beginning here, that Mississippi was not a detour, but a redirection, and that once returned to the other path, even for good reasons, I would probably never return to this one. This turn in my life had come unexpectedly, but with a certain grace I could not deny. I believed that it was time to embrace this interruption, to part with the old pathway and step forward decisively on the new, making the same kind of break my parents had made that eventually led them to the risks of Korea. I had once heard JP define *joy* not as having all your needs happily met or having your potential fulfilled but "being in the will of God," and I believed that I was.

But it was painful giving up a certain idea of selfhood and all Middlebury meant to me. Now I would have to reformulate my idea of success and the meaning of my gifts. I was hardly leaving ambition or my proud perfectionist self behind in Vermont's green mountains. In Voice of Calvary too I saw an arena for my competitiveness, drive, gifts, and high ideals.

That afternoon I let go of Middlebury for good. My parents were supportive, but my grandfather—a devoted Middlebury alumnus—could not understand. Yet once I made my decision, I did not look back. "Jesus didn't commute from heaven to earth on a holy escalator," I told visitors, giving them the Voice of Calvary mantra. "Jesus dwelt among us; he became one of us. The way we make God's love for the least of these visible is by living among them. 'Them' and 'us' becomes 'we.' Their needs become our needs. If schools are bad, our children suffer too. If crime hits, our homes get burglarized too." I wrote to a friend, "The problems of poverty are deep, and only people with a deep commitment can get at deep-seated problems."

I felt ready to go the limit with my own deep commitment. It was too late to be a civil rights freedom rider. But even as I knew I could still be a radical for justice and reconciliation, I didn't really know what that would demand.

# 4

# THE UPRISING

*I*n the summer of 1983, almost a year after making my decision to stay in Jackson, I earned a diploma from Belhaven College, a local Presbyterian school, and Lem Tucker promised me a Ministries staff position starting in the fall. I in turn had made a five-year commitment to him. With two years under my belt and no plans to leave, my good progress toward the elevated status of a long-termer made me feel I had made the right decision in leaving Middlebury behind.

Spencer Perkins, however, had emerged again to confound me. This time he did it through his marriage.

Under a latticed archway, the husky bruthah in a gray tuxedo spoke his matrimonial vows into the eyes of Nancy Horst, the tall, outspoken, and noticeably white woman who had grown up in Pennsylvania in a conservative Mennonite family, worked in Nicaragua, and sung next to Spencer in the choir for the past year. Spencer and Nancy were the first interracial couple at Voice of Calvary to marry and stay in Jackson.

In Mississippi interracial marriage was a cultural taboo that dropped jaws and drew stares from both whites and blacks. Many black people saw it as a betrayal of racial loyalty. I heard that it took a while even for JP and Mrs. Perkins to warm up to the idea of a white daughter-in-law and that it was JP himself who had originally inserted the unsympathetic words about interracial marriage into the Ministries policy manual. Everybody, it seemed, had their racial limits, even JP, and Spencer had an astounding talent for challenging them.

With this latest move Spencer became even more enigmatic to me. It wasn't like he was "going white"—Spencer had recently opened up the Battery Clinic, a small business that sold recycled car batteries and did car repairs on Lynch Street, working in an all-black, eight-to-five world. Why would he choose to complicate his future leadership possibilities and credibility among black people and with his parents? How did he reconcile his seeming black militancy with marrying a white woman like Nancy? I had no idea. Spencer and I had still never talked.

The heat that summer was intense. In my first days in Jackson someone had joked that Mississippi had only two seasons—summer and January. Starting around February, levels of heat set the rhythm, from lukewarm to warm to hot. Mississippi summers wrung you out and showed what you were made of, and I was about to be squeezed to the very core.

To the naked eye of seekers of racial harmony, Voice of Calvary was a stunning interracial panorama. But hidden in the lush integrated scenery, the lurking volcano called Jamaa was about to erupt.

Unknown to me, the ways of white folks had been carefully observed during the entire eighteen months since Spencer had asked his startling question. Spencer had rightly referred to us as "all you white people." There were a lot of us. And what were we doing here, he had asked. Well, we were in charge, all over the place.

Phil Reed was doing most of the church's preaching, teaching, and administration. My friend Tressa was now in charge at Thriftco, and whites were running the housing operation and the health center. Lem's program directors at the Ministries were mostly white, as was the church's leadership board of elected elders.

Spencer's Jamaa gang didn't like what they saw. In their eyes it was time to practice "holding each other accountable."

A few days after Spencer's wedding a Jamaa member stood up during sharing time at a worship service. There was a noticeable edge to her voice. What she said shocked me.

She said Voice of Calvary had a problem. She said its name was racism. She said it was time to root it out, and meetings were being organized to do so. Jamaa still contained the blacks I was most unsure of. Here I thought we had been on the right track. To hear a charge of racism from their lips made me tremble.

A week later Jamaa called a meeting in the brick house we called the Youth Center. As I walked in, my heart pounded like a bouncing basketball. *Be cool,* I thought, *this surely isn't about me.*

I cautiously took a cross-legged seat on carpet faded by the feet of hundreds of neighborhood children. A standing-room-only crowd of church members spilled through French doors into the next room. This was not an officially sanctioned meeting, but I saw nearly all our key leaders—Phil

Reed, Lem, the elders, the Ministries directors. Spencer, away on his honeymoon, was noticeably absent.

The meeting started, and I quickly realized that I had misunderstood the sharing time's charge of racism.

Black folks were not upset. They were *enraged*. To hear them talk, Voice of Calvary had become a slave plantation run by white do-gooders.

One sistah lit right into Tressa. "How come you runnin' Thriftco? How long you been here? Two, three years? Sittin' over there, high and mighty, runnin' thangs like you own the world. Don't you think a black person could do it? All I see when I go over there is white folks workin'. Why's that? Y'all come here and take over. That's what white folks do. You ain't hired a single black person over there. They all white volunteers."

I had been one of those volunteers. I'd even managed the warehouse. But I didn't say a word. Neither did Lem, who had made Tressa the store manager. He sat silent, stoic and tight-lipped.

Other blacks chimed in, adding their own stories of how Thriftco favored whites and discriminated against blacks. *Black folks must have been talking to each other,* I thought, *the way they're ganging up so quickly. Or is this just the way a mob forms?*

White stay-at-home moms were next up for chewing out. Among them was one of the sunniest, smiling-est people on the planet, Sarah Myers, whose husband, Herb, was the health center's beloved physician. Mennonites like Sarah oozed niceness. She was active in the church and on her street. But you'd have thought she was a plantation mistress sipping mint juleps all day long.

"Whi'folks have all kinds of benefits we don't have," snarled a black church member. "Black folks don't have the option to have Momma stay at home with her kids. Both of us have to work. That's not right. It's selfish too, just looking after your own. If whi'folks cared about reconciliation, they'd get jobs like we have to."

One of the other white stay-at-home moms tried to reason with the mob in a soft tone. "This is a choice me and my husband have made because we think it's best for our child. We have to make a financial sacrifice to make it happen. And . . ."

"Naw, naw," interrupted a sistah. "I don't wanna hear that. Y'all got other resources you can fall back on. Parents, inheritances, savings. All that stuff white folk always got. It's not a choice; it's an option. That's racism."

Other black church members nodded their heads. "That's right. That's right. Say it, girl."

Gerald Gains, who grew up dirt poor and was a budding black professional, was one of the gentlest and kindest people in the church. He always sang the choir lead on "He Has Done Great Things." But now he jumped in too.

"A white family once invited me over to their house for dinner. You know what they served me? Quiche! Black folk don't eat quiche! That offended me."

Obviously our definitions of the R-word were very different, because black folks were throwing it all over the place. Thriftco was racist; white stay-at-home moms were racist; and now . . . quiche? To me, it was below-the-belt insulting.

Phil Reed had been quiet, and whites seemed mostly in shock and disarray. My old boss, Warren Godfrey, who was white, now a local college professor, made a couple of gutsy protests that were shot down.

But Harold and Betsy Roper, now they were different—irritatingly so. Harold was a bookish computer programmer, and Betsy was a social worker. To me they sounded like an amen corner of black wanna-bes with their ingratiating praise of anything and everything any indignant black person muttered. Here they were again, nodding their white heads as if to say, "I feel your pain, girlfriend. This is not a black thing, because I definitely understand." Beneath their cries of empathy I felt I heard their skin screaming even louder, "Out, out, cursed spot of whiteness! Why wasn't I born black like you? Oh, I am racist through and through."

The most fearsome presence in the room for me, though, were several black women. I had always enjoyed my times with Spencer's sister, Joanie. She was the administratively gifted director of the Harambee School, and I respected her keen analytical mind and writing talent. Joanie had always been warm to me. Once, riding at the front of a bus together, she talked up Donna Wheeler to me, trying to match me up with Miss Runnin' Things. Joanie laughed when she saw me blush. She had a fun-loving, gregarious side that could get a grizzly bear eating out of her hand. But suddenly tonight, Joanie and several other black women turned on a tell-it-like-it-is, head moving side-to-side volatility that would have sent that same fearsome bear scurrying back to his cave. Theirs were the sharpest attacks, the most cutting words, the widest flaring eyes, the most poisonous venom.

I tried to remain self-controlled and unemotional. But my insides were roiling. *Puh-lease. Get over it. Just 'cause you're black and loud doesn't mean truth is on your side.*

Suddenly, overnight it seemed, our black comrades had become our accusers. And they weren't playing fair tonight. Their ground rules were: Be loud. Then get louder. Interrupt. Don't confront anyone privately. Do it publicly, in their face. If the result is humiliating and traumatizing, well, truth, justice, and accountability have been served. *Does it hurt a black person when they talk to each other this way?* I wondered. *Does it sting like these words do? Do they somehow just shake it off? Or do they just reserve this particular venom for white folks?*

"I ain't studyin' that stuff about kindness," countered one sistah when the rough tone of the meetings was brought up. "This isn't about kindness. This is about justice."

The Reconciliation Meetings. That's what those in charge began calling the series of confrontations that began that June night in 1983. But it felt like an uprising to me, led with the self-assurance of revolutionaries whose time had come. Their decision to meet every two weeks was a very scary thought.

Back at home my white roommates were as dazed and confused as I was, and we had another intense debate about our role here as whites. I was already dreading the next meeting. Nobody was forced to attend, but we knew if we chose not to, the consequences for us might be worse. Whatever the fallout, this uprising was clearly going to touch us all.

---

❖

---

On the day of the second meeting I woke up with a pit in my stomach, like I was headed into the slaughterhouse for white folks. That night a formidable new player took the stage.

Dr. Ivory Phillips (no relation to Arthur) was a relatively new church member, and the Reconciliation Meetings' organizers quickly tapped his gifts. Ivory was a professor at Jackson State University and author of a book ominously titled *White Power and Black Powerlessness.* Rail thin, with a large head and hands, closely cropped hair, a slightly hunched back, and piercing eyes, it soon became clear that his unpretentious manner cloaked the heart of a rugged fighter. The doctor became the unofficial moderator and chief prosecutor of the Reconciliation Meetings. He wasted no time setting terms for the dissection of race at Voice of Calvary.

"Blacks can be racially prejudiced," Ivory explained methodically, "but they cannot be racist because they lack the power to systematically eliminate, humiliate, segregate, marginalize, or discriminate against another race. Racism is prejudice plus power."

"You got that right," said a black church member, with others nodding in agreement.

I fidgeted in my seat as the implications sank in. *He's saying there is no such thing as racism. There is only white racism.* Spencer and Nancy were in the room now, back from their honeymoon. Were the doctor's truths what Spencer was driving at with his explosive question—"What are all you white people doin' here"?

The doctor went on. He said there were different strains of racism. One was "active racism." *That's the Klan,* I thought. *Outright, giving-black-folks-the-finger discrimination. No whites here can be nailed on that charge.*

The lecturing continued. "Then there's *institutional racism*—racism that's built into systems that put black folk at a disadvantage. It runs on a perpetual engine set in motion hundreds of years ago." I was clueless how institutional racism may have infected Voice of Calvary, although I was sure that I would find out.

But what the doctor said next filled me with dread. "Finally, there is what we call passive racism." He said it like he was stating an obvious law of nature. "*Passive racism* is that pervasive force by which no white person has to do or say anything actively racist to continue the hurtful effects of institutional racism. Merely by virtue of being born white, your skin attracts privilege, advantage, and benefits that are unavailable to black people."

More black heads nodded. More *amen*s filled the air. Whites looked severely agitated. The definition of *reconciliation* was morphing before our eyes.

Before these meetings "good white people" were those who lived in black neighborhoods, worshipped interracially, or at least committed some energy to justice for all. But in the doctor's new racial gospel, racism was catch-all and condemn-all. Racism had become hereditary guilt, the natural orientation of the white will, and every one of us was an accomplice whether we knew it or not. Racism came with white skin—it was written into our DNA.

Until now, not all white people had been directly implicated by these meetings, but now we were all guilty. *They think all whites are racist. They're saying I am a racist. How do I go forward, living here among people who think this?*

I glanced around the room. The faces of my white cohorts had a deer-in-the-headlights look as if, out of nowhere, an oncoming truck was about to crush our life of common cause and smear our interracial hopes and dreams on the highway.

Phil Reed looked like he'd just been handed a pink slip.

Mild-mannered Sarah Myers was pale and tight-lipped.

Tressa, always spirited and animated, looked defeated.

Lem had said very little to show where he stood and how this might all shake out at the Ministries. Donna was his assistant, and her eyes were full of hopelessness, like she was trying to understand, but didn't.

So far Spencer had said little, but to me his few words and body language put him squarely inside the oncoming vehicle—with the doctor, Gerald, Joanie, and those fierce sistahs. From their amen corner, Harold and Betsy acted like all of us whites deserved to get flattened.

A week later the third meeting turned the heat up yet again. It was dominated by a loud discussion about why whites were in so many leadership positions.

"Voice of Calvary ain't about developin' white folk, but us blacks," a sistah snapped. *OK, but is it necessary to add that bitter edge to your observation?*

She growled onward. "Whites here have so much more education. Y'all can go anywhere and find no doors closed. Y'all need to step aside, and we need to step forward."

After the meeting I walked home alone down St. Charles Street. My insides churned. Walking this dark urban sidewalk would have sent millions of Americans into panic attack. Yet everything I passed was familiar and natural—the houses of friends, neighbors on burglar-barred porches, the booming sound systems of passing cars, even the drug-dealing, car-stealing family's infamous gray house. This was home; I loved it here, but now it wasn't loving me back.

Had I misheard God's voice, calling me to stay here? Had I let this place get too close to me? I had let Voice of Calvary's people change the course of my life, and now those I respected and admired had rejected me. It was a knife-in-the-back stab of betrayal, and that is a wound from which one rarely recovers. How could this body of people not be torn apart by this?

The sistah's words pierced deep into my heart—"You whites need to step aside." *Don't you know we're on the same side? Don't you see all this fuss about black and white has nothing to do with reconciliation? Don't you give a flip about my potential, about the gifts I bring to this cause? I just want to serve, that's all.* My eyes filled with tears. I could not understand, and they couldn't care less.

As I settled into my bed a few minutes later I sensed a door closing that would diminish my opportunities, and the weariness of race overwhelmed me.

*I know who racists are. Racists wear hoods. Burn crosses. Use the N-word. Shave their heads and make the Hitler salute. Racists kicked and stomped JP. Humiliated Spencer at the white high school. Moved out of west Jackson when blacks moved in. Whi'folks. Them. Not me.*

*Don't they know I'm good white people? Don't they care that my parents broke from all that country-club privilege? Doesn't my father's Freedom Summer commitment count for something? What about my cross-cultural badge of honor from Korea? What about all I gave up to stick around here—the Middlebury diploma, my future ambitions? If I ain't on black folks' side, who is?*

Ivory Phillips was wrong.

Black folks had power on this turf—the power to suddenly condemn all of us as whi'folks and never to release us from the curse. Reconciliation with black folks felt like getting sentenced to an eternal, humiliating boot camp that had never produced a single white graduate. And this boot camp wasn't run by truth. It was dominated by those whose truth had the louder voice and held the sanctified status of "black oppressed victim."

As I closed my eyes that night to fall asleep a seductive voice surfaced and took a firm foothold in my mind: *Leave, Chris. You're not wanted here. These black folks are so damaged. Let them vent their ridiculous anger on somebody else. You've got better things to do with your life. You can't do justice for all here, and don't waste any more time thinking you can.*

There were six meetings in all. I skipped two of the last three to relieve the tension. Other whites skipped some too. The outcome was obvious. Spin-the-bottle never stopped on me, but the charge of racism was leveled at us all.

It had taken less than two months for the Voice of Calvary world as I knew it to crumble. *Why not, I thought, why not leave?*

# 5

# AFTERSHOCKS

---

$\mathcal{A}$s the Reconciliation Meetings and the fateful summer of 1983 ended, the inner voice shouting at me to flee retreated for a while into a simmering whispered temptation. As Lem and I had agreed earlier in the spring, I joined the Ministries staff in September and began grinding out newsletters and grant proposals upstairs in the Fellowship House. *Getting outta Dodge,* as I thought of it, was still a definite option, but it was not at the forefront of my mind.

For one thing, I wasn't personally attacked in the Reconciliation Meetings and even skipped two nights to avoid becoming a target. I had no idea how my ego would have handled a demotion or loss of power. My stubborn determination kicked in too, passed down from what had sent my parents to Korea and kept them there for sixteen years through all kinds of trials. I had given Lem a five-year commitment, and I wanted to try to keep my promise. My new job was fulfilling, and I logged long hours for no extra pay. But I also realized I didn't have anything better to do. I had turned away from the old Middlebury path. After two years here I had something invested in staying, at least long enough to see how things shook out.

Over September and October I watched the flood waters of the Reconciliation Meetings sweep over every nook and cranny of Voice of Calvary life.

Tressa resigned, and Lem replaced her with a black store manager. He swapped white directors for blacks at the housing program and the health center, and he surrounded himself with an all-black leadership team. Was Lem being led by conviction or political necessity? I didn't know.

In the church congregational life became more color-conscious and visibly black in focus, guided by Ivory Phillips's so-called new racial truth: Whites will always dominate unless an intentional effort is made to affirm and value black leadership.

The abrupt shifts in power and the summer's lingering atmosphere of accusation and bitter disagreement left many people angry and wounded.

Then the departures started.

One white member stood up during a church sharing time in October. "I thought Voice of Calvary was about racial reconciliation," he said bitterly. "I thought wrong." He said his family was leaving the church.

Both whites and blacks began to trickle away, often naming the Reconciliation Meetings' mean-spiritedness as their reason. The whites seemed to feel they would no longer be allowed to use their gifts to the fullest, and the departures of black members proved that not all black folks agreed with the way the meetings were carried out.

The exodus began to feed my hopelessness about Voice of Calvary's interracial future.

Was racial residue too overpowering to keep blacks and whites together more than a few years? Were we too immature to handle a grown-up relationship? Maybe black folk needed a separate space to organize, unify, and establish dignity and power. Was the role of whites to go prophesy to our own people?

While I rejected the doctor's diagnosis of condemn-all racism, I was forced to rethink my racial ideals.

At the time he asked it I had seen Spencer's question as an aberration, as one black man's opinion. But now it was painfully clear that there was a residual fault line running right through the heart of our own Voice of Calvary family. I had come as the solution to racism, not the problem. But the problem was no longer out there. This was personal now. I didn't trust these black people. They didn't trust this white person.

So what did I have to show for my time here? It dawned on me that I didn't have a single close black friend, no one to interpret things differently for me, no one I could safely confide in and spill my guts to. For two dadgummed years I'd lived, worked, and worshiped with black folks, most everybody grinning, and all along they had resented us and been talking to each other about how they felt. And now that I'd seen the real them, I didn't know if I cared to know this angry alien people.

---

But while I brooded, Spencer was having his coming out party.

In November an election was held to bring racial balance to the church's elder board. Two ominous names were on the ballot: Ivory Phillips and Spencer Perkins. At a congregational meeting, church members were invited to ask questions of the nominees. Spencer sat with his arms folded on the table, wearing his typical don't-dare-mess-with-me look of self-assurance.

My old boss, Warren, stood up. Warren was always smooth and articulate in public, and he had three years of seminary under his belt. He calmly began to cross-examine Dr. Phillips. He read quotes from Ivory's book, challenged them, and asked piercing questions about Ivory's theological credentials. Then Warren turned to the next nominee.

"Spencer, what is your position on the inspiration and authority of Scripture?"

Without hesitation Spencer shot back, flicking the question aside like an irritating insect. "That issue's irrelevant in the black community. Black people take it for granted that the Bible's from God, and we don't require a sophisticated explanation."

Enough said. With a few choice words, Spencer abruptly shifted the spotlight from his unschooled theology to his interrogator's racial motives. Warren was visibly stunned.

Both Ivory and Spencer were confirmed as new church elders. The doctor had a prominent new platform for his racial gospel. And Spencer gave Jamaa a potent new voice in the church's formal power structure.

Spencer's sudden rise had baffled me. It dawned on me that all along he must have been a key player in a blacks-only world.

Of course, I knew separate racial universes existed outside of Voice of Calvary. I briefly glimpsed this other world when I walked into all-black mom-and-pop restaurants and heard the patrons talking and joking loudly. When they noticed me they suddenly stopped, then continued in a quieter, more guarded way until I left.

But the Reconciliation Meetings proved that a separate world also existed inside our tight-knit interracial life. There was a space whites and blacks shared, and there were the places of our distinct discourses. My most honest, in-depth conversations about race were inside my all-white household. I suspected that, in all-black spaces like Jamaa, the Reconciliation Meetings had been hatched through intense give and take.

There, it now seemed, all whites were assigned to a kind of racial predestination that declared, "This is how whi'folks be: They always got to run things, be in control, act holier-than-thou, come in first, and when things don't go their way, throw the white privilege card and run. White folk can't shake all that any more than a beaver can stop damming up a stream."

What hope was there for Voice of Calvary's future if our shared world could not become greater and our parallel universes lessened? If every conflict was viewed through different lenses, leading to an inevitability of opposing conclusions? If blacks and whites looked at the exact same situation and evidence, and came to completely different interpretations of it?

Another devastating aftershock from the meetings hit the church in December. Die-hard Phil Reed—church pastor for seven years, stalwart symbol of the equal citizenship of whites at Voice of Calvary—turned in his resignation. In a letter to the congregation Phil wrote: "In the presence of competent and willing black leadership it is wrong to have a white pastor at Voice of Calvary."

All signs pointed to "Church Split Ahead."

How could the resignations and demotions not fuel more white hopelessness? In a place where leaving was always desertion, how could the departures of whites not fuel more black resentment, more *I told you so*s, more certainty that whites would run when the heat got too hot? Why not just say "the heck with each other"?

By the end of 1983 my old mentor Warren was gone from the church.

All of the Ministries programs and major departments were in solid black control.

Spencer was moving up in public prominence.

I was dog-paddling, desperate for some hope that this whole enterprise wasn't about to unravel.

I braced myself for a complete black takeover, wondering what it was all going to mean for me.

# 6

# PUZZLING SIGNS

---

*T*he palace had been stormed, the revolution won. The Ministries leadership was swept clear of whites, and Phil Reed had tendered his resignation. The next obvious step for the uprising's black victors was to turn to the church and purge whites from influence.

A church meeting was called in January 1984, and I expected a search committee to be appointed to find Phil's black replacement.

A black church member quickly spoke up. "Look, as far as I'm concerned? Phil should stay as pastor. As long as his preaching gets a little more black."

Laughter broke out. This sounded like the loose old days, the pre–Reconciliation Meetings Voice of Calvary, where blacks and whites joked easily about cultural differences.

Other blacks spoke up, and they were insistent. "We want Phil to continue serving us as pastor," said one sistah who had been vocal during the meetings.

Phil's resignation was soundly rejected, and a white man was reaffirmed as senior pastor by his volatile flock. I was bewildered.

Another church meeting soon followed, and our new racial philosopher-in-residence, Dr. Phillips, made surprisingly conciliatory public statements. "We will not deemphasize white," the doctor declared in his usual matter-of-fact tone. "We will just begin to value the qualities that blackness brings to the body." Wasn't this the guy who declared all whites racist? *Would somebody please spell out the rules to me here?* The longer I was around these black folks, the less I understood them.

Not only were blacks not sending whites packing, or relegating us to the sidelines, but many whites seemed very determined to stick around in spite of the cost to their ego.

Tressa continued working at Thriftco under the new black manager.

Phil Reed accepted the boundaries set by the new racial truths, which included two black elders joining him on a pastoral team he would chair.

A steady stream of members was still departing the church, and severe wounds and unresolved tensions remained. But the church split I had feared wasn't happening.

✦

Donna Wheeler also chose to stay. From the prestige of being Lem's top assistant, she had been replaced by a black person and moved to a gofer job in charge of the Ministries' mailings. Her new desk was upstairs in the Fellowship House, right across from mine.

The unsavory first impressions that had made Donna *Miss Runnin' Things* in my mind made those first weeks rather uneasy. As neighborhood folks would have put it, we got on each other's last nerve. Still, I respected her.

Several years before, a man with a gun and stocking cap over his face had barged into Donna's house, demanding money from her and her three roommates. When he let down his guard, Donna had bolted out the door, screaming for help. The intruder chased her, then fled. The women were so rattled they slept at other houses for weeks. But none of them left for greener pastures.

Not only was Donna gutsy, but we had something in common. She told me she was terrified during the Reconciliation Meetings. Yet she accepted her demotion with a gentle grace and remained on good terms with Lem. Unlike me, she had always lived in interracial households in Jackson and was close to many of Jamaa's blacks, especially a friend named Marlene Hardy, who grew up in Mendenhall.

I knew that Donna had served as JP's assistant for a couple of years. But during a conversation in March Donna told me that Spencer had also been a friend for years.

"Are you kidding?" I said. "Big bad Spencer Perkins?"

Donna chuckled. So I wasn't the only one who perceived him that way.

"Yeah, me and Spencer go way back. In fact, you know how the elders are reorganizing household groups? Spencer and Nancy are starting a new group, and they've invited me to join."

Household groups had always been a powerful glue in our church. Meeting weekly in homes, people studied the Scriptures, spilled out joys and struggles, and prayed for strength and divine guidance to face the tough challenges of the neighborhood. It was also one of the primary ways that "holding each other accountable" happened.

"Hey, Chris," said Donna suddenly. "Why don't you join Spencer's household group?"

Gulp. *Are you talkin' to me?* If Spencer was in charge, other Jamaa members were sure to be in the group. This was like being invited to a swimming party with polar bears.

"I don't know, Donna. I'll have to think about that," I said, knowing that I definitely would not have to think about that.

Yet within a couple weeks, I got another invitation, this time from teddy bear Derek, who now lived across the street from me. "Come be with us in the group," he encouraged.

But the thunder from the Reconciliation Meetings still echoed in my ears from seven months before. And boarding this boat would mean more than sharing a ride with Spencer—Mr. Militant would be right behind the wheel.

Yet if any group held out hope of widening my shared racial world with blacks, this might be it. Everybody joining, I learned, was a long-termer, and they were evenly mixed racially. As I guessed, several members of Jamaa were signing up. But I had to admit, they seemed awfully benevolent these days.

Maybe I was headed into another storm of racial disappointment. But my greater fear was missing out on something significant or being labeled as too racist to give it a try. And the boosts from Donna and Derek meant a lot to me.

It was finally time to get up close and personal with the man whose question still haunted me.

# 7

# BIG BAD SPENCER

The first meeting for the new household group was set for April. It would be my first time inside Spencer and Nancy's light blue Valley Street house.

As I sat on a long black vinyl couch in the spacious living room my heart pounded the familiar thump-thump-thump from the Reconciliation Meetings. The tribal spear and shield on one wall were, I guessed, from Spencer's Kenya trip, the one that had inspired his bold Harambee Creed. There was a colorful painting by Derek of a bunch of smiling neighborhood kids clowning on a street. On my way in I'd seen a photograph in the hallway of a teenager with a big Afro shooting a picture-perfect jump shot. I hadn't known Spencer played ball.

More than fifteen people surrounded me, all survivors of the Reconciliation Meetings. The blacks in the room all held the exalted status of "indigenous."

There was JJ, already jousting with singer-songwriter Dean, who had driven over in his aging brown van. I knew Gloria Lotts, who was a member of Jamaa, as a youth worker at the Ministries.

There was a big Perkins contingent. While Joanie was in a great mood tonight, laughing and at ease, her diatribes still rang in my ears. Besides Derek and Spencer was their aunt, Lue Shelby, Mrs. Perkins' half-sister. Lue, who at twenty-seven was two years younger than Spencer, was about the same age as Joanie.

Besides Dean, whites in the room included Donna, Nancy, her sister Dorcas, and Phil Eide, wearing his latest pair of run-down Hush Puppies. I was happy to see Tressa beside him. They'd gotten married about the same time as Spencer and Nancy. I wasn't thrilled to see Harold and Betsy Roper, former members of the white amen corner.

Mr. Militant sat in a rocking chair with a fat, olive-green Bible on his lap. I cocked my self-defense systems into full alert.

Spencer broke the ice. As usual, his voice and manner were confident and direct. He quickly proposed a boundary for the group's purpose. "Why spend so much time on Bible study?" he asked. "I been involved in Bible studies since I was knee high to a duck. I ain't int'rested in bein' part of another group where we nod our heads at one more nice truth, go home, and our lives don't change."

To my surprise, Spencer's words immediately struck a chord with me. I had been in too many church settings where people went around a circle and shared "what this passage means to me," as if Christianity was between them and God, and Scripture didn't put the same claim on us all. My problem wasn't knowing more. It was acting on what I already knew, in community with others. *OK, Spencer, I'm listening.*

"We already know waaaaay mor'n we're doin'," he continued. "Let's look at the Bible for what it says instead of tryin' to fit it into how we already live, instead of justifyin' ourselves. If we're not doin' it, let's just admit that, instead of changin' what it says. Let's see if we can help each other do it."

Spencer's presence was magnetic in this smaller environment. I could imagine him "runnin' thangs" behind the scenes with Jamaa.

He made sure everybody got pulled into the conversation. "Glor-i-o," he asked at one point, "wha'chu think 'bout that?" He seemed to value everybody's gifts, directing pointed questions to specific people as if tapping their expertise. "Harold, does that pass your scholarly test?" He listened closely to what people said. He reigned comfortably over the diversity in the room, with no air of racial "us" and "them."

I marveled at the way he warmly invited controversy and disagreement, and seemed unfazed by it. But at the same time, he lightened up the atmosphere. His teasing made people laugh at their own foibles. "Betsy's always got the right answer. Let's hear from her." He would respond to someone's overly idealistic statement with, "You ask much, Grasshopper," a reference to a then-popular TV show about a Chinese monk in the Old West. And sometimes he would answer sarcasm with a quick "tschhhhh" sound through his teeth, delivered deadpan, as if he had just slapped the speaker's face. But then he would pause, unfolding a thin, wry smile.

Spencer's standard for dialogue was patiently but insistently demanding. Pat answers were unacceptable. He was his father's son—exuding authority, stirring you up, making you think. He was hard-nosed about truth and had strong opinions. But I didn't expect his softness with people.

After just one hour in his presence Spencer completely disarmed me. But the fact that his high expectations for the group included me didn't match my previous image of him at all.

His considerable skills steered us toward consensus. Before we left, each of us agreed to four simple commitments.

We would meet every week.

No one would skip a meeting unless it was unavoidable.

We would tell our life stories to each other.

We would read Scripture together, try to come to one understanding, and discuss its implications for our lives.

I underestimated what sounded like a completely harmless beginning. Because we had just bound ourselves—across lines of race and class—to an ongoing conversation around a text that would begin to interrogate our lives. I didn't grasp what might happen if such ordinary commitments were taken seriously within a small circle.

I was simply relieved that the race card didn't get played.

Over the following weeks our Wednesday night meetings on Valley Street found a rhythm. There was no rush to get started. Eventually Spencer rallied us, offering a brief prayer. Then two people told their life stories, each taking a half hour or more. After that Spencer moderated a sharing time—talking about how our weeks and lives were going. The two hours ended with spoken prayers for one another.

Telling life stories had an impact I never imagined. We gained a compassion for each other as persons, shaped by particular families, episodes, and communities.

Donna knew Southern California suburbs and beaches, and won straight A's. Tressa knew cows and polka dancing, and won a milking contest in college.

JJ's roots were in an underworld of absentee fathers, the gang at Velma's Purple Pantry, and noisy rows of shotgun houses—duplex shacks with three rooms on each side. Dorcas and Nancy grew up in a stable Mennonite family of nine, gathering over lively dinners of freshly picked corn and tomatoes blessed by the soft-spoken prayers of their father, a church bishop.

When I heard Harold and Betsy's stories, I softened toward them, and I removed them from the suffocating box I'd put them in during the Reconciliation Meetings. I came to respect their outspoken advocacy as heartfelt compassion for the underdog. I watched Betsy's eyebrows lift in empathy as Gloria told her story.

Nobody had had an underdog life like Gloria. Her parents, both chronic alcoholics, had died when she was a child. She was split up from her brother and shuttled between foster homes. Life got so bad once that she hunted for food in garbage cans. Later her brother was murdered. In searching for love in the wrong places, Gloria said, she had gotten pregnant the previous year. But Gloria's trials formed sinews of faith and resilience within her. Neighborhood kids flocked to her sparkling smile, and her car was always packed with "chil'rin." At regular Voice of Calvary sleepovers, Gloria counseled with "my girls" as she braided hair into the wee hours.

She knew what it was to live without options, out of power, not having control, to fight against a world full of destructive forces. Her life gave her a way of seeing Scripture, and seeing God, that I needed too.

But nobody's story gripped me like Spencer's. I finally glimpsed both the forces that sought to keep us apart and what brought us together at Valley Street, beyond all likelihood.

What war stories were to nations, stories of JP and the Perkins family had become to Voice of Calvary, so familiar and mythic they had lost their edge of brutal reality. But the night Spencer told his story, it became sacred personal property, raw and graphic, like listening to the soldier who gripped his gun in the sand while weapons blasted and men died around him.

My first memory of race being an issue wasn't until I was sixteen, reading the book *Roots*.

Spencer's was when he was six, in 1960. The family was driving east, leaving California's comforts for Mississippi's dangers. At a Texas rest stop, Spencer and his brother slept on the hood of the car while everybody else slept inside on the seats. "Me and Philip thought we were so lucky, sleepin' out under them stars!" Spencer said with a chuckle. Only later did he learn his father had been turned away from a whites-only motel.

In Korea I had grown up as an honored minority.

In the black "qua'tahs" of Mendenhall, a name left over from "slave quarters" days, Spencer told of the black children in his parent's Bible classes arguing about the meaning of Jesus' command to love your neighbor.

"That don't mean whi'folks," one kid would say.

"Yes, it do!" another would shoot back.

For Spencer the answer wasn't clear. "I'd never seen a single act of love from the whites who lived across the tracks," he said. He put his dilemma to his parents.

"I'll never forget what Momma and Daddy said. They told me loving my neighbor meant especially loving white people."

My high school years had been magical. Spencer's had been filled with terror.

In 1966 his parents sent him and Joanie to integrate all-white Mendenhall High. It was his first up-close experience of Mississippi whites. "And you know what they say about first impressions," said Spencer. "It was lasting."

White students would look at him and sing their taunt to the tune of the "Battle Hymn of the Republic." Spencer could still quote their words:

Glory, glory segregation,
We don't want a nigger nation.
Bury all the niggers in the Mississippi mud,
The South shall rise again.

"I never had trouble findin' a seat," he said, chuckling. His little laughs seemed to be a way of deflecting pity.

"There was always a circle of empty seats around me. I got called nigger, oh, 'bout fifty times a day. The white lady who collected lunch money, she never once took it out of my hand. When students bumped into me in the hallway, they wiped their hands in disgust. Like they'd been contaminated."

The experience was horrible, he said, "Somethin' I wouldn't wish on my worst enemy." Students either insulted him or were silent. The fact that no higher authority ever intervened—no teacher, no principal, not a single adult or parent—greatly deepened the pain.

"But I never doubted what we were doing," he said. "I always understood that I was on a mission."

What had raised him out of bed every morning for two years, knowing the pure dread of the day ahead? What qualities of patience and determination, loyalty and courage were formed within this man before me?

Many, many times I'd heard JP tell of being ambushed by highway patrolmen in 1970, being nearly beaten to death by them in a Brandon, Mississippi, jail and Mrs. Perkins coming to visit him the next morning. Only tonight did I discover that she took Spencer with her.

Spencer spoke of JP walking into the waiting room—his shirt splattered with blood.

His father's bulging eyes—"'bout to pop out of his head," he said. The knot on his head "the size of a softball."

"I'll never forget the humiliation on Daddy's face." He paused, containing his emotions. He wasn't chuckling now.

Spencer said that when he and his siblings visited JP in the hospital later, Joanie took one look and ran out the door, screaming, "I hate white people! I hate them all! I will always hate them!" As he spoke Joanie was quiet, staring at the floor. I had never heard this story, and I felt a sharp new compassion for her. *Here she is,* I thought, *still hanging in with white folks after all these years.*

Spencer watched his father struggle to forgive his persecutors. He told of his own struggle to forgive.

But life in the "qua'tahs" wasn't all troubles and pain. He told hilarious tales about stealing watermelons and racing cars, about his triumph as an all-state point guard on Mendenhall High's basketball team and winning the 1971 state championship.

I finally understood why Spencer had been so invisible until the past year. For him, he said, the point of faith wasn't knowing about God but doing the will of God—and it was always better to act on a little than to know a lot. He said he had chosen to be on the sidelines because he wasn't ready to get serious about what he believed. But a couple of years ago that had begun to change. What followed was Jamaa, his rise to eldership, and now leading our household group.

Part myth, part militant, part enigma for so long, Spencer was metamorphosing before my eyes. In spite of the huge distance between his story and mine, I saw the similarities between us. Another preacher's kid, uprooted by renegade parents at age six, just like me, and taken to a frontier land. Someone else raised with boundaries blurred between family and the cries of the world, by parents who labored against the odds, when change was not promised. Like me, he was determined to make something of his legacy. His story bound him to me.

This Valley Street crew was surely nothing remarkable to behold. There were no buns of steel; no one was dressed to kill. We were no assembly of the glamorous, the powerful, or the envied. But something profound was stirring among us.

Our separate worlds and loyalties were narrowing, and our shared world was widening. We knew and mattered to each other more as individuals. We had heard each other's stories of joy and pain, and we saw treasure in these fragile earthen vessels. In Spencer I now beheld a gifted leader who seemed to grasp well before anyone else what a motley crew could become. He was not just permitting this to happen; he was willing it.

It was astonishing what could happen when people endured a crisis, stayed at the table, and hung on for dear life. *How strange,* I thought, *that it took a racial revolt to bring Spencer and me onto common ground.*

# 8

# DNA MATCH

---

*N*one of us in Spencer's household group could be accused of being self-satisfied. Our church had barely survived a racial explosion. We lived in a neighborhood most people feared. And in June 1984, after we finished telling our stories, we accepted Spencer's challenge to be pushed even further.

We began with a study of the Sermon on the Mount. We chose it because it was Jesus' most extended teaching on the "here and now" lifestyle and, of course, because it was difficult.

The Sermon began with the counterintuitive "Blessed are you" Beatitudes that seemed beyond reach—like being poor in spirit, and meek, and taking joy in being reviled and persecuted. Dean quickly put the Beatitudes to a simple tune, and we kicked off every meeting with Dean's guitar and our new theme song.

The Sermon painted an unsettling picture of God's kingdom breaking into everyday life.

Bending over backward to mend things with some jerkface, even if the jerkface had wronged you more? *Riiiiiight.* Don't worry about tomorrow? Surely that didn't mean no insurance policies, did it? Oh, here's a good one: You get sued for ten grand, you're sure the law is on your side, but instead of going to trial, you offer your opponent twenty grand if he'll settle out of court.

What do you do with this stuff? In neighborhood terminology, Jesus "done slung a rod." His engine just blew. But the list went on.

Giving freely to those who ask? Our church would run its reserves down to zero in two weeks. Not storing up treasure on earth—that didn't mean no burglar bars, did it? And doing regular heart exams for anger and lust? I was born with a quick temper and lively hormones. Could I get a waiver on this one? "Narrow is the way that leads to life," said Jesus. No kidding. In other words, "Good luck."

Yet the Sermon, we saw, held out an audacious promise.

The popular ways of looking, said Jesus, won't get you the joy and peace everybody longs for. But if people dared to turn their wills over to God's kingdom, Jesus promised that we would bring light to the world, inherit the earth, find comfort, get filled, obtain mercy—and even see God.

✤

Over the next several weeks we were overwhelmed with clarity and unity.

When the Sermon got in our faces about the dangers of trusting in money and possessions instead of in God's provision, we each agreed to give away ten percent of our incomes to our church each month and to ask each other whether we had done it.

Then we agreed to give an additional five percent of our salaries to a group checking account. Joanie called it "the kitty," and we used it to help a family whose house burned down and a household group member who hit a tough spot.

To deepen our friendships, we began a schedule of one-to-one meetings during the week. We celebrated life's joys together—when Gloria's baby son was born, we welcomed Kortney as a great gift, our group's first child.

Weekend projects bonded us further. One Saturday we painted a rental house owned by Phil and Tressa, filling the day with teasing, dreaming, and take-out fried chicken, sweet tea, and biscuits. "Ya gotta eat 'em with syrup," Spencer insisted.

Good eating together was becoming such a ritual, we even coined a name for it. In the neighborhood, as an action, to "th'ow down" was to do something with exquisite style, enthusiasm, and excellence, such as "The Lakers th'owed down last night against the Celtics," or "Lue, you th'owed down on them greens." For us a th'ow down became an event where good food—and plenty of it—was served. "Good food" did not mean tuna casserole and carrot sticks, but barbecue, for example (defined in Mississippi as slow-grilled, sauce-swabbed ribs or chicken), or soul food, meaning vegetables cooked until well dead, and then reincarnated with hamhocks and seasoning into an afterlife of high-fat bliss.

Through our increasing activities and th'ow downs, we were courting each other, sizing up what kind of match we were and even "talking noise" (boasting) like we might be bonded for the long haul. For us the Sermon was not a call to individual heroism but to build a community of friends.

✧

Yet over these intoxicating weeks, I still kept my guard up. A huge question remained unresolved for me: the issue of the white DNA of privilege and racism raised by the Reconciliation Meetings.

Gradually, hard truths had begun to surface for me, not through confrontation but indirectly. My growing friendships with black people who were beginning to matter to me softened me up enough to revisit the agonizing summer of 1983. For one thing, comparisons within our household group had made the litany of historic racial difference intensely personal.

Both Spencer's kin and mine, I realized, had crossed a hazardous ocean passage to arrive on American shores. But coming as strangers by choice or force was the difference between the Mayflower's glory and a slave ship's humiliation.

Early decades in America were often a degrading interlude for Italians, Irish, and maybe even the Norwegian immigrant ancestors of Phil and Tressa. But none of them would have swapped the benefits of whiteness they eventually inherited for centuries as national untouchables.

Our white kinfolk had freely passed down capital, networks, and know-how through a string of generations, while Gloria and JJ's ancestors were willed away in inventory lists along with mules and pigs. The day that Spencer's grandmother died in a sharecropper's shack from malnutrition, it was not unlikely that my grandparents were enjoying a quiet family dinner with china and silver set on a crisp white tablecloth. And while I was the latest in a long historical line to graduate from college, Spencer was the first Perkins to go beyond high school. Even as we tried to level the ground between us all on Valley Street, black advances were only sixteen years removed from Dr. King's assassination.

All our ancestors had endured natural disasters, economic depressions, and family breakdowns. But any deprivation that Rices, Eides, or Horsts had on this soil, Perkinses, Lottses, and Shelbys had a hundredfold more. For us there was so little to forget or forgive in comparison. For them Jesus' seventy times seven barely scratched the surface.

To write all this off as ancient history, with no continuing grip on determining our existence—that was impossible in the intimate space of the Valley Street living room. I finally admitted that whiteness still dealt privilege. Even at Voice of Calvary. Even for me.

Part of my privilege, I saw, was that for me dealing with race was optional—I could take it or leave it. I could cross town, move into an all-white world, join an all-white church, find a job where everybody on top had skin like mine, and for the rest of my life I probably wouldn't have to deal with race again. Unless I *chose* to. But Joanie and JJ had to deal with the everyday struggles of race whether they wanted to or not.

I was learning how they faced overt barriers, like the talented black plumber in our church who had all kinds of obstacles thrown in the way of getting a plumbing license.

They also faced endless subtleties. Everyday matters like cashing a check could be an ordeal for Gloria, who got treated letter-of-the-law by the same bank teller who never asked me for two forms of ID. I didn't have to ask myself questions like "Is this lady doing this because of my skin color, or does she snap at everybody she encounters?" Black people could run but never hide. There was an overwhelming weariness to it all.

No overt bigotry had handed whites our dominance before the Reconciliation Meetings. But now I believed that racial DNA had driven us to unconsciously take over, aided and abetted by subtle allies.

Elitism was one accomplice, revealed by church elders who were not only mostly white but seminary-educated, thus ruling out the factory worker–prayer warriors in our midst. The Ministries had required staff members to raise funds for their salary from outside donors, yet whites invariably brought better-moneyed networks than blacks. How could Gloria's funding possibly keep up with mine?

I began to see the shifts of power after the meetings differently. If you're used to living at the top of the food chain and suddenly have to make room for new contenders in the feeding ground, it can feel like a humiliating demotion.

Yet all these breakthroughs could not budge the heaviest boulder of all.

I carried a deep grudge toward the blacks who dictated the atmosphere of the meetings. Black rage was legendary. But there was a quiet, icy white anger that could be just as lethal.

For me watching the feeding frenzy on white skin privilege was like seeing kindred spirits turning rabid and attacking their own pack. To be *dissed* in the neighborhood was to be disrespected, called nasty names in public, and—worst of all—your momma ridiculed. The Reconciliation Meetings were one big diss. Whites got smacked upside our "know-it-all" heads and assailed with mean names while we groaned on the ground. Racist. Do-gooder. Power-hungry. Privileged. Sons and daughters of racist mommas. That's how it felt to me. And all that orneriness was excused in the name of justice, the sacred altar upon which any notion of compassion and loyalty could be so easily and brutally sacrificed. Accepting hard truth from a friend was difficult enough. But taking it from a jerk? Nah.

To accept the truth of my privilege felt like legitimizing their behavior. Bargaining was better: *I'll admit my privilege . . . if.* If you come to me, get on your knees, and apologize for all the mean stuff you said about Tressa, and stay-at-home-moms, and quiche, and promise to never diss us like that again. The alternative—forgiveness—seemed blatantly unfair.

---

But a conversation with Spencer and Nancy started me on the road to release.

One evening after a household meeting, I joined Spencer, Nancy, and Donna at a nearby restaurant's late-night breakfast bar. While Spencer mixed his scrambled eggs and grits together, we got on the subject of the Reconciliation Meetings.

I took a risk. "I've got to tell y'all. One of my biggest hang-ups with the meetings was how blacks expressed themselves. Angry. Abrasive. Demanding. I can't get over that."

Spencer listened patiently. Then he responded, using an example from South Africa, which was still in the grips of apartheid. "OK, the white government says, 'We won't negotiate with blacks until they stop usin' violence.' But what conditions are blacks protestin'? I ain't sayin' black violence is justified or right. But it's not irrational. It's a reaction—to deep injustice. You can focus so much on how people voice their criticism that you lose sight of why they're so upset."

Nancy was Spencer's equal in being outspoken and articulate, and she jumped in. "Chris, believe me, I understand how you feel. But black folks mostly have a different style of conflict than we do. They get in your face, they let it all out—and it's over. They're more honest and blunt than we are. I think you've got to give room for that difference."

Listening to Spencer and Nancy, Joanie came to mind. As long as she had showed her warm and fuzzy side, she was my "some-of-my-best-friends-are-black" soul sister. But when she had gotten honest about race in the meetings, I wrote her off as a militant foe. I had put a huge condition on my relationship with black folks: If they didn't say things just so, I wasn't listening.

I still saw problems in the atmosphere of the meetings. They had exposed a deeper layer of anger and bitterness. They had not only killed the cancer but some of the patients too. The reaction to the disease, I believed, could become dangerously toxic itself. Surely forgiveness didn't mean letting all this off the hook.

But to forgive did mean holding on to people even when you thought they failed you and would probably fail you again. It meant that even with their weaknesses, I still needed these black people. Because that was the only way they came. It was the only way any of us came. I had to release myself from their anger so I could be free to see their truth.

It was painful, doing that. Because I saw why I detested and resisted owning my privilege. It was like suddenly discovering that my lineage, the DNA of my being, had been pumped full of tainted performance-enhancing drugs. It degraded my accomplishments, diminished my successes, and polluted an innocence that had told me that all I had were well-deserved prizes won by virtue of my individuality—my savvy, discipline, brains, guts, and hard work.

I realized that I had subconsciously struck a deal: I'll do justice for all, as long as I can look in the mirror and see the squeaky-clean face of goodness. Innocence. Helper. Giver. One in control. Solution.

But the recipients of my "righteousness" saw blinders over my eyes. Like a horse shielded from a disturbing, unseen world around it, those blinders obscured race's subtle consequences and sent me trotting forward in directions that mostly suited my self-image of goodness. Hey, I was big fan of justice for all. As long it didn't limit justice for me.

I wish I could say that I had recognized these uncomfortable truths earlier, during the Reconciliation Meetings. But what first met me as blatant bias only became truth for me when it was embodied through new friends who, I now believed, had my best interests at heart—friends like Spencer.

One night I finally pieced together why he and I had seen those meetings so differently.

Before the meetings, he said, he wasn't secure enough in Voice of Calvary's whites to climb into the same foxhole with us. He held back. He resisted responsibility. "To me, the meetings were a showdown between God and race," he said. "And all my life it seemed like race always won."

That summer became a test for him, not only of Voice of Calvary's deepest beliefs, but his own. After the smoke cleared, he saw the whites who stayed through different eyes, and he was taken further than he expected to go.

"Y'all whites who endured to the end? Y'all had been tested in the fires," he said. "These were the people who could help me turn my hurt and anger into a passion for reconciliation. I knew I could go into battle with you."

I finally understood what a high price the meetings had exacted from our black members and how deeply they had been forgiving all these years simply by choosing to stay in relationship to whites and to be in the same church with us. They too had been pushed to give more than they wanted.

The dominant theme of the Reconciliation Meetings was the truth about whites—what we needed to do to be faithful to authentic reconciliation. But what I learned from Spencer was that whites could change, pay millions in restitution—even slap Dr. King's face on the flag—and still there would be no new racial relationship. For that to happen, black people had to be changed too. In our shared racial world Spencer was saying there was something for him, and black folks, to gain in the exchange as well. The costly price of a new racial relationship was for all of us to be transformed.

Nobody had said this during the meetings, and I certainly never expected Spencer to open my eyes to it. Some sought truth only so far as it served their self-interest, others even when it led them further than they wanted to go. I saw that Spencer was one who went where the truth took him—regardless.

All this time black folks like Spencer and Joanie had hung onto white folks "in spite of," and I had been tempted to run at the first sign of real conflict. I felt cowardly and spoiled. But I had passed, with some reluctance, from despair into hope. And I had been, in a sense, converted.

## PART TWO

# Toward the Promised Land

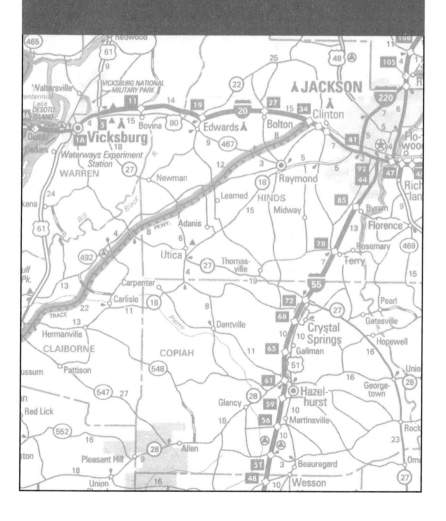

# 9

# PURPLE COMFORTER

---

*A*fter just three months together as a household group all of us could already see a major block in our path: We were still living more like geese than ants.

We were flocking into formation on a regular basis—pooling some money in the kitty, tackling common projects, showing glorious glimpses of togetherness. But once we hit the ground of our everyday lives, it was back to puttering around in proximity. Just gathering everybody for a work project was a challenge. We had reached a consensus that we could live the Sermon only so far without breaking through to a whole new lifestyle plateau—becoming a colony.

We called it *community,* and to us that meant intentionally unifying our lives by living in the same houses and sharing our resources. It did not mean forming a new church. Voice of Calvary church was our lifeblood, and we were only one part of it. But we in the household group had begun an intimate journey together, and we saw this more intense version of community as the greatest test of our seriousness about living the Sermon. The idea of doing it began to routinely surface in our discussions.

At a meeting in mid-July Spencer settled into his favorite chair and put his trusty Bible on his lap. As usual, he kicked things off with a terse, high-minded question. "What is God's will for you personally and for this group?"

A number of us attempted to answer—Donna, Lue, Tressa, and me. I made a reference to Acts 2, which had become our shorthand for the unified life of the first Christians in Jerusalem, described in the Book of Acts: "And all who believed were together and had all things in common; and they sold their possessions and goods and distributed them to all, as any had need. And day by day, attending the temple together and breaking bread in their homes, they partook of food with glad and sincere hearts, praising God and having favor with all the people. . . . There was not a needy person among them."

We had come to see this intense daily life of voluntary unity as propelling the Sermon's radical lifestyle beyond the life of Jesus. And living this way could happen again, we believed—here and now.

But Spencer was not satisfied with the quality of the responses to his question. He pressed again. "Why is this question so hard? What is the will of God for Christians, y'all?"

Nancy took a stab at it. "I think the will of God is preaching good news to the poor and liberty to the captives. We do specific things to bring that about."

Spencer liked that. He was ready to make a statement now, referring to Jesus' first public message in Luke 4:18. The words Jesus had read from Isaiah were as familiar and revered at Voice of Calvary as the pledge of allegiance was to Boy Scouts:

> The Spirit of the Lord is upon me,
> Because he has anointed me to preach good news to the poor.
> He has sent me to proclaim release to the captives and
> recovering of sight for the blind,
> to set at liberty those who were oppressed, to proclaim the
> acceptable year of the Lord.

"The way we know God's will is by Jesus' example," Spencer declared. "And Jesus said to preach good news to the poor, which is that the poor can come into God's kingdom on earth. Preaching to poor people means makin' their life better, here and now. The will of God is copyin' what Jesus said in Luke 4."

Nancy spoke up again. "I used to think God's will was for me to be a secretary. But God's will is more than an individual's work unto the Lord."

Spencer liked that too. "It's easier to think God's will is limited to our specific little jobs and lives, like Nancy's sayin'," he said. "We're at a point where we need to go further than we've ever gone before. How do we live out Luke 4 y'all, here and now, together?"

"If we keep goin' down this road," warned Derek in a singsong voice, "we gonna be trapped into livin' in com-mun-i-ty."

Derek was the most gung ho for the idea. But none of us needed convincing about the benefits of sharing houses and resources.

Voice of Calvary had enjoyed relationships with many intentional Christian communities throughout America that had a rich social impact far disproportionate to their small numbers. Washington D.C.'s Sojourners community ran an urban outreach center and influential national magazine.

Another prophetic publication, *The Other Side,* was mostly hatched from a Christian community in inner-city Philadelphia. And rural Georgia's Koinonia community had birthed Habitat for Humanity, which was spawning worldwide home ownership for the poor.

I for one was also aware of communal influence from a variety of historical traditions—the Franciscans and their friendship with the poor, the architecture and design of the Shakers, and the impact of Israel's kibbutzes upon national formation and character. Three of my heroes had based their work in intentional communities: Mahatma Gandhi, shaping nonviolent revolution from an ashram; Dorothy Day and the Catholic Worker movement; and Mother Teresa and her order of sisters, the Missionaries of Charity.

But if anyone in our group knew this history best, it was Harold Roper. What met the eye with Harold was a thin, blond curly-haired geek with glasses. But if the subject was French existentialism or the New Deal and rise of the Democratic Party, Harold was the man. When his brain was in high gear, he had a habit of nervously picking at his teeth.

"How do we help poor people be whole people?" he asked, pulling his hand away from his mouth. Harold seemed to be trying to bring together the ideals of intentional community and bringing good news for the poor. "Sometimes when we help the poor through our church, we hurt them instead."

A constant Voice of Calvary frustration, this hit a raw nerve with Phil Eide. Phil and I were quickly becoming best friends. He appropriately hailed from the state whose inhabitants were dubbed Minnesota Nice. He was wildly popular for his live-and-let-live nature. But he and Tressa were still licking their wounds from helping Joyce, a struggling mother on welfare. She had ultimately pushed them away because of the responsibility they had expected of her.

"Harold's right," said Phil. "Joyce wasn't ready to become whole."

Spencer wanted to go even further. He had a remarkable skill for getting at deeper dimensions of motive and resistance.

"I think we're afraid of the real answer to Harold's question," he said. "If we were really serious about helpin' the poor become whole, it would mean allowin' too many needy people to become truly part of us."

A scary thought indeed. Add living with people like Joyce to the long list of reasons not to live in community. I pictured Joyce down the hallway—constantly needy, sucking me dry with endless needs and requests.

"All I know is, right now I'm just taking care of me," said Nancy.

"Me too," echoed Joanie. "But if we're willing as a group to give up everything, I'd give it up too."

Joanie paused, and suddenly had a look of shock on her face. "But what about the things I love so much? Would I have to share them with y'all too? Like my purple comforter?"

The room exploded into laughter.

Every one of us had our "purple comforter" fears about living in community, from teeny to gargantuan. People sticking their noses in your business. Surrendering your paycheck to the kitty and arguing about how to spend "our money." Losing privacy. Endless meetings. Other people's awful cooking. Early-morning-ugly women in their curlers. Men who didn't put the toilet seat back down or even lift it in the first place.

Spencer pressed Joanie. "Do you think community's gonna happen? Is that the direction we're goin'?"

"Yes," she said quickly, with resignation, like she knew it was right, but wasn't too excited about it. It was precisely the way I felt.

The challenge of uniting community with justice for all was still bothering Nancy. "My expectation of what the poor think when I try to show love to them is that they see my material things and then they feel they can't be a part of me."

Gloria spoke up. More than any of us, her own difficult life had taught her what the poor most desperately needed. "When Nancy said 'love,' that really hit me," she said. "Love is the key thing. It needs to be our motive—wanting the best for others. If that drove us, we wouldn't be so worried about where this is leading and how we draw the poor in."

For me Gloria had put her finger on the heart surgery each of us needed in order to move toward authentic community. Spencer seemed to agree. "Love is wantin' the other person to have what you have," he said. "If I love somebody, I'll give 'em what's mine."

This train was still moving too fast for Joanie. "I think of people living in community. They remind me of tramps," she said, as everybody burst out laughing again.

Joanie had a point. For most of us, at the top of the reasons not to live in community was living like cultish weirdos.

When the idea first came up, the image that had jumped to my mind was *hippie commune*. I pictured long-haired children with names like Bountiful, Peace, and Sunset running barefoot in organic gardens tended by adults in tie-dye who drove beat-up Volkswagen buses, ate tofu, smoked weed, and swapped spouses in leaky log cabins.

At one large community some of us had visited dogs ambled through a vast cafeteria dining room like strays, and members lived in cramped, dormitory-style rooms on hallways where children from different families shared a single room with bunk beds.

Another problem was that the communities we knew of were almost exclusively made up of white folks from the "haves" side of the world. And most community dwellers tended to be so serious, with interminable meetings addressing earthshaking policy questions like "What would Jesus do about stereos in our rooms?" Too much reading of their magazines made me deeply appreciate what *People* magazine brought to the world. Sure, I admired Gandhi, but he swore off sex with his wife, had weird bathroom routines, and was a vegetarian extremist. In our household group th'ow downs with good barbecue were right up there with changing the world. Mostly it was our black members who offered this gift of lightening up. Many had lived poor for most of their lives, and they weren't about to go back to no air conditioning, meatless meals, and life without cable TV. They were teaching me that you could do justice for all and enjoy life at the same time.

It was time to wrap up.

"If we decide to do something, we have to do it together," Spencer reminded us, absolving himself of any blame for this crazy move in the direction of community. But Spencer had an uncanny ability to press us all forward.

He asked a final question. "Is it fair to pray, 'Lord, help us get to the point where we can do your will'?"

Lue's answer cut me to the heart. She had won me over through the small things—cooking a mean pot of collard greens, never forgetting a birthday, and revealing the rural roots she shared with her half-sister, Mrs. Perkins, when she played the piano in a molasses-slow, down-home country style. Lue was soft-spoken. But when she spoke, it was worth listening to.

"We need to decide if we really want to do God's will," she said. "If we want to, but are afraid, or lack courage, it's legitimate to pray, 'Lord, I believe. But help my unbelief.'"

Spencer nodded. He liked that too. "We've come to a good point," he said. "What steps do we take to become the kingdom of God? Right now I'm confused—and usually I don't like that. But now it feels good. We've come to a place where we have to pray, and we have something specific to pray for."

"All I have to do is give up everything," said Joanie glumly. She still couldn't shake the tramp idea, it seemed.

Betsy had the last word that night. I thought she spoke eloquently for many of us. "This is the first time in my life that I thought I had something to lose by this kind of idea."

We ended with eyes closed and hands clasped in prayer, led by Spencer. There was no need to remind anybody that sometimes communication with the divine is simply a scream for help.

Over the rest of 1984 we groped our way forward.

People came and went. Dean left the group for personal reasons and dropped out of the church. JJ began to float in and out. Derek married a Pasadena native, Karyn Farrar, and they planted themselves there to help JP and Mrs. Perkins in their work. New people from the church joined us, decided our direction wasn't for them, and left on good terms.

In the spring, feeling confident enough to set down some roots, I had taken out a loan and bought a small duplex not far from the Fellowship House. Somehow this move reinforced my nagging doubts about our lives in the household group: We were still scattered, all living in our separate little boxes with our individual sets of stuff, hustling to pay our bills, fix our meals, frustrated that we didn't have more time to minister, and reluctant to give more to the "Joyces" without friends to join in the risk and challenge.

I was wondering more and more about my assumptions about how we were supposed to live, about the intense individualism that still seemed to drive us. Money, and the energy and time it took to get it, was a big obstacle to living more for others. Who said ten adults needed ten different cars, toasters, refrigerators, and bigger and bigger houses with more and more stuff to fill them?

"Materialism is a trap," said Spencer one night. "You'll never be able to do somethin' for somebody else if you're always focusing on yourself and gettin' more."

Four elements began to converge into a common vision for our household group. First, racial reconciliation. Second, bringing good news to the poor, what we thought of as justice for all. Third, growing into the demanding but freeing way of the Sermon. And finally, privileged and unprivileged doing all of this side by side, leveling the ground between us.

In October we stumbled upon a name for our group—a symbol for us of all four of these elements.

In the New Testament Book of Acts, we had learned of the Mediterranean city of Antioch. There the new Jesus sect was first called Christians, and a peculiar practice set them apart—Antioch's believers breached the wall between Jew and Gentile, Hebrew and Greek in their midst. The apostle Paul adopted this interracial phenomenon as his base for taking the gospel story to the world. But Antioch was also a place of pain. There, as described in Galatians, Paul confronted the apostle Peter about his cowardly retreat from table fellowship with new Gentile believers.

A year after our church's own painful confrontation, we took the name *Antioch* for our group. Our journey had also been a drama of struggle and resilience. We too held great hopes for touching the world. We already were.

In January of 1985 Voice of Calvary was visited by an olive-skinned South African, a veteran of the antiapartheid movement named Graham Cyster. Graham preached one Sunday about his long crisis of faith after seeing people shot by police during demonstrations. "I had gotten to where I could not trust white people," he admitted. "And I was almost hoping I would not find a place like Voice of Calvary. Because then I could say whites were beyond hope. But here I have found a corporate resurrection of my dream and vision for the torn country of South Africa."

As Graham's voice boomed through the sanctuary, he posed the questions that we in Antioch longed to answer. "Did God really intend for the church to be a place where the walls are broken down between black and white, rich and poor? Did God really intend that to be incarnate reality— or is God playing games with us? Because if Christ gave us an ideal we cannot follow, I suggest that we abandon it right now. And we can all go out, join the rat race, make as much money as we can—and live like the devil himself."

Antioch did believe that a new kingdom reality could be incarnated, further than we had ever imagined. But none of us was eager to surrender our purple comforters. Our long list of fears held us back. We kept approaching the communal idea and backing away.

We believed. But we would need help with our unbelief.

# "ONE OF US"

s 1985 rolled in I still found my understanding of a white person's place in a black community and in an organization dedicated to black community development shrouded in a dense fog. My confusion went back to those debates with my white roommates about whether whites were a temporary work crew, a permanent supporting cast, or fellow citizens. The black leaders that Lem appointed after the Reconciliation Meetings were still firmly entrenched at the Ministries. The pathway for a white person did not seem to point upward. And given my new understanding of the white tendency to take over, I was mostly content to be a member of the supporting cast.

In late January the director of development, who was my boss, announced that he would soon be leaving Jackson. A couple of days later, Lem called me into his office. Color-coded charts and graphs lay on the table where we sat.

"Chris," said Lem in his nasal twang, "we're going to start looking for a new director of development. A black person."

"Sure, Lem. Makes total sense." *Maybe he thinks I'm gonna be hurt by this,* I thought. *Someone like me might ordinarily be promoted to director. Nice of Lem to soothe my feelings.* But he wasn't finished.

"Until we find the right person, Chris, I want you to be the acting director."

I was stunned. Not only was I decidedly white, but he was talking about putting a twenty-four-year-old in charge of raising an annual budget of over half a million dollars. Strike one on race, strike two on competence.

But saying no to a challenge like this was not within my determined makeup, and being in over your head, of course, had never disqualified anybody from a job at the Ministries. I didn't need time to contemplate this offer. "OK, Lem, I'm on board," I said.

Lem had just given me my first shot at truly consequential responsibility in life. It was a decision of considerable trust and risk, for I was the first white person to be promoted into top leadership at the Ministries (even if temporarily) after the meetings. But the image of Tressa being chewed out after taking over at Thriftco was haunting. How would black folks at Voice of Calvary receive this?

Over the next couple of months, in spite of many blunders, I discovered that I was fairly talented at this kind of work—communicating with the public, organizing people, and administrating. By grit and by grace, the funds came in.

Through my new seat on the Ministries' policy-setting management team, I found that my flair for organizational and strategic thinking was far better than I ever realized and that my temper was far worse. But my peers were forgiving, and my friendships began to deepen with the other program directors, all of whom were black.

One of my favorites was Lawrence Hayes, who directed Voice of Calvary's housing arm, which renovated houses for rental and purchase to neighborhood residents. With his thin frame, blue overalls, and construction boots, Lawrence became a regular and welcome sight in my office. "Got a minute, man? Oh, baby, Lem slung a rod yesterday, didn't he? Givin' us those monthly report forms to fill out? Man, I ain't got time for that! Look, bruthah, lemme show ya some sketches here." I loved it when Lawrence called me bruthah.

Because of my new responsibilities, I also drew close to Lem. During a fundraising trip in February Lem began to open up to me about the excruciating days in 1981, after he succeeded JP as president. I thought back to the gripe session after I first arrived.

"Those were some of the most painful days of my life, Chris," he said. "People were saying all kinds of awful things about me. My temptation was to strike back.

"But I coined a phrase that I have tried to live by ever since. 'He who has the greatest truth must have the greatest love, which is the greatest proof.'"

Lem's proverb was a high road to take with disagreement and difficult people. For me it summed up the weakness I still saw in the Reconciliation Meetings: so much truth, so little love, leaving so many unconvinced.

But maybe there was a high price for holding such ideals. I wondered about that a few days after we returned from the trip.

Lem led me into one of his old offices, pulled back a piece of paneling, and pointed behind it. "One time I got so angry with someone, Chris, I punched this hole in the wall." This guy concealed a lot of emotion behind his poker-faced exterior.

✥

In April I was working late in my office one night when Donna showed up. Her desk was still near mine.

She had her usual radiant smile. We greeted each other, then I returned to my work. One of my gifts—and weaknesses—was intense concentration. I wasn't the type to quickly drop a task for the sake of conversation. But as Donna busied herself with some kind of artistic project, I noticed her thin graceful fingers. I found them strangely attractive.

A couple of nights later, Donna showed up again.

*Her house is only a two-minute walk away,* I thought. *It's probably just easier for her to work here than take stuff home.*

This time I decided to put my work aside, just for a couple of minutes. We started talking and just kept on.

During household group's early weeks, when Donna had told her story, her idyllic life had sounded so different from my missionary kid upbringing. She'd had it all—growing up in an all-American suburb with loving parents, days at the beach and boy-watching, great grades and high school accomplishments. But there was a horrific tragedy at the heart of her golden California life.

While she was away in Europe on a senior class trip her parents and two brothers headed out on a family vacation. A few hours from home her brother Mark began to feel carsick. Donna's dad pulled onto the shoulder, and Mark stepped out. Seconds later, on the highway behind them, a truck driver nodded off at the wheel. His tractor-trailer veered onto the shoulder and plowed into the car with Donna's parents and brother Richard inside. All three died instantly. Only Mark survived.

Tonight our talk turned to how Donna handled the accident. "You had planned to go to Pomona College, right?"

"Yeah," said Donna. "It was a prestigious school." That sounded familiar.

"But I was concerned about Mark. He was only twelve, and I wanted to be available to him. I enrolled at a state university instead, so I could live at home. I felt so embarrassed, going to an ordinary school instead of Pomona! But I planned to transfer after a year.

"Well, I got serious about my faith, got deeply involved with like-minded people, and after the year was over, all that was more important to me than Pomona. One thing led to another. After I graduated I came to Voice of Calvary as a four-month volunteer—and you know how long four months can stretch around here."

I chuckled. "Donna, do you remember when I first arrived here? Direct-ing me over to the Study Center—rather bossily, I might add? Or the banquet a couple weeks later, when you directed me to pick up chairs?"

"Actually, no." She laughed and brushed her shoulder-length brown hair behind her ears. I noticed the elegant lines of her neck and shoulders.

"I thought not. You seemed so high and mighty to me then."

She laughed again, and our eyes met. Suddenly I realized my brief work break had turned into an hour. "Hey, Donna, let's pick this con-versation up again soon. I've got to get back to work." We said good night, and she left.

But I found myself continuing to think about her.

How did the warmth and vibrancy I saw in this woman emanate from the senseless ashes of tragic death? I admired how at only eighteen she had made such mature, unselfish decisions. And I realized that there was so much more I liked after four years of observing her in Voice of Cal-vary's small world.

Every Sunday I saw her joyful, handmade banner hanging during our worship services and watched her sing soprano in the gospel choir's front row. She'd been the first to invite me into the household group, and after all our meetings I'd learned she was the strong, silent, and stable type, with a hard-earned humility. I remembered Spencer's comment at group one night. "Now, Donna, when she first came here? She thought she had to run things. She's come a long way—she's all right now," he said, chuck-ling. "We brought her down a notch."

Sure, she was twenty-nine, five years older than me, but those years (including her three more in the neighborhood) had only given her more character. She'd endured all the tests of time at Voice of Calvary with quiet determination and grace—from the armed intruder to the Reconciliation Meetings to demotion from her position as Lem's assistant. While some people gradually reveal themselves as so much less than what meets the eye, with this woman there was so much more. I was surprised to learn that, like me, she loved a cold beer.

Over the next couple of weeks I found myself noticing Donna, shoot-ing secret glances at her slim figure and taking it all in. I was finding excuses to get to the office every night, hoping she'd show up and give me another chance to talk with this woman whose zest for life, steadiness of faith, and pleasing curves were becoming very attractive to me. It finally occurred to me that she probably had the very same scheme.

One night in May she told me about her plans to leave the Ministries and start nursing school in Jackson. The catalyst, she said, was a trip to Haiti the previous year. Seeing poverty there touched her, and she wanted to acquire skills that put her closer to people who were hurting. I told Donna I was behind her all the way. I didn't say how much I was going to miss our late-night rendezvous.

A month later, after Donna started nursing school, we went out on our first official date. Over a day of blueberry picking we finally voiced our affections for each other. By August I was regularly walking Donna home from Antioch's weekly meetings on Valley Street, and we were spending as much of our time together as we could wrangle from our busy schedules.

A very enjoyable part of my busy schedule was my work with Lem and the other management team members. For the past few months we had been meeting weekly at Lem's house for informal, early morning discussions on the usual theme of making a difference in the neighborhood. There were about ten of us, including Lawrence and Joanie, who ran the youth program. It rarely occurred to me that I was the lone marshmallow in the group of black people.

Lem's plan was to hire a black director of development by January. I accepted the logic of strong black leadership and wondered what Lem would ask me to do next.

One afternoon late in October, nine months since I had started as acting development director, Lem called me into his office. "Chris, you're doing a great job," he said. "I think it's time that we removed the 'acting' from your title."

I was completely taken by surprise. Being a temporary white replacement was one thing. But making it permanent? I wasn't sure what had just been placed on my chest—a badge of honor or a big fat bull's-eye. Would this decision pass the critical gaze of Voice of Calvary's bruthahs and sistahs?

My answer came at the next management team breakfast at Lem's house. Lem had told me nothing about the agenda. When he opened the meeting, he blindsided me again.

"Everybody knows that when Chris came on as development director, it was understood that he was 'acting' and that a black director would be hired."

Bruthahs and sistahs were munching their doughnuts, nodding their heads, looking me over.

I had no idea what Lem was going to say next.

"Well," said Lem, "this week I asked Chris to become permanent." *Did I just see somebody gag?*

Lem continued. "This morning I want to discuss the role of white people at Voice of Calvary. And Chris is our guinea pig." He looked at me, grinning.

I immediately was flooded with painful memories of the Reconciliation Meetings' spin-the-bottle game. The guinea pig image wasn't exactly comforting.

*Is Lem having second thoughts,* I wondered, *putting his finger in the air to see which way the winds about white folks are blowing?*

I sized up my black colleagues around the table. We'd had our family feuds, but I considered my relationship with each one to be peaceful. Yet there was a lot they could use against me. Many times they had seen my temper flare in management team meetings. What I considered my stubborn perfectionism, they often seemed to see as irritating judgmentalism. I was always the youngest person at the leadership table, and maybe my immaturity showed. Most of all, at least four leaders in the room, including Lawrence, had gained their positions because of the Reconciliation Meetings. I knew this group would hold nothing back.

I was right. They weren't shy. Every person at the table had something to say.

Joanie spoke up first, jumping to my side like my defending attorney. "Chris doesn't have anything to prove," she said. "And y'all know how tired I can get with all these white folks. As long as Chris is accountable to black leadership, he serves us well." I was grateful for her honesty, and her trust.

Don Govan, a living saint who directed our Crisis Care Center with his wife, Helen, weighed in next. "We've all got our struggles," he said. "But I've seen Chris wrestle with race. This brother's earned his way into leadership."

Babs Salu, Thriftco's manager, spoke up in his Nigerian-accented baritone. "Chris's department brings in the appropriate funding—correct? What more needs to be evaluated than this?"

They all made me feel very good.

But from across the table, it was Lawrence whose words meant so much, knowing he'd grown up on a dirt road near Mendenhall, raised by a grandmother who labored as a maid in white folks' homes for pay that had made him angry and determined to rise above his circumstances. I knew Lawrence didn't coddle anybody. It was his words that extended what seemed so long in coming. "You know, y'all, I don't think of Chris as white. He just seems like one of us."

*One of us.* Those words immediately settled into my soul like they were desperate to take up permanent residence there.

*One of us.* It wasn't a black man's "bruthahman" palm slap to a white wanna-be who craved a skin color change, or a celebration of my racial hipness, or my being "down with the homeys."

*One of us.* I received the words as the highest compliment that a black person could pay to a white person but, much more, as a declaration of hope.

Hope that in a nation and a world that so often assumed ethnic and racial predestination, we were not locked into narrow allegiances or the fates of our upbringing but could transcend them and become allies in a cause of higher truth.

Hope that know-it-all do-gooders who ride in on high horses can get knocked off; wipe the dust off; stick around unsure of their place; endure some humiliation, hazing, and maturing; and get helped back up by the very ones who had shoved them off. Because there is a war to be fought together, and we need every soldier we can get, once we get some sense in their heads.

Hope that blacks can dig deep and set white folks free. I had been longing for that freedom, and I saw that black people held a profound power to deny or supply it, to bestow or withhold empowerment, to pronounce forgiveness or to bridle their tongues, to encourage camaraderie or to stifle it, to keep us strangled in the grip of the past, or to release us to serve the future while never forgetting.

These black folks were such a peculiar people. Phil Reed had resigned, surrendering power, and the next month black folks gave it right back to him. During the meetings they had jumped all over white folks for running things, and now they welcomed me onto the top rung as a peer. It was as if once they saw you humbled, they wanted you on the side of justice, at full strength. Yes, they wanted an end to white control. But they didn't want white folks on any guilt trips either. Once you endured their tests they almost acted as if you had never done anything wrong. Were they on my side for good now? And was it because they felt I was on their side for good?

There was something I had to do to reach this point. But there was also something that only they could do. *One of us.* I had wanted to hear words like that for a long, long time.

I felt that I had graduated to a new place of confidence, into full citizenship. And it was Lawrence who handed me my diploma.

# 11

# SECOND THOUGHTS

---

*I*n the fall of 1985, I settled into my promotion to development director and full-fledged membership in the management team with a fresh vigor. Raising the funds to keep the Ministries moving continued to be a daunting challenge.

Courting Donna, however, mostly gave me great joy. For over four months, I had been eating dinner at her house almost every evening, and we were learning more and more about each other's idiosyncrasies and passions. I loved the outdoors, but the big picture, not the details. The sight of a rufous-sided towhee and blooming crepe myrtle could delight her every time.

One night over dinner at her house Donna divulged some new information with serious implications. "Chris, did you know that I have some money?"

"Yeah, right. Is that why you live in this millionaire palace in the 'hood?"

"No, I'm serious. It's not a huge amount. But when my parents died, I received an inheritance from an insurance policy. I've never drawn a salary from the Ministries."

It was clear that Donna didn't live on much. She owned a small two-bedroom house, drove an ordinary car, and dressed plainly. But in the Voice of Calvary world her inherited wealth made her a member of the highly privileged.

I probed a little deeper. "So how does having this money make you feel?"

"I've always been uncomfortable with it," she said. "I struggle with how to be a good steward of it."

For me this was one more item on my admiration list for Donna. Inheriting money as she did, a lot of young people would have indulged themselves with pleasure and acquiring stuff. Her restraint and modesty magnified to me how she had resisted her options all these years and high-lighted the risk she was taking to join Antioch's journey toward sharing more and more together. And hearing her tell how she had used her re-sources to assist others at Voice of Calvary made my respect for her grow.

But in Voice of Calvary's family of haves and have-nots, her money raised all kinds of issues about fairness, which could be very sticky if Anti-och ended up living in community. And it would become my sticky issue if we ended up getting married.

From the day Donna and I went blueberry picking, the prospect of marriage was implicit. She was closing in on thirty, so I was sure it was on her mind. And it was certainly my goal to determine if Donna was "the one"—even if I, at age twenty-five, wasn't in a rush to figure that out.

The more I pondered it, the more conflicted I felt. As attracted as I was to Donna, part of me resisted her. If she had been studying to be a doctor instead of a nurse, it might have been another matter.

A very persuasive part of me saw a more glamorous, exotic, up-and-coming woman by my side—a lawyer, maybe, or a published professor with a Ph.D. That part of me still craved connection to a Middlebury kind of world, but in a more progressive and legitimate way. *Even if the pres-tige and glory weren't yours,* I reasoned, *you could marry into it and have it reflect back on yourself.* "Aren't the Rices a cool couple? Chris works in a tough urban area, and his wife is one of the most well-known doc-tors in the city." That's the kind of thing I wanted people to say of me, not "Oh, your wife patches up bedsores?" If I couldn't graduate from a place like Middlebury, at least I could marry someone who did. The very things that made Donna so attractive to some parts of me made other parts of me cringe. And besides, Ivy League coed types headed for Ph.D.'s did pop into the neighborhood as volunteers from time to time, so there was still hope.

Donna certainly had the brains to be a doctor. But her desires seemed much less complicated, and purer, than mine. Four months into the re-lationship I was already waging a familiar internal Middlebury-versus-Mississippi battle, trying to discern between legitimate and illegitimate voices. Was she "the one"—or should I wait for another (better) one?

In the Antioch sphere too the task of discernment was intensifying.

We were a solid circle of eleven friends now, along with two little ones, all of us together from our beginning: Phil and Tressa and baby Erik, just born in August; Gloria and Kortney; Spencer and Nancy; Harold and Betsy; Joanie; Lue; Donna; and me. A rapid courtship between Dorcas and Graham Cyster was leading them toward marriage, after which they were moving back to Capetown to start an interracial community in the face of apartheid.

Throughout 1985 we had continued to meet, solidify trust, contribute to the kitty, and wrestle with the future. Sharing one house, we estimated, would only require half of our incomes, leaving the rest to invest in ministry to the neighborhood. If anyone had doubts about the ultimate ideal of living in community, they weren't verbalizing them.

But we still backed away, again and again.

Besides the familiar lists of fears, we didn't know of any models that proved that our particular vision was possible. While the other intentional communities we knew of were inspiring, their inability to incorporate black folks was disheartening.

Spencer put it well one night that fall. "Whites will take to community quicker than blacks," he warned. "More whites have achieved. They've seen that the American dream is a dead-end street. They can understand an alternative to materialism better. Black folks haven't had the chance to see that yet—we're just startin' to make some economic and social gains."

"If the whites dominate," Nancy warned, "blacks won't trust it."

Another obstacle was the plodding nature of community itself, where decision making was as slow as pouring cold molasses. No executive could impose a new direction whether people liked it or not. We relied on persuasion and unity to make all our decisions. Once we came to one mind there would be power to it, but all of us would have to agree to community simultaneously and unanimously.

Still, the truth was that we didn't need any more information to make a decision. We had discussed all the big issues over our twenty-month group courtship. Apart from the impossibility of omniscience, everybody pretty much knew who they were getting in this deal and what was at stake. We simply lacked the perennial leap of faith, the gumption and guts to take the plunge. It boiled down to Spencer's challenge from our very first meeting: Would we embrace what we believed to be true—or would we settle for less than what we believed was best?

By the end of December most of us were heading out of Jackson for the Christmas holidays. I was going to Oklahoma City, where Mom and Dad had moved after leaving missionary service in Korea.

The night before I left, Donna shared her fears about community with me. "When I get off by myself, I think about how much I like life just like it is. Being able to have dinner when I feel like it. Just having a sandwich instead of joining a crowd of fifteen for dinner. After a busy day at school, I guess I like coming home and having a quiet house."

I nodded. My resistance too boiled down to the huge issue of giving up control. But Donna summed the other side of the equation just as well.

"You know, Chris, when we all get together, I get dissuaded out of my fears. I think how we're going to work it out and how much we're going to gain. When I look at the overall picture, I can get excited." She smiled. "I'm trying real hard to keep that outlook, Chris."

We parted with a kiss and a long embrace.

As Antioch scattered for the holidays, all of us were contemplating community, with most of our struggles out in the open. And though we did not speak of it much, Donna and I were contemplating marriage, with many of our fears about that plunge still unspoken.

# 12

# ROBINSON STREET

fter the holidays in January Antioch had its first meeting of 1986.

In a stunning move Gloria immediately called everybody's bluff. "Well, I'm ready to make the move into community, y'all." There was a steely determination in her voice. "I'm tired a talkin' about it. I say, let's do it." Nobody before had ever dared to cross this line.

There was no need for a long debate. It was either "I will" or "I won't." Around the circle, one by one, each of us responded to Gloria's decisiveness.

In the succession of affirmatives I heard before my turn to speak, there were plenty of *yes, but*s—"Yes, but I'm scared out of my wits." I knew this would be my answer too. But in the end, everybody said, "I will." We needed someone with the guts to spur us forward, and Gloria was the one.

We didn't even consider consulting anyone about our decision. Not Lem, not Phil Reed, not the elders or management team or JP. All these people were familiar with Antioch's journey. All along we had been letting them know what we were up to.

Besides, we said, what more did we need to act besides the Sermon and the clarity that had brought us to this threshold? No mentors had guided us. Nor did we look to the centuries of wisdom accumulated by other communities of Christians. As far as we were concerned, the movement of God in history since a miraculous birth in a Bethlehem stable proceeded from the Sermon, to the first-century Acts 2 community, to JP, to Voice of Calvary, to us. What higher authority was there to report to than our own amazing unity and our certainty about the meaning of existence in a world where God's kingdom could actually break in? All this bordered, perhaps, on arrogance. But perhaps without such brashness, we might have never gotten to this point.

Eighteen months after Joanie had fretted about living like a tramp all of us had come to believe there was much more to be gained than lost by living together. The Antioch household group would now become the Antioch community. Even Spencer was satisfied. Whatever happened from here onward, he couldn't be blamed for it.

We agreed to begin searching for a location to move into together, either one huge house or a couple of houses on one street. We knew it could be up to a year before we could find such a place. I, for one, looked forward to a last breath of independence.

"Well, I'm pretty excited," I told Donna as I walked her home after the meeting. "But this is going to make things intense for you and me, isn't it?"

"Yeah, talk about pressure on a relationship."

"Sort of like living with ten chaperones, right? Overseeing our every little move?"

She laughed.

*And if you and I break up,* I thought, *staying in community will be rough.*

---

&#8258;

---

While Gloria was the first to call Antioch's bluff, Providence was next.

Only a week after we decided to look for a property Spencer got a call from a real estate agent who said he had just the right place.

Two blocks south of Spencer and Nancy's house, Valley Street abruptly ended at the four-lane Robinson Street thoroughfare both favored and feared by white commuters from Jackson's western suburbs. Straight ahead across Robinson, smack-dab in the middle of the neighborhood, was a deteriorating property that had just come on the market. Behind a long disheveled bank of thick pine trees and overgrown bushes, looming at the top of a gravel driveway, stood a huge old white farmhouse that had been ransacked by vandals. Twenty yards to the right stood a second one-story house of gray brick. It was in even worse shape.

Each of us had driven past these houses hundreds of times and never really noticed them. Now what we saw was stunning.

On one of those warm, clear, sunlit days that can always interrupt a Mississippi January, the eleven of us marched through knee-high weeds looking at broken windows and peeling paint, and knew that we had found our promised land.

Our eyes gleamed, and our voices burst with zeal as we sidestepped broken glass and swarmed inside and around the two houses.

"Y'all, come here! Come here!" cried Nancy, who was standing about twenty yards behind the Big House.

I jogged up to where she was and looked where Nancy was pointing. "Oh . . . my . . . gosh."

There was a vast area of at least five acres of wooded land and grassy lots behind the two houses. "Nancy, I see walking paths, gardens, a baseball field forming before my eyes," I said.

Spencer emerged from the trees. "Y'all, this property touches the backyards of an entire city block. It even borders Central Street on the back. There's at least a dozen pecan trees back there. Those babies are gonna be loaded in the fall. Can y'all buh-lieve this?"

Donna was beaming. "I counted a peach tree, a pear tree, and a fig tree. There's blackberry bushes back there," she said. "This place was unbelievably landscaped at some point."

Tressa was champing at the bit. "I can't wait to get on a tractor and pull up those old stumps by the house." I could see her now, Erik in a backpack, Kortney on her lap, running that tractor into high gear.

"The Small House gives us room to grow," said Harold.

"And until we need it," chimed in Betsy, "we can rent it out with the houses we've already got." We were already calling the four houses that we owned between us "our" properties.

Phil Eide was a skilled carpenter, and had worked in housing renovation for years. He walked up briskly, pointing a thumb back at the Big House. "We knock down two walls downstairs—that gives us one big living and dining area. I climbed up into the attic. We tear that roof off over it, raise up a higher one, stick on a second story. It'll give us ten to twelve bedrooms in this house. Piece of cake."

"This place looks like a paradise for the children, y'all," said Gloria.

"This is it, you guys," I said. "This is it."

Joanie nodded. "You know that's right. Let's jump on it."

"How soon can we get it?" asked Lue.

"Looks like everybody's on board," said Spencer. "Let's give a day to prayer about it and reconvene tomorrow to make a final decision. Is this crazy or what?"

The $97,000 asking price for the two houses and all the land wasn't cheap for west Jackson when you knew that solid three-bedroom houses went for around $30,000. Phil projected that we'd need another $75,000 to renovate. But for buying paradise, this was a steal. The property far exceeded our hopes. That week we signed the contract.

Now financial decisions and sacrifices had to be made, and they came surprisingly quickly and painlessly over the next several weeks.

Everybody saw the legal issue of the property's ownership as a mere technicality. No one cared whose names were on the deed. We were becoming one family, so the property was everybody's. The only question was how to best leverage a loan.

When the bank required collateral, Donna volunteered to back it up with a major chunk of her inheritance. I kicked in a couple of thousand dollars I had received after my grandfather's death, and Phil and Tressa and Harold and Betsy kicked in several thousand more. The Ropers, the Eides, and Donna became the property's legal owners, and nobody questioned the fact that they were all white. The trust between us had come a long, long way.

In our discussions around these decisions the idea of deciding what would happen in case someone left or our community didn't work out never came up. There was no talk of anyone owing or being owed. The very idea of such a prenuptial agreement was insulting. Hey, we were together forever, right?

With all of Voice of Calvary's interlocking relationships between church and Ministries, Antioch community's decision was a major development within the family, with a large potential ripple effect. Toward the end of February Lem sent Antioch a memo, saying he was thrilled about our decision. He raised some questions, saying he was sure we had thought of them. Well, Lem, not exactly.

LEM: What is the plan for Voice of Calvary at large benefiting from this move, and what will Antioch's relationship be to the Ministries and church? Will Antioch be a "minichurch"?

ANSWER: Antioch is of our church, by our church, for our church. We are not launching a competitor to it nor an organization like Ministries. But we are creating a powerful new organism within the Voice of Calvary family, and we don't expect its bubbling passions to be contained within Robinson Street.

LEM: What is your plan for health insurance, death insurance, disability, retirement, emergency savings, liability insurance, etc.?

ANSWER: Uh, let's see, how about this, from the Sermon—"Therefore do not be anxious about tomorrow, for tomorrow will be anxious about itself. Let the day's own trouble be sufficient for the day."

LEM: What is the best legal structure? A corporation? A partnership?

ANSWER: Well, this question had never even occurred to any of us.

In our later discussions with Lem, he didn't get the precision he'd hoped for. His questions weren't unreasonable, and I felt he wanted to see things move in an orderly and harmonious way. But such details seemed too ordinary and obsessive to people who were hypnotized by a bigger picture. For us the macro trumped the micro. Endless lists of *what-if*s could not be answered in advance.

This was about vision, and for Voice of Calvary the power of vision was sacred. You didn't let the facts overwhelm the possibilities of imagination.

For us it was vision that separated Caleb from fellow Hebrew spies in the Book of Numbers, who reported fearsome giants in the unconquered land across the Jordan River. Caleb saw those same enemies as mere grasshoppers, and vision transformed a vast desert filled with foes into a promised land flowing with milk and honey.

It was vision that launched Mahatma Gandhi and weaponless Indians on the 1930 Salt March against the mightiest colonial force on the planet and sent the 1964 civil rights marchers across the Edmund Pettus Bridge toward legions of armed Selma, Alabama, state troopers, who brutally beat them.

Vision was Voice of Calvary's most precious commodity. It propelled Spencer and Joanie to keep going to that white high school for two years, thrust JP out of his hospital bed to preach reconciliation while the wounds of his persecutors were still fresh on his body. Vision moved up-and-comers like Lem to west Jackson, got Gloria through the heartaches of her upbringing, glued Donna to the neighborhood, and transformed me so that I chose Mississippi over Middlebury.

A proverb in the King James Bible said, "Where there is no vision, the people perish." But with vision, the ill-advised became everyday normal; unknown possibilities pushed the envelope of reality; and foreboding obstacles and sacrifices became like mirages in the light of further greater destinations.

The thrill of romance has rushed many a soul into marriage who didn't have a clue what they were getting into. And so it was with Antioch. With only warm thoughts of each other and the glorious blue sky over our future, we knew it was time to elope. To make haste, run from our individual homes, tie the knot, and become a community. Forget the questions, full speed ahead.

---

&#10070;

---

With paradise ours now, we immediately got to work.

The large house on the hill was dubbed the Big House, the second one the Small House. On every Saturday in March and many evenings during the week we eagerly met on Robinson Street to tear down walls and move out the refuse. Phil was our beaverlike renovation leader; Tressa darted around like a trout that had found cool water; and even bookworm Harold got skilled with a crowbar. Our high spirits made the huge dumpsters that we filled look like mere wheelbarrows. The joy and camaraderie of our work together had a sacred quality to it, as though we were shaping a palace destined to hold a new racial order and the Sermon's new kind of kingdom.

One day, as I worked in front of the Big House, a big, nice-looking silver car pulled up in front. An attractive middle-aged white woman in a pastel pantsuit stepped out. She was smiling but looked a little nervous at being in west Jackson. She introduced herself to me as the granddaughter of the property's original owner.

"The wood in this house is all hand-picked pahn," she told me in her cultured Southern accent. "Granddaddy picked it all himself. You won't find a single knot. He designed the high ceilings and porches on three sides to keep the house cool in the summer. When it rains, there's no need to close the windows because of the porches." *Open windows? Ma'am, these days in this neighborhood, we fear break-ins more than heat.*

"It was built in 1891, you know."

"Are you kidding? It's almost a hundred years old?"

"Yes. It was almost designated a historical landmark. It was a typical well-built farmhouse for its time."

I gazed over at the front porch with its elegant posts, simple white railing, and three seven-foot windows and shutters running from the floor to the ceiling.

I learned that her grandfather had been a prominent business owner in Jackson, who established a farm on what was then the city's outskirts. Two details struck me. She said three black families had lived on and farmed the land, and that her grandfather was a stalwart member of a downtown church—a church that had, I knew, officially segregated blacks from the congregation during those years.

I chuckled to myself. *How would Granddaddy feel now if he knew about the new racial history that was going to be made on this ground?*

She never asked who would actually be living in the house, and I didn't offer.

"You don't mind if I come back and get one of these English boxwoods, do you?" she asked as she left, pointing to some bushes in front of the house. "They're very rare-ah, you know."

# 13

# BIG MOVES

*O*ver the spring of 1986 saws buzzed and hammers pounded away at Robinson Street. JP blew into town in March, and Spencer took his father around the new Antioch property.

Spencer seemed very eager to please his father. "He's fired up, man," he told me, grinning. "JP really thinks we're onto somethin'." Even Spencer often referred to his father as *JP*, as if referring to the founder of Voice of Calvary instead of *Daddy*, a voice and presence looming over his life.

JP's excitement didn't surprise me. He often described his purpose in founding Voice of Calvary as community. For him community meant forming an intense cadre of people making deeper and deeper commitments and insisting on complete fidelity to "the vision." Robinson Street offered the perfect recipe for JP's appetites: empty land to subdue and develop, buildings to renovate and fill with activity, and dedicated people with truckloads of vision to do it all.

But I also detected a strong dose of fatherly pride. Antioch, and Spencer's leadership within it, stood in sharp contrast to a major failure earlier in Spencer's life, something that Spencer talked about openly.

In 1980 JP had been influential in appointing Spencer to run the Thriftco clothing business. And why not? His son had a business degree from Belhaven College, and it was a perfect opportunity to prove himself, to grow into further responsibility at age twenty-six. But Spencer had failed miserably—financial and staff management, organization, and detailed oversight were not his forte. When JP decided to entrust the Ministries to a second generation of leadership in 1981 it was Lem—not his oldest child—whom he deemed ready to take over.

But Antioch was an achievement, with Spencer at its forefront. JP liked nothing more than seeing commitment growing deeper. And we and Spencer were already being noticed. A big Jackson newspaper article appeared in April, oozing with optimism about our impending move into community.

Antioch, wrote the reporter, was "consciously turning their backs on the selfishness and materialism of the American dream in favor of a faith-centered life of giving in and getting along with each other."

Spencer claimed we would succeed where others had failed. "Our emphasis will be on relationships, more than issues. When you're more committed to the relationship than to an issue, it's tough to break you up. There are going to be little problems about living together, but everybody is committed to working them out."

Nobody doubted that JP saw Spencer as his future heir. It was far too early to tell how that might play out. But the Voice of Calvary confederation now consisted of three interdependent entities: the Ministries, the church, and a fledgling Antioch that had JP's blessing. Community could become a strong base for pushing Spencer into further influence and his rightful inheritance.

As daffodils added yellow bursts to our overgrown primeval-looking land, Spencer and Nancy's energies were drawn to their newborn son, Johnathan Spencer, whose April birth expanded Antioch's rainbow of children to biracial, black, and white.

Donna and I were still courting, now for almost a year. When Mom and Dad visited late in April, they were excited about Antioch's plans, but elated about Donna, whom they put on a Florence Nightingale–sized pedestal. Yet I was still conflicted about her.

Events on another of her trips to Haiti in June began to dissolve my doubt. She went to visit friends doing development work in the countryside. But when Donna's plane landed in Port-au-Prince right after a violent political coup erupted, her friends couldn't get to the airport. Undeterred, Donna managed to locate a missionary veterinarian who invited Donna to stay with her. She and Donna spent the next few days dodging burning-tire blockades set by vigilantes and engaging in relaxing rural activities like cow castration.

In a letter Donna told me she "ate up being in the middle of all this action." I realized how much I underestimated this self-effacing, adventuresome spirit who made great chemistry with my own missionary-kid roots. I named my resistance to her as that same part of me that had longed for the prestige of Middlebury and hated seeing the doors close on my ambition during the Reconciliation Meetings. It finally occurred to me that while I had had one idea of who I should marry, in Donna I was being offered something much, much better. Yet I still hesitated.

But when it came to Antioch, I was ready to roll. With renovations on the Big House moving more slowly than we hoped and the Small House finished, in August Antioch took out a loan and bought a third house, making Spencer and Nancy its legal owners. The Duplex had two stories, six bedrooms, and two expansive apartments. It was only twenty yards from the Small House, and having it allowed us to finally make the big move into community.

✤

The first week of September, five years to the month after my arrival in Mississippi, a new era dawned in our lives when the Antioch community spent our first night together in the Small House and the Duplex. Sharing a checkbook, menus, refrigerators, and bathrooms, every decision could have seemed like a crisis.

Instead, we were like honeymooners. Much-feared details hardly mattered. Each day was about who you were with, and mutual admiration was at an all-time high.

Our unmatched array of furniture gave our houses a decorating style best described as Early Ragtag. Within a couple of weeks a path had been traced in the grass between the Small House and the Duplex.

Each single person and couple had their own room, while we shared kitchens, living rooms, and bathrooms. By the time I squeezed all my stuff into my bedroom at the back of the Small House, it looked like a furniture storage closet. I had to quickly get used to the smell of Joanie's late-night boiled shrimp. Spencer was already teasing Donna about the crumbs she regularly left on the counter. Thrifty Tressa had a thing about washing out and saving every little plastic baggie. Nancy's pet peeve was wet balled-up dishrags.

Spencer was blunt about his likes and dislikes. I had always assumed the proper place for storing ketchup was the fridge.

"I don't like my ketchup cold," he announced, and it turned out he wasn't the only one. Ketchup found its home in the cupboard and became an early symbol for me about choosing my battles and being willing to give in.

Weekly grocery shopping was like a military operation. Two shoppers armed with a detailed, aisle-by-aisle list methodically filled two carts each. Antioch became a puzzling but celebrated customer at our favorite local supermarket.

With breakfast and lunch on our own, dinner became our nightly town square. We shared the day's news amid a noisy flurry of chaotic food passing, animated conversation, and energetic children that stunned our frequent dinner guests. I volunteered to make coffee after one early meal, and soon everybody was referring to "Chris's coffee ministry." "Forming a co-op" became shorthand for everybody pitching in to do the dishes.

The men all chose to clean up; the women all chose to cook. Cooking for fourteen-plus was intimidating at first. The cooks had to have thick skins.

Spencer would tell you exactly what he thought. "Donna, I'm just curious. How come you didn't season this more?" If a casserole was on the menu, the main attraction for our black members was stated like some generic form of goodness—"Where's the meat?" Some people unabashedly sorted through the dish to fish out treasured chunks while the less carnivorous looked on in disbelief. But cultural comfort zones got stretched, and signature dishes emerged: Nancy's chicken spaghetti, Donna's ham and potato casserole, Joanie's taco salad, Lue's greens, Betsy's stroganoff, and Gloria's anything. She even had me eating liver when she disguised it in a savory sauce. While Spencer was fussy, Joanie liked almost anything. She even piled on the red-hot pickled cabbage called kimchi when my parents visited, and Mom cooked Korean for the whole crew.

From Harold's healthy computer programmer salary at a large company to my anemic Ministries contribution, all of our paychecks went into a single account. I bravely volunteered to oversee the communal checkbook, and payments included Antioch's three house notes, the huge renovation loan, utilities, food, medical bills, and our church tithe. The individual houses people still owned from before community were all managed by Phil as Antioch rentals, and the income went into the community's separate "Antioch Properties" account.

Some communities, we knew, frowned on any personal money. But we preferred some individual freedom. Who wanted to ask permission to buy ribs for lunch? The best blend of communal ideals with individual preference and responsibility, we decided, was a personal stipend system. Every adult, without regard to salary, received the same stipend of $150 a month, plus $50 for each child. Personal stipends paid for clothing, eating out, going to movies, hair work, vacations, Harold's endless Coke and Twinkies, my pipe tobacco and beer, and cable TV for those who wanted it in their rooms. Since nobody wanted to sign up for a car every time they went on an errand, and because we thought cars would stay in better shape with individual ownership, we settled on each person who had a car note paying half and Antioch the rest.

A stickier financial issue was the money people had before we moved into community. It was agreed that no one should tap these funds for their individual benefit, and Donna channeled all her investment interest into Antioch's account. Her generosity impressed me: After a month in community she made an outright gift to Antioch of a large chunk of money to help pay off part of the Robinson Street loan. This greatly reduced the monthly note and made all of us better off.

Gloria's prediction about community being a paradise for children proved to be true. Our financial sharing freed Tressa to stay at home and care for the three boys. With "aunts," "uncles," and "cousins" in ready supply, the children never lacked someone to perform for, blow on their little round bellies, or watch out for their safety.

A glow of wondrous unity seemed to shine on Robinson Street. I loved strolling with Donna on a crisp October Sunday, picking bulging pecans off the ground, dreaming how it would all look back here in ten years.

In November we celebrated the birth of Antioch's first baby girl, Catrice Lauren, and I marveled to hear her whimpers and cries from Harold and Betsy's room next to me, the closest I'd ever lived to a baby.

Spencer, Harold, Phil, and I regularly sat up until midnight at the Duplex, talking about growing old together and changing the world along the way. Those first three months were heady indeed.

---

❖

---

At Thanksgiving Donna came with me to Oklahoma City to my parents' house. I arranged dinner for the two of us one night at a high-priced restaurant. She had salmon, I had roast duck, and the rest was a muddle because I was trying to frame the right words for the right moment.

My internal battle had been decided for about a month. I finally saw how crazy I'd be to pass on asking this woman to become my wife. But now I had to spit out the words.

In a trembling voice, I popped the question.

Donna's face lit up, and she couldn't stop smiling. I suspect she said a "Yes!" for every time over the last year that she thought I had been going to propose and didn't.

Mom and Dad were overjoyed. The next day Mom told Donna that she still had her wedding dress from 1956. "I'd love for you to wear it, Donna," she said.

*Uh-oh, how was this going to turn out?*

Donna maintained calm, but her eyes betrayed her. Number one, she had never seen the dress. Number two, she was probably comparing her slim figure to my mother's. Fortunately, Mom had weighed a bit less on her wedding day, and fortunately, Donna loved the dress. I was glad not to see a showdown. My dearly beloved mother was notorious among her children for getting very big bees in her bonnet.

⊹

When Donna and I got back to Jackson, Antioch cheered our big news. But only a week later, just as one honeymoon was being planned, Antioch's came to an abrupt end.

Lue and Gloria walked into the dining room at the Duplex where the rest of us were gathered. Lue said they had an announcement to make. "Gloria and I have decided to leave community," she said.

What? Maybe I was out of the loop, but I had no idea this was coming. I was dumbfounded.

"Why?" asked Spencer. He seemed as shocked as I was.

Lue and Gloria looked at each other, then Lue spoke first. She mentioned a meeting a couple of weeks before, when she had brought up how she and Gloria were going to be alone in Jackson over Christmas while everyone else had families to go to.

"When I asked for some extra money so Gloria and I could make Christmas special, everybody broke out laughing, like I was joking. That really hurt, y'all. Things aren't fair around here, especially for Gloria and me, not having family like the rest of y'all. Besides, I can do better financially outside of community."

*C'mon now,* I thought. *Who said doing better financially is why we're even in community?*

"I mean, some of us are doing okay in community, money-wise," said Lue. "Like Donna."

My heart skipped a beat. It was my first time hearing of such a tension. Donna sat quietly at the table, like she wasn't going to respond. So I jumped in. "What do you mean by that?"

"I mean that Donna's got more options than the rest of us. It's not really fair, you know."

Lue didn't say it with meanness, but her comment bothered me. In our meetings no one ever said they felt Donna or anyone else should turn over all their resources to the whole group. And what about the money she'd invested in the property?

"How can you say that, Lue?" I said, my voice rising. "Donna lives on her stipend just like the rest of us. I think you've misjudged her."

I was not objective. My bride-to-be was the target, and this made it sound as though what really mattered about Donna was her money. At the same time, it was true that some of us had more options than others. *Fairness* suddenly had an empty ring of impossibility to it. Could Gloria and I ever have the same options, given our backgrounds—even living in community?

"Well, I just think things aren't equal around here," said Lue firmly.

Others tried to persuade her that she wouldn't do better financially outside of Antioch and that, like the rest of us, she needed community life for her spiritual growth. But her mind was made up.

Gloria was subdued through this whole exchange. I could have been wrong, but when I was defending Donna I felt like my words had made a difference for her. At the end of the conversation Gloria said her mind wasn't made up yet.

Afterward I wondered if others felt the same way as Lue but had never said so. I already knew how much living in community intensified comparisons between people, because I was prone to it myself. No matter who you were, there were endless ways to see yourself on the losing end, constantly reminded that someone else got their way more often, had a nicer car, had a child who was more advanced or got more attention, got listened to for their opinions more, or had found a marriage partner while you were single. Unfairness stared you right in the face every day around the dinner table. Living so intensely together, comparison could be dangerously and divisively habit-forming.

The next day I was relieved when Gloria announced that she had decided to stay at Antioch. She said she believed in what we were shooting for and that she knew how good community was for Kortney.

But Lue was gone before our first Christmas together.

I was very disappointed. I would miss Lue's quiet companionship, her knock-out greens, her faithful birthday cards, her slow steps shuffling through our house. She stayed in the church, so at least I could count on hearing her play the piano on an occasional Sunday in her down-home style. But her empty room left a depressing hole in the Small House. Spencer's prediction that everybody was committed to working out our "little problems" was destroyed.

Lue's departure was an early lesson about resolving conflict in our midst. In our first weeks together, led by Jesus' words in Matthew 18, we had affirmed the practice of going directly to housemates when you had a problem with them. Either you did this, we agreed, or you brought your problem up in a meeting, to seek everybody's help. Otherwise, the rule was to suck it up. Go fuss to God about the person in private. But don't go behind anyone's back and gossip to a third party. That undermined unity and trust—we called it breaking community.

Clearly, now, disagreement could lurk in the midst of apparent peace. Without truthful self-disclosure, conflict could take a toll on our friendships. By the time Lue aired her problem, it was too late for it to be resolved. Whether Antioch would grow from this or not remained an open question. I wondered if other fires might be smoldering in our midst.

❖

Soon after Lue's departure Spencer's brother Derek and his wife, Karyn, moved back from Pasadena to Jackson to live with us in community. Having my old friend back took the edge off my sorrow over Lue's departure. He even got several of us hooked on Saturday night pro wrestling on TV.

By February 1987, after six months in community, there was plenty of evidence to weigh the pros and cons.

Losing privacy and sharing money, two of my big fears, had been easier than expected.

But I hated how a simple fix-it job requiring a screwdriver became thirty minutes of searching for the blankety-blank communal toolbox, thirty more minutes hunting for the blankety-blank screwdriver that somebody never returned to the blankety-blank toolbox, and thirty more minutes of fuming and forgiving—followed by two minutes of twisting in the screw.

Sharing bathrooms brought out the worst in us. There was something particularly atrocious about cleaning up all that scum that surely, I told myself, wasn't mostly mine. Cleaning bathrooms was one of the best arenas for competing in the self-giving ways of the Sermon, but nobody in this case seemed eager to come forward.

People had different standards for the kids too. How much screaming and crying was too much, especially at dinner? Should the boys be allowed to do high jumps off the couch? When was it okay for someone else to tell your child no—if ever? Some Antioch members came from the no-nonsense, spank-'em-when-they-disobey school of thought, while others favored the they're-only-kids-give-them-room-to-grow approach. Differing styles quickly surfaced, and opinions were never voiced quietly.

Our biggest setback by far, though, was losing Lue. Were other fault lines growing in our midst? Were everybody's motives really on the table?

Yet for me any of community's problems and lingering questions paled in comparison to its benefits.

While the houses of fellow church members continued to be burglarized, our constant coming and going made Antioch a safe zone. Financial
sharing freed up Tressa to care for Antioch's kids and Derek to minister
to young bruthahs on the streets. Spontaneous little moments like raking
leaves or forming a dish co-op were sanctified by a unified purpose that
bound us into an intimate racial and spiritual order. On a cloudless weekend in February all of Antioch grabbed crowbars and hammers and tore
off the back roof of the Big House, framing up a second story. The property I surveyed from up there still looked like the promised land to me.
Nothing was committed to paper between Antioch's members—no policies, no job descriptions, no rules. What more did we need than trust and
vision?

With our April marriage only two months away Donna chose Tressa
as her maid of honor, and I chose Phil as my best man. He was the one
person I would have picked if I had to be stranded with someone on a
desert island, the kind of guy who would wake up and fend off a tiger
with a stick in the middle of the night, fall quickly back asleep, and forget to tell you about it the next morning. Not only was there nothing Phil
wouldn't do for you, his lips simply could not form the word *no*.

To trust and vision, add loyalty.

# 14

# DIVORCE

---

*E*ven though I lost my voice for the better part of the day and had to whisper my vows to Donna, our wedding was perfect. All the best qualities of Antioch's early communal life were incarnated for me on that glorious sunlit day in April 1987. At least it seemed that way.

The night before the wedding the Big House's nearly finished huge common room swarmed with friends from Antioch and church, working in high spirits to boil chicken, set up a big yellow tent in the yard, and decorate the property. Though we were having our party and reception at the Big House, we were being married in a church building that Voice of Calvary had bought nearby.

The clichés were true: Donna was radiant. Mom's wedding dress returned to public glory; the choir blessed our vows; and Donna's Uncle Ken—a Lutheran minister—led a long series of prayers. After my dad pronounced us husband and wife, Donna and I exited the church into Derek's gigantic vintage black Cadillac (stocked by Tressa with a bottle of champagne), and Derek chauffeured us over to Antioch. As Spencer oversaw the sacred rite of grilling chicken, the whole church assembly descended on Antioch's green oasis for a th'ow down. "Chris," said Joanie with a smile, breaking me into laughter, "that was the prayin'-est wedding I've ever been to."

Phil and Tressa were by our sides at the altar and much of the day. But once again, as with Lue, I had no clue about all that had started to stir inside my friends.

---
✥
---

A couple of weeks later we were discussing Antioch's finances at a meeting, and someone made a snide remark about Tressa needing to contribute more. "After all, she's just a stay-at-home mother."

Nobody said anything. Maybe everyone was writing off the comment—
"Oh, that's just so-and-so. You know how they are." Or maybe we were
all too chicken or just preoccupied. But nobody challenged the remark.

The next morning when I ran into Tressa at the Duplex she was steam-
ing. She tried to unload some of her feelings on me. "Can you believe
what was said in that meeting about me last night? Me being 'only a stay-
at-home mom'? Not doing more to contribute? Like managing Johnathan,
Kortney, Catrice, and Erik—four children under age three—all day is a
vacation or something? If only some of these lazy people around here
could be in my shoes, because if . . ."

Now as I look back on the moment, I wish I had reacted with compassion instead of self-righteousness. I wish I had found a way to listen.
I wish I had been a confessor who had at least tried to lead my friend into
forgiveness and reconciliation.

Instead, I cut Tressa off. "Don't you think you tend to be a little gos-
sipy? You're bordering on breaking community."

I knew what was going on, what might be behind the comment, that
Phil and Tressa were having tensions over children with another Antioch
couple. But I didn't want to hear about it.

"That's what you think about me, Chris?" she snapped. "That I'm a
gossip? Thanks a lot." She stomped away.

Maybe Tressa was bothered by details that didn't matter as much to
others, but if I'd been more compassionate, I'd have seen that she had the
closest daily intersection with two of life's most volatile issues: money and
children. She had taken over running the Antioch checkbook. And she
was at home all day caring for the children—and that had to put much
more communal messiness in her face than mine.

A thick skin was necessary to stay happy around Antioch. If stipends
didn't get out on time because another bill was paid instead, Tressa got
the heat. And if I had been a parent at the time, I might have understood
how emotional differences over children can be. Tressa was one of the
most giving persons I'd ever known. She knew, just knew, exactly what a
suffering person needed and delivered it: a meal, a listening ear, an errand
that needed to be run, just about anything. But she helped best when it
was on her own terms, in her own space. Some people at Antioch took
on too little responsibility, and some, like Tressa, took on too much.

One weekend in June Phil and Tressa went camping. After they returned they summoned Donna and me to their room.

Phil was sitting on the bed with his head against the headboard. There
was a look of resignation in his eyes. Tressa lay on her stomach next to
him, her arms wrapped around a pillow. Her face seemed peaceful.

Donna and I sat down cautiously.

"Guys," said Tressa quietly, "we're leaving Antioch."

I felt myself begin to tremble. Tears welled up in my eyes, and I couldn't stop them. Soon all of us were blubbering like babies.

"I can't do anything right in Antioch's eyes," Tressa said through her sobs. "I just find myself constantly disagreeing with how decisions are made. I have headaches and stomach pains all the time. I hardly sleep at night. It doesn't take anything for me to go off on Phil."

I dabbed my eyes and managed to squeeze out some words. "Phil, what about you?"

"I have to choose between Antioch or Tressa. I think it's obvious which choice needs to be made."

"Why does it have to be so hard?" I cried out. "Why?" I said it again, and again, and again. My cry was more to God than to anyone present. *It* was doing the will of God, living the Sermon, being the new kingdom, just simply trying to live in peace with one another. Why did all that have to be so hard? Why? I had no answer for my question.

"I don't know if we can ever be friends again," I said. "You're rejecting the most important part of my life."

When I said that, it was fact to me, not judgment. No matter how much we might want it to be different, I sensed our relationship could never be the same. There was no way to compare the intimacy of life in Antioch with life outside. They were two worlds lived at different depths, even within the same church. I didn't feel anger toward Phil and Tressa. Just hopelessness and dread about our future.

Antioch called an emergency meeting a couple of days later, and Spencer proposed a compromise. "What about living in the Small House, y'all? You can live there by yourselves while we try to work things out."

But Tressa had hit that point of no return where every molehill was Mt. Everest, where a little misunderstanding over dishes became somebody's skirmish in ominous warfare. Trust was gone; the differences were irreconcilable.

I was out of town the day the Eides moved back into their old house at the end of June. I was relieved. The pain was too great.

---

Losing Phil and Tressa instantly left a great void in our midst. It was like waking up, feeling a strange sensation beneath the covers, pulling back the sheets, and discovering that one of your legs had been cut off.

How could Antioch possibly survive without this part of us? Without that patch of blue sky Phil put over our life every day? Tressa had been a constant anchor for me, from pouring Kool-Aid at Good News Club, to our laughter in the sweltering Thriftco warehouse, to drawing hope from her, watching her stick it out after the Reconciliation Meetings.

I recalled an old conversation with church members Herb and Sarah Myers. They had lived in an intentional community in Pennsylvania that eventually broke up. But they had stayed close to each other afterward. "It was very painful," Sarah had said. "But we kept reminding each other that we still cared for one another."

A week after Phil and Tressa left I told Donna I was going to visit them. "I'd go with you," she said, "but I'm a little afraid to see Tressa. I'm afraid of more conflict." So I went alone.

The few blocks to their house seemed so far now. It was strange, the whole idea of "their house."

I told Phil and Tressa what Herb and Sarah had said. "I've thought a lot about that," I said, choking up. "I just came to tell you that I love you." We embraced.

Phil and Tressa did all they could to ease the transition. Phil consulted with us about property issues. They offered to keep their names on the Robinson Street loan until we worked out an alternative. And they didn't ask for the money back that they'd invested in the purchase.

But their departure put more stress on everybody who was left. There was the same amount of work but fewer hands to do it. We lost Phil's income, and making our rental properties profitable was intimidating without his skills. There were so many ways Antioch could dream only because we had Phil and Tressa's resourcefulness.

The rest of us drew closer together. Gloria nobly volunteered to do child care, Nancy to run the checkbook, and Betsy to manage our properties. We closed ranks, held tight to our vision, and pressed forward.

Gradually, "us" and "them" began to poison my thoughts toward my old friends. It soon felt like a divorce, with all the fault on their side.

Stepping into communal life was an implicit vow for the long haul, maybe even for life. I never imagined Phil and Tressa would leave, no matter how tough it got. Why didn't they give Antioch a chance to change their minds, we asked each other in our meetings. What one-sided version were they telling our friends in the church?

We didn't examine other questions, like why trust got erased so quickly, or why nobody realized how serious the conflicts were, or didn't intervene before it was too late. We chalked it up as Phil and Tressa's fault that they hadn't spoken up more. There was no thought that their leaving pointed to any weakness in our midst. We never discussed how to continue caring for people that had disappointed us. Acting as if we loved Phil and Tressa whether they stayed in community or not required far deeper reservoirs of grace than we had.

It never occurred to us that maybe community wasn't for everybody. *Novice* wasn't in Antioch's vocabulary, the idea of starting out admitting your inexperience and need for guidance, and going through months or even years of seasoning in community, before determining whether this was your call.

We had dived into community as raw beginners. But we doled out opinions, challenged each other, and churned out decisions like we had already won the gold medal of community living. People who left were "uncommitted"; they were deserters who settled for softness. Spirituality for us was something you gutted out, even if you belly flopped. Living the Sermon was about trying harder and doing more, a matter of raw truth and rugged obedience. If it seemed demanding, well, suck it up, because God is demanding too. There was only one choice besides being radical, and that was being more radical. But to retreat into your own little house with your own little money and your own little life? That betrayed everything we had learned together.

Deep down, though, there was another reason it all hurt so much. With Phil and Tressa, we had tasted the most wondrous delicacies of like-mindedness and camaraderie—seeing the sunrise after the storm of the Reconciliation Meetings, watching Robinson Street's dumpsters transformed into mere wheelbarrows. It hurt so much because we had shared so intimately.

But my stubborn pride was very good at concealing my underlying affection. *Fine,* I thought. *Go. We'll manage.* In some ways Antioch, and I as part of it, had developed the same harsh, demanding edge as the Reconciliation Meetings. I grew distant from Phil and Tressa.

Living in a community of friends like this presented an awful dilemma. The very place that offered the greatest joys, highs, and possibilities was also the place that left you most disillusioned and disappointed with others. It was dangerous, I saw, opening yourself up to others this way.

At least I had a break to look forward to. Donna and I had been planning our October trip to Korea for a long time. With Antioch's approval, we tapped into "Donna's money" to pay for the trip. I couldn't wait to show her the beloved land of my youth. Our big departure day came, and Derek drove us to the airport.

As we stood in the check-in line, Derek told us that he and Karyn were moving to Minnesota to finish up their college degrees.

"I know it's rough gettin' the news like this, right before your trip," he said. Was I ever going to be not surprised when I heard that someone was leaving?

Derek had never seemed completely content at Antioch. He never seemed comfortable about not contributing financially, even though everybody agreed they wanted to support his neighborhood work. The blow was greatly softened by the fact that Karyn and Derek had left Jackson before the community started and that they had only been with us for nine months. They weren't leaving over any great conflict, and I felt sure that my relationship with them would remain friendly.

But the cumulative impact of the departures was disturbing. Over our first sixteen months the Antioch community had lost five adult members. Vows of persevering "in sickness and health" seemed built on shaky ground indeed.

# 15

# COMMUNION

---

*D*uring Antioch's Super Bowl party in January 1988 we screamed, jumped, and high-fived for a good three hours, watching Washington Redskin Doug Williams trying to become the first black quarterback to win the NFL championship. The house shook with each of his four touchdown passes, and when the Redskins won we celebrated a little notch for racial progress. The laughter and partying was a welcome relief from 1987's disappointments.

Even with losing five core members, we didn't try very hard to replace them. Our relationships had been forged over a years-long, intense journey together, and we knew it would be hard for others to join us now. We were open to welcoming others and reached out to several people in particular, but we didn't actively recruit. We still had a brash confidence about our vision, and there was plenty to do, scrambling to keep afloat. Besides, Antioch wasn't the end-all to our lives—we were part of the larger Voice of Calvary body and its mission.

We went ahead with ourselves, and in spite of Antioch's storms and frailties we began to rally, guided by Spencer's interpretation of our pain. During an Antioch meeting in February he pulled out his Bible and read us a parable of Jesus from Luke 13:6: "A man had a fig tree planted in his vineyard; and he came seeking fruit on it and found none. And he said to the vinedresser, 'Lo, these three years I have come seeking fruit on this fig tree, and I find none. Cut it down; why should it use up the ground?' And he answered him, 'Let it alone, sir, this year also, till I dig about it and put on manure. And if it bears fruit next year, well good; but if not, you can cut it down.'" The vineyard owner, said Spencer, was God, and the vinedresser caring for the tree was Jesus. Antioch was like the fig tree.

"Diggin' and tillin' around the fig tree, I see that as studyin' the Scriptures, prayer, and worship. For most Christians that stuff's as far as their faith goes. But we've learned those things are only a means to an end.

"Because then there's the manure—the crap, the heavy stuff, the growin' pains. All the hard times that go into makin' us a representative of God's kingdom."

*Yeah*, I thought, *I can make a ten-page crap list in a minute.* From the Reconciliation Meetings, to facing my white privilege, to all of Antioch's departures.

"Remember this, though," continued Spencer. "Later in this same passage, Jesus compares God's kingdom to a tiny mustard seed that grows and becomes a sturdy tree—a place where birds can make their homes in its branches.

"The reason why churches are usually such a poor representation of God's kingdom is because they avoid the manure. And when the manure is avoided, well, you might as well be cut down! Too many of the branches break. And birds can't build their nests in weak trees like that.

"Jesus started with his twelve disciples, a bunch of misfits, and he had three years to turn them into the kingdom. They started out small and insignificant, but eventually, after much pain and suffering, they became a sturdy tree."

He paused, looked into our faces around the room, and brought the parable home to our own small and insignificant circle.

Consider yourself warned: If we think that by keepin' Christ's commandments we'll gain some kinda selfish gratification—that we'll be able to look at ourselves and feel good about what we're doin'—don't bet the ranch on it. These commandments demand a sacrifice. A giving of one's self that most Christians are not willing to give.

I won't pretend that I know what the kingdom of God looks like for Antioch. All I know is that the seed has been planted. When the tree is ready, when it's strong enough, God will send the birds. So if anyone asks me, "What is Antioch?" my answer will be: "Antioch is a little seedling in Christ's vineyard, struggling to become a productive tree in God's kingdom."

It was ingenious to me, Spencer finding a way to turn Antioch's manure into an asset. And if redeeming manure is what it took to gain a wider ministry, well then, amen, brother, amen. Because Spencer and I had begun to dream of teaming up to work at the Ministries.

❖

For three years, I had served as director of development under Lem, and our relationship had been close enough to ask him to be one of the groomsmen in my wedding. But things had been eroding over the past year.

I had become disenchanted with raising money for an organization that I believed was too top-heavy. But that wasn't how Lem saw things at all. Some staff members had resigned, and I felt Lem had done too little to respond to their criticisms. I thought he needed more accountability, but he didn't. I had pressed him to move me from being development director to bringing a now-defunct Study Center back to life. Lem had finally approved the move, months ago. But I felt he was dragging his feet on making it happen. And now we had begun battling over whether or not he would hire Spencer to join me.

The Battery Clinic wasn't doing very well, and I knew that Spencer had so many gifts that weren't being tapped, including teaching and writing. He'd started penning some stories about race and growing up in Mendenhall, and he had marvelous talent. I felt he wanted to step further into his legacy too. As our friendship grew, so did our vision for teaming up.

As the training arm of the Ministries with a national reach, the Study Center had enjoyed a huge influence over the years. Spencer and I wanted to revive it together, and I believed so much in Spencer that I was willing to have him be the director, with me working under him. Spencer was already Antioch's de facto leader and a key leader on the church's elder board. Being Study Center director, with a seat on the management team, would make Spencer a major player in all three entities within Voice of Calvary's confederation—the Ministries, the church, and Antioch. It was exactly what I hoped for.

In March Lem and I met in his office to discuss a proposal from Spencer and me, outlining our plan.

"So, Lem, what about Spencer?"

Lem was wearing one of his best poker faces ever. I suppose hiring the founder's outspoken eldest child and heir would have threatened even humble St. Francis. I sensed the need to strengthen my arguments. "Look, Lem, it's like the NFL draft. You go after the best athlete you can find to strengthen your team."

Still, he looked at me with that blank stare. But I really believed what I had just said.

"Chris, I'm not convinced Spencer has the gifts to make this work."

*OK*, I thought, *Lem's starting his "neither yes nor no" game.*

Was Lem thinking of the Thriftco failure? I'd seen Spencer's many other gifts arise within Antioch's journey, and my administrative abilities perfectly complemented his visionary, conceptual, and teaching and writing talents.

But Lem's mama didn't raise no fool.

Lem was by the book, Spencer was unorthodox. Lem was organizational and methodical, Spencer was communal and spontaneous. Lem could have never gotten Antioch off the ground, but he had stabilized all kinds of projects. Spencer failed at managing Thriftco and thrived in leading Antioch. I had benefited greatly from both of these gifted leaders. But they were the proverbial clashing odd couple. On top of this I had made it very clear how much I disagreed with many of Lem's decisions. Putting Spencer and me over the Study Center was like the czar putting Lenin and Marx over the national education department.

Lem, however, was in a delicate position. Saying no to Spencer would mean rejecting a Perkins. What would JP think? And Antioch's life was likely to have a big influence, whether or not Spencer and I worked with the Ministries.

"We need to do further assessment, Chris," said Lem as he ended the meeting.

*Assessment of what?* I thought. Lem wasn't clear about that, and I walked away angry. My impatience with him was growing. But I was determined to get Spencer hired.

In mid-April I wrote Lem a long letter, venting all my frustrations of the past year, apologizing for some of the things I'd done and said, and pleading for us to make a new beginning.

I didn't hear back from Lem in April. Not in May. Not in June either.

Was he sending his response back via a carrier ant? I was seething. Granted, Lem was busy and constantly on the road. But I'd done my bit to make peace. It was his turn now.

---

✤

---

Lem had command over whether or not Spencer and I would work together. But Antioch had an indisputable power as well—the power of friendship and unity.

In June, on a whim, Spencer, Harold, and I drove twenty-fours hours straight to a conference at a sprawling Christian community near New York City called the Bruderhof.

At first it seemed to be a spotless colony of clones. The men all wore blue shirts, black pants, and suspenders. Women darted around like German peasants in long dark skirts and polka-dot scarves. Ten rosy-cheeked white babies crossed our path in a deluxe baby buggy pushed by a smiling caregiver. "Greetings!" she said cheerfully. When we walked into their state-of-the-art factory and saw robot welders, we felt an extremely strange sensation, as if they'd crossed Mercedes Benz with the Amish.

Our guide told us of the Bruderhof's roots in pre–World War II Germany, their persecution by the Nazis, and their escape to Paraguay, and then to the United States in the 1960s. Four U.S. locations boasted a total of around two thousand members, all of whom functioned as one community with one common purse and a motto: "whatever the need."

Our breakneck driving feat, combined with Antioch's interracial membership, made us instant celebrities. People at the Bruderhof kept saying they didn't know of any communities—past or present—that had successfully unified whites and blacks. One person from a community in Los Angeles was curious about who Antioch patterned ourselves after. "What books did you read?" he asked me eagerly, as if he were looking for cool models and community gurus. "Did you read the Rule of St. Benedict? Dietrich Bonhoeffer's *Life Together?*"

My answer, I'm sure, was rather disappointing. But I was rather proud of it. "Uh, books. Let's see. Well, mostly just the Bible, actually. Mainly the Sermon on the Mount. That was about it really."

When we met with one of the Bruderhof's elderly leaders, he seemed like one of those wise, white-bearded masters in a kung fu movie. "Ah, finding unity around raising children. Yes, my brothers, this is a hard subject indeed. It is difficult to be objective about your own flesh. Tread carefully. Seek the path of the interest of the other."

I kept waiting for him to say, "Remove the pebble from my hand. Then you will know the true secret of community." Much as I appreciated him and his community, I was still pretty sure we had it all figured out.

After we returned to Jackson Lem finally responded to my April letter with memos and a meeting. I got part of what I wanted when, a month later, he hired a new development director, and I moved to the Study Center half-time, spending the rest training the new person. Now I could focus completely on getting Spencer there with me, regardless of the iciness of my ongoing interactions with Lem.

⟡

By November life in the Big House had established a familiar rhythm. We had added five new bathrooms to the old farmhouse, and all eight adults and three children, including Donna and me, had moved into 1831 Robinson Street's ten bedrooms and two floors. Shortly after, Spencer and Nancy had welcomed their new daughter, Rebecca Jubilee Perkins, forever after known as Jubilee, or simply Juba. We all settled into our lives together, learning the intricacies of our bedroom intercom system that made it easier to get phone calls to the right person and to talk to each other without trooping up and down the stairs. It wasn't uncommon for two-person conversations to be heard by the entire house.

Joanie's voice might cackle over the monitor from her room: "Glo, you watchin' channel fohty?"

"Naw," Gloria would answer from the monitor in her room.

Joanie: "Check out Denzel." As in Washington, the good-looking black actor.

Pause, as Gloria would flip the channel in her room. Then Gloria, audible the to entire house: "Ouuuuuuu, girl!"

We left each other messages on a huge blackboard on the top of the hefty mahogany hutch in the foyer, messages like "WHO TOOK MY EBONY MAGAZINE?!!! RETURN TO JOANIE." We picked up our mail from the wooden-framed cubbyholes on the hutch and avoided looking at the box labeled "BILLS." It was always full. My pet peeve was trying to find that dadgummed screwdriver; I always started with the hutch's cluttered drawers, fumbling through ancient church bulletins, Teenage Mutant Ninja Turtle toys, and Spencer's fishing bobs.

Holding weekly meetings was an easy task—after the children were in bed we all commuted to the downstairs guest room, right off the house's expansive foyer near the front door. The meeting began after everyone filtered in and Spencer was able to quiet us down, this not being what might be considered a tightly run ship.

The atmosphere was often light, playful, and peaceful. One night, at what seemed like a typical meeting, we sounded new depths with each other. Spencer began by asking, "You're leadin' the discussion Wednesday mornin', right, Harold?" Besides business meetings, we were doing a weekly 6:00 A.M. Bible study.

"Got it," Harold said.

"Chris and I will take the kids Wednesday night," Donna added.

"Yes!" exclaimed Gloria, pumping her fists. On the parents' night off Donna and I did activities with the kids while moms and dads enjoyed free time at or away from the house. This was especially popular with Gloria, who was doing the weekly child care.

"Nancy, how are your folks fittin' in?" Spencer asked. Nancy's parents had moved to Jackson from Pennsylvania for a year. They were living in the Duplex, helping us out in important little ways (like painting the Duplex), and enjoying their grandchildren.

"Mom and Dad are fine. But I get scared seeing Daddy climb that ladder every day," said Nancy, smiling.

"Hey, did everybody see Spencer's article in *Christianity Today?*" I asked, holding up a copy and reading the magazine's headline. "Look at that y'all: 'The Pro-Life Credibility Gap.'"

Cheers and clapping broke out. Spencer originally penned the piece to work out his anger over a racial incident that happened in our church during a meeting of Jackson pro-life supporters. He gave a copy to JP, who sent it on to the editor of *Christianity Today,* who was a friend. With a circulation of 150,000 pastors and church leaders, Spencer had hit the big time.

"Listen to this, y'all," I said, reading from the article. "'When white evangelical Christians stand against abortion, the first thought that comes to the minds of many African Americans is "What's in it for them?" Whatever it is, it must be something bad for us.'"

"Say it, Spence!" interrupted Gloria, addressing him the nickname we sometimes used.

"'Right or wrong, the fact that black Christians would even think like this demonstrates the ungodly mistrust that exists among the people who are supposed to represent a God of love. There is a huge credibility gap between us—a deep lack of trust. The historical gulf that lies between blacks and "right-wing" Christians is so deep that it's hard for some to imagine being on the same side of any serious issue.'"

Joanie was stunned. "They really published all that?"

"OK," I said, "one last sentence. This is a humdinger."

"'Why should blacks not assume that as the ghettos become larger and more dangerous, the Christian anti-abortionists will not move farther and farther into the suburbs, taking little or no responsibility for the social consequences of the lives they helped to save?'"

"Ouu, Spencer!" said Gloria. This was the talent that I knew Spencer would bring to the Study Center. With an article published in an influential platform like this, Spencer was going to be very hard for anybody to ignore, including Lem.

"OK, y'all, enough already," Spencer said with a grin. "Betsy, how we lookin' on the money?"

Antioch's finances were always tight, but somehow we squeezed by. Our forecast of freeing up thousands of dollars a month had met the reality of losing members and their incomes.

"Well, I've paid all the bills," said Betsy. "Everybody gets stipends tomorrow." More claps and cheers. "Of course, our rental properties aren't helping," Betsy continued. "Almost everybody's behind on their rent."

"That's why we call it the Antioch housing ministry," Donna laughed. "You want free rent? Apply for an Antioch house!" Everybody cracked up. Antioch's property management had become a regular theme of communal comedy.

Spencer finally reined in the free-for-all. "I thought we'd just check in with each other tonight."

From time to time we put community business on hold and caught up with each other's job situations and states of mind. It could be difficult. Betsy had some serious health problems, a complicated situation that often took up a lot of our energy as we tried to figure out what she needed and how to help. It could be very discouraging for her, for Harold, for all of us.

But this night, as we went around the circle, we stripped off the masks and shared our inner thoughts and experiences and found a particular joy together.

As we finished up our sharing Spencer had a sudden inspiration. "Y'all, I think somethin' special is happenin' among us. Our unity tonight kinda reminds me of when we first decided to move into community. Let's mark this moment. Let's celebrate Communion together."

On this night, for the first time in Antioch's history, we did what Christians had done all the way back to Jesus with his disciples, the night before he was crucified. Admittedly, the way we did it was a bit unconventional, some might even say sacrilegious. But I received it as a sacred inspiration.

We didn't have any wine, and a couple of members didn't drink it anyway. We didn't have the standard Protestant grape juice either. We did have Coke and Kool-Aid, but that seemed profane.

Instead, Spencer gathered chunks of white bread and cups of milk. His theology was simple. Celebrating peace with God and each other wasn't about what we were imbibing. It was about who we were doing it with and Who was at work over our life together.

"Wine was the purest, cleanest thing they had to drink in those days," he said. "Milk's kind of like that for us. Pure. Wholesome. God-given through the creation. Let's mark this moment of unity."

We passed the bread and milk, proclaimed Jesus' death and resurrection, and ate and drank.

In the common room a few feet away a colorful banner the women had quilted hung over our dining room table. A big radiant-looking house on an urban streetscape had a fat red heart planted in its center. On the banner were words from Psalm 133: "Behold, how good and pleasant it is when brothers dwell together in unity."

Whatever high sent the psalmist tripping into poetic extravagance must have been like what I felt that night. It was a high that no drug, no sex, no earthly treasure could touch. Moments like this made any pain worth enduring and spawned weeks of adrenaline. The manure had cleared away, leaving a sweetness in our midst.

Before we parted we grasped hands and closed our eyes. Some weeks we prayed so poorly that our words seemed to hit the ceiling and drop with a thud. But that night I felt like they shot to the heavens like a rocket.

Two weeks later I had an early Christmas surprise for Spencer. "Spence, Lem gave in today. You're on board with the Study Center. You start in January." True to Spencer's even-keeled nature, we did a gentle high five.

I didn't know why Lem caved in. Maybe it was politics, or maybe it was a sincere act of graciousness, going back to his old proverb: "He who has the greatest truth must have the greatest love, which is the greatest proof."

My private reaction, however, was rather irreverent. "Spence. You ever hear what Lyndon Johnson said about a political enemy of his?"

"I don't think so."

"After Johnson appointed his foe to his cabinet, he said, 'I'd rather have him inside the tent pissing out, than outside the tent pissing in.'"

We broke into laughter. Our new office would be in the building behind the Fellowship House, right underneath Lem. So what if he wanted to keep an eye on us? The Big House was our real base of operations. Living together in community had never been enough. Spencer and I wanted to touch the world.

## PART THREE

# Yokefellows

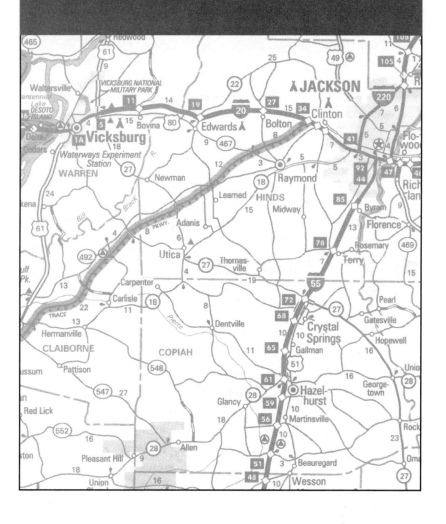

# 16

# BOOT CAMP

he day after New Year's 1989 Spencer left the Battery Clinic and joined me on the staff at the Ministries. He exchanged his eight-to-five world of mostly all bruthahs for a full-time job leading America's racial tribes into intimacy and equality.

Lem had appointed me Study Center director, but Spencer and I proclaimed ourselves a two-man platoon of equals, and we leapt into action. Soon our new recruits arrived: two dozen college students of many ethnicities who converged on Jackson for our three-week program, Winterim. As I had in 1981, they had come to help the poor.

But Spencer and I had mapped out a more subversive plan—a three-week boot camp designed to lead these young people through the same racial conversion that Voice of Calvary's blacks and whites had experienced. Never ones to aim too low, we also intended to change forever how they thought about being Christian.

The battle for their hearts and minds had already begun when we brought them into the neighborhood and housed them communally at the Study Center. As I knew from my own experience, one night of hearing gunshots was enough to jolt anyone out of complacency.

During orientation on Monday morning Spencer proposed a new way of thinking. "Christianity ain't between you and God. It's about joinin' in God's agenda and becomin' part of a new people—a body that together witnesses God's truth to the world. And central to that is us together livin' in a way that is good news for the poor." The students were wide-eyed, in shock it seemed.

I laid out the assigned reading, including *The Autobiography of Malcolm X*. "This one's gonna upset you. It upset me too. But open yourself to the truth that's told here. Why did Malcolm X think the way he did about white folks? What history formed him?"

What better drill sergeant to bring in next than Ivory Phillips, the prosecutor of the Reconciliation Meetings? The doctor did two half-day lectures. He was relentless.

The first morning Ivory rattled off a thousand years of history in three hours, from African kingdoms to the Black Panthers. White students looked like they were panting from heat exhaustion. Ivory could have done the next day blindfolded. For three more hours he dissected the litany of racial viruses—racism in its active, institutional, and passive forms. I wondered if the students were as shaken up as I had been, hearing that stuff for the first time.

We kept pushing the pace.

The core curriculum, well honed over nearly two decades, was JP's famous three "Arahs": relocation, reconciliation, and redistribution. Over the next three days we hammered away at our recruits.

The theological basis for relocation was the Incarnation—God entering the messiness of humanity as a human being, as Jesus the Son, in order to reveal who God is, and to save humanity. To bring God's life to the least of these, we too were called to follow Christ's example—foregoing privilege and becoming one with their world.

Pastor Phil Reed and his wife, Marcia, were relocation's ideal instructors. White transplants from pleasant Midwest upbringings, they had each lived in the neighborhood for over a dozen years. With carrot-colored hair and bright eyes, Marcia looked like your normal PTA mom from the suburbs. Toward the end of their talk she started into a story. "Several years ago, Phil was out of town doing a seminar at the state prison, about 150 miles away. Me and the three kids were home alone.

"During the night a man crawled into the house through the bathroom window and assaulted me in my bed."

Marcia stopped and started to tear up. Phil wrapped an arm around her shoulder. "I . . . I . . . managed to fight the man off with kicks and screams. The children heard everything. They were terrorized." Marcia continued to choke back the tears. "Thank God . . . that man ran from the house."

Marcia stopped again, gathering herself. "By the time Phil got home a couple hours later, many of our neighbors and church friends were at our house, looking after the children, comforting me, praying together with us.

"When Phil and I embraced, when I saw his face, I knew what he was thinking. I said, 'Phil, God has called us to this community, and we are not leaving. This is our home.'"

Marcia couldn't go on. There were many moist eyes in the room, including mine.

Phil began to speak. "Y'all, I learned two things that night. The first thing I learned is that it is the women who are the true heroes of relocation. The second thing I learned is that God, through God's people, can take better care of my family than I can."

*And one more thing, Phil,* I thought. *If middle-America Phil and Marcia can incarnate God's love in the 'hood, why can't these students?*

✤

The next day Spencer and I did reconciliation. We had never spoken together on the topic publicly before, and it showed.

Spencer's big hands fumbled with his notes like he was trying to handle a loose football. He read awkwardly from a manuscript, in a halting but confident voice.

He spoke of his quandary growing up in segregated Mississippi and told the stories that had become so familiar to me now—the white high school, JP's beating in Brandon.

He told of watching JP struggle with his faith afterward. "I was in the background," he said, raising his voice, "rootin' that my father would conclude we wouldn't have nothin' else to do with white people!" His face was stern and angry.

"But that's not what happened. The stuff we had learned in the Bible won out. And I had to learn about forgiveness."

He told of Nelson Mandela, befriending and speaking truth to his white jailers in South Africa during the apartheid years. His voice rose sharply. "What good is it if you love them that love you?" he said, expanding on Jesus' words from the Sermon.

> Look, even dogs and cats do that! Even the animals take care of their own! But when you do good to those who despise you, who spitefully use you, great is your reward in heaven.
>
> Y'all, sometimes I wish Jesus had never said words like this. But that's the kind of forgiveness we're supposed to practice.
>
> You see, for Christians, forgiveness isn't optional. Your neighbor is especially those people you don't get along with so well. Especially those people who you ignore and don't like. Who ignore you. Who live over there and you live over here. Who don't trust you and you don't trust them. Those are the neighbors of the world. And it takes a powerful commitment to be able to step across racial and cultural barriers to demonstrate that kind of love.

Who's the person or group that's most difficult for you to love? That's your neighbor, y'all.

Spencer glanced at me and sat down.

*OK, Chris, here we go,* I thought. I stepped to the podium, my heart pounding.

The biggest racial conflict in the New Testament, I said, is told in Paul's Letter to the Galatians. It happened in a city called Antioch, between Paul and Peter—both apostles, both self-confessed Jews, both key leaders in the new sect called Christian.

"The church in Antioch became Paul's headquarters to the world," I said. "That church broke a forbidden boundary between Jews and Gentiles in an unprecedented way—in common worship, in common leadership, in everyday life. Eventually Peter visited Antioch to check out this new interracial phenomenon.

"I can imagine Peter warming up to the cross-cultural excitement," I said with a chuckle. "He's learning how to clap on two and four." The students laughed.

"Peter is eating nonkosher barbecued rib tips for the first time; he's licking his fingers; he's loosening up and shouting, 'Amen!' during the worship service. I imagine Peter enjoying himself, seeing the wall between Jew and Gentile coming down.

"But then Peter's homeboys showed up from the Jerusalem church. They took him aside and they said, 'What are you doing, Peter? We clap on one and three. We don't eat pork. We don't eat with Gentiles. Don't you know what a mess this is gonna lead to? Upsetting our traditions? Sharing power? My God—even interracial marriage?'" The students were eating it up.

"Well, Peter's long-held habits of superiority and separation won out. He retreated from fellowship with his new Gentile brothers and sisters.

"How did Paul respond? Did he say 'Well, maybe Peter's right after all. Maybe this interracial stuff is just too messy'?

"No! Peter's offense was so serious to Paul that he confronted Peter publicly. To his face. And he told Peter that the 'truth of the gospel' was at stake.

"That's exactly what's at stake in racial reconciliation," I said. "The truth of the gospel."

I quoted our church's slogan, a verse from Ephesians 2, speaking of Christ and the wall between Jews and Gentiles: "For he is our peace, who has made us one, and has broken down the dividing wall of hostility."

I looked up from my Bible. "But, y'all, even when walls come down, we've still got work to do. We've got to step over the rubble. That's the hard work of racial reconciliation—stepping over the rubble."

Seeing the audience gripped by my words was an empowering moment. I felt my relationship with Spencer, and the journey behind it, added an authority to my voice as a white man.

"You see, laws change, walls come down, but our old habits stay intact. We have become very comfortable with our side of the wall.

"Hear this: Integration and reconciliation are not the same. You can force schools to integrate. But parents can always move to another neighborhood. You can force neighborhoods to accept all races. But you can't force neighbors to become friends. You can force legal justice and political change, but you can't force brotherhood and sisterhood.

"Dr. King once said he would never be satisfied with court victories for racial equality. He was after a new relationship between the races—what he called a 'beloved community' and 'redeeming the soul of America.'"

I described my own experience of stepping over the rubble, of coming to Mississippi as "the solution," and my gradual, painful racial conversion.

"Hey, I knew 'My Country 'Tis of Thee,'" I said. "But I didn't know 'Lift Every Voice and Sing.'" I told how Spencer's question burst my romantic bubble, of my terror during the Reconciliation Meetings, of blacks and whites enduring with each other, of my rebirth of hope through the small group with Spencer.

Spencer took the podium after me again, and me again after him. We delved into the nitty-gritty of black-white dynamics, of working for justice and reconciliation, offering lessons from our experiences.

After our hour was finished a white student raised his hand. "Who's that guy that you referred to—Mandela?"

Spencer looked like he was going to reach out and grab the boy by his collar. "Wait a minute, you don't know who Nelson Mandela is? South Africa's most famous black leader, up with Desmond Tutu? Y'all are gettin the best education money can buy, huh?" Spencer said, chuckling. "Y'all, this is a good example of passive racism. There's stuff you don't know because it doesn't affect your life.

"And y'all black students in here—the ones who didn't know all that stuff about the civil rights movement we saw last night in the *Eyes on the Prize* video? You should be ashamed of yourselves. Everybody knows who Dr. King was. But the movement was way more than that."

As always, Spencer was an equal-opportunity critic.

⚜

The next day's last "Arah"—redistribution and its focus on economics—was prime territory for Lem's talents.

Lem and I might still be butting heads over Spencer's role in the Study Center, but visitors rarely knew what was going on behind the scenes.

Lem slapped a chart up on an overhead projector, showing the disparity between rising black income and declining black wealth. Another diagram showed the money flow in and out of poor communities. "A dollar circulates in west Jackson once or twice before it leaves. In north Jackson it's more like ten times. That's why we need to create community-based enterprises.

"Redistribution isn't about Robin Hood, taking from the rich and giving to the poor," said Lem, breaking his trademark grin. "This is about moving poor people from dependency to empowerment, and that involves a radical sharing of our lives, skills, and resources. But redistribution is also a huge public policy issue. What are the implications of the Old Testament Year of Jubilee for public economics?

"You know, theologians love to talk eschatology and soteriology," he said. Being a seminary graduate, Lem knew his "-ologies." "But what you don't hear about is what Voice of Calvary calls 'poorology.'"

He launched into a long Scriptural survey of God's concern for the poor. When Lem finished it was just the end of the students' first week.

On Sunday our Winterim recruits joined us at church for a glimpse of the transcendent interracial worship life that only existed because of a history together, because of all the day-to-day practices and commitments laid out the previous week. For the next two weeks we sent the students into the unromantic grunt work of tutoring children, sorting clothes at Thriftco, and gutting houses slated for remodeling.

We had many conversations with Jacquiline Gates, a white student from an affluent family who attended a prestigious university. We asked Jacquiline to write an article about her Winterim experience for our new Study Center publication, "The Lamppost."

Jacquiline opened her article with a raw confession. "When I first arrived here, on a barely conscious level, I associated black men with rape and black women with 'help.'" Over the next three weeks, she said, she was converted. Through the hugs, drawings, and junk food gifts of neighborhood children. Through the words *justice* and *oppression* leaping out of the Scriptures for her for the first time. Through long and frank talks with Voice of Calvary people. "I'm simply grateful," Jacquiline wrote, "to the God who saw fit to rescue me on the streets of the inner city." Making stories like this happen was why Spencer and I had teamed up at the Study Center.

As Winterim ended I noted the ease with which Spencer had moved from an all-black job world to take on the endless stream of questions from curious and naïve white people, questions like "How do black women do their hair?" He was a patient teacher; he had a gift for this work, and his transition amounted to a monumental reinvention of himself at age thirty-four. My respect for Spencer was even greater than before.

In February we had to choose someone to do some graphic design and photography for "The Lamppost," and Spencer insisted on having Mr. Harvey do it. "C'mon, man," I argued, "that doesn't make sense. Johnny's gonna mess it up."

Tall and lanky, around sixty, always adorned in a loud tie and maroon beret over a shiny bald head with a fluffy gray beard, Johnny Harvey worked out of a small studio on Capitol Street near a graveyard and a fast-food fried-chicken place. On Saturdays I'd often see him, in his beret, barbecuing in the small potholed parking lot next to his burglar-barred studio. When I had been development director he was always calling for business.

"Come on, bruthah, I know you got some work for me," the familiar smooth voice would begin as I picked up the phone. "Business cards? Some staff photos? You gotta be puttin' out a newsletter by now, bruthah."

But I held Mr. Harvey off. There were graphic artists and photographers who were quick, professional, and reasonably priced. And then there was Mr. Harvey: once a stellar performer, he was slow, unreliable, and a bit ornery, plus he had a growing case of Parkinson's. A photographer with shaky hands? Johnny Harvey was too much pain and no gain.

But Spencer and Mr. Harvey went way back. Spencer loved Johnny and always took his calls. I'd hear Spencer chuckling, fussing, going on with Mr. Harvey about city gossip, politics, and white folks. "Now, Johnny, you know that wasn't whi'folks' fault!" he'd say, hooting with laughter.

If it hadn't been for Spencer, I would have written off Mr. Harvey, as well as most of the old Battery Clinic gang who were regular office visitors.

Donna's and my car (my hoopty was long gone) had a problem in February, and against my better judgment, I took Spencer's advice and gave the job to an old buddy of Spencer's from Mendenhall. He fixed the problem and then, I learned later, made the longest test drive in history by taking my car to Mendenhall for the weekend. When Spencer and I finally found it, the back seat was littered with beer cans.

After that it grated on me to no end that Spencer still sent work to his friend. Between him, Jacquiline, and Mr. Harvey, I marveled at how Spencer navigated between the worlds of race and class. Whether it was a Waspy white know-it-all or an ornery bruthah, Spencer seemed to find the goodness in any outlaw.

# 17

# LEM'S TRUTH

*W*hile Spencer and I stoked the Study Center fires, Lem was
being catapulted onto a national stage, courtesy of JP.
When JP had first moved to Pasadena, he had started a national organization called the Foundation for Reconciliation and Development.
The Foundation was JP's vehicle for spreading the spirituality of the three
Rs to the United States and the world. JP had an enormous following
among hundreds of Christian activists nationwide who based their work
on his teachings and whose inner-city efforts were beehives of social transformation completely absent from the media radar screen.

But these leaders and their churches and organizations were mostly
unknown to each other, and for about a year now JP and his Foundation
board had been laying the groundwork for a national association to unite
them. Lem had participated in these discussions, as had Spencer and I at
various times. We were rooting for the idea: An association could weave
the tender isolated strands into a focused, formidable movement, lever-
aging far more influence on behalf of the nation's poor.

In February thirty urban developers met in Chicago to discuss the idea
of forming the Christian Community Development Association, which
came to be known as CCDA.

Lem was chosen to moderate the dialogue about forming the association, and he did a masterful job. I was like the younger brother who
couldn't stand his sibling at home but swells with pride watching him
become the hero of the big football game. The participants enthusiastically voted to start an association.

There was no doubt that JP would be CCDA's chairman, and now Lem
was poised to work by his side as its president. If JP was the movement's
Moses, Lem had become its Joshua, positioned to shepherd it beyond JP's
lifetime. This promised to extend Lem's influence, make Jackson CCDA's
home base, multiply Voice of Calvary's national influence, and propel our

Study Center forward as training arm for the entire movement. Spencer and I were pumped.

Back in Jackson, though, Lem and I continued to butt heads. I was still pushing for Spencer to be director and for more freedom from Lem's control. Between tense meetings Lem and I had exchanged a series of argumentative memos.

In early March we had a long and especially difficult meeting in Lem's office. I sensed that Lem was losing patience with me. It seemed like we'd been in an unending two-year argument, with no resolution in sight.

Late that night I sat in my upstairs bedroom with Donna at the Big House, trying to recover. "I feel so demoralized and drained, Donna. I'd probably be fired by now at most places, for the stuff I've said to Lem."

"Yeah. It's hard to imagine those days when you and I were so close to him."

Suddenly Harold's voice cracked over the monitor. "Chris, Lem's here to see you."

My face dropped. "Oh, great. Donna, am I in, like, very big trouble?" She looked concerned.

I plodded downstairs. Lem was in the living room.

"Sorry to drop in unannounced, Chris," he said. "Can we speak somewhere, just the two of us?" *Gulp.*

"Uh, sure. Come on upstairs."

I ushered Lem into our room. Donna gave a quick greeting and left. Lem took a seat on the couch. I sat on the bed. *Here it comes,* I thought.

Lem was quiet for a few seconds. Then he spoke. "Chris, I just came to make sure everything is OK between us. I don't have all the answers. But our relationship is important to me, and I want you to know that."

His words pierced the edgy atmosphere between us. I let them sink in during several more seconds of silence.

"You've taught me a lot over the years, Lem. You gave me my first shot at real leadership, you know." He smiled.

"I guess sometimes we just live putting one foot in front of the other, don't we, Lem? Walking with the light we have? Hoping we're doing what's right?"

He nodded. "Hanging on to each other even when we disagree—I think that's at the heart of reconciliation, Chris. I've lost track of the number of arguments I've had over all my years here. But somehow we keep on keeping on."

We talked for a few more minutes and reaffirmed our friendship and commitment to one another. I walked him downstairs to the front door, and we embraced.

"Good night, brother," said Lem.

"Good night."

Later I thought how Lem probably had several intense disagreements every week that left him alienated from someone. I remembered Lawrence telling me how he and Lem had had it out at the office once, how Lem showed up that night at his house with a peace offering—a gallon of ice cream. I thought of the months after Lem made me acting development director. They were fond memories, days of drawing close and Lem opening up to me. I thought of the proverb he shared with me then: "He who has the greatest truth must have the greatest love, which is the greatest proof."

*Tonight, Lem, you had the greater love. And maybe you always have.*

A few days after our talk Lem went in to see a doctor about abdominal pain and was immediately hospitalized. The diagnosis was frightening: Lem's insides were being eaten up by a ravenous cancer called American Burkitt Lymphoma. He began a massive course of chemotherapy.

The news numbed me. The entire Voice of Calvary family was distraught and bewildered. Lem had been as energetic as ever, striding through the parking lot, working long hours. Suddenly he was fighting for his life.

The church scrambled to support his wife, Ellie. All-night prayer vigils were held at the church and at the hospital. We begged God to heal Lem.

He began to bounce back. Some proclaimed that a miracle was happening in our midst. But then Lem's condition worsened. Family members flew in as the church gathered to pray again. Lem swung back, then he declined again.

Hospital rules allowed very few visitors to his room. But in April Spencer joined the church elders to lay their hands on Lem and pray over him. I asked Spencer about the visit.

"Physically, Chris? Lem doesn't look good. He's puffed up, man. I barely recognized him, it's that bad. But there's this aura about him. He said he sensed God's hand clasping his hand. He said, 'I can't let go, and God won't let go.'"

It was difficult to stay focused, worrying about Lem. At least now I knew how much I cared about him. Maybe this crisis would melt our hearts in the right places, clear the air, and give Lem and me a fresh start. I prayed that such a day would come. I longed to hear his nasal voice again, beckoning me into his office.

✣

As our Voice of Calvary family drew tightly together, Lem was getting worse. In May he was transported to a cancer center in Richmond, Virginia, to receive more advanced treatment and to be closer to family.

We were told that Lem, with a great presence of peace, was reciting Psalm 23 to those around him: "Yea, though I walk through the valley of the shadow of death, I will fear no evil. For thou art with me, Thy rod and thy staff they comfort me." In June he fell into a coma.

I never saw Lem again after he entered the hospital in March.

He died on June 16, 1989, at age thirty-seven.

Spencer, Nancy, Donna, and I drove fifteen hours straight through the night to the funeral in Virginia. It hardly mattered that I'd had three months to prepare for this moment. I shook with sobs as I watched Lem's body laid into the ground in a driving rain.

Some jumped to easy answers. "Lem's work was finished, and the Lord called him home." If so, why? Lem was on the precipice of a major new national role. His influence was only beginning.

Did this have to do with a particular kind of life? I knew of other reconciliation leaders in our circles, dying at the height of their careers.

A man named Ron Behm, who coauthored a groundbreaking book called *Your God Is Too White*, had been shot to death by his adopted son. Thom Hopler, another evangelical racial pioneer and author of an influential book titled *A World of Difference*, had died at age forty-two of a sudden heart attack while he was jogging. There were other stories since the 1970s of emotional, physical, and family breakdown among former civil rights activists.

Who could measure the internal toll of pressure and stress of idealism meeting reality? Was there an insidious, invisible dimension of evil in confronting race? Was fighting racial and social division on the frontlines a hazardous occupation, the psychological and spiritual equivalent of waging war? Had Lem just taken on too much caring, too much responsibility for the world, with too little rest—too much trying harder and doing more?

"What sense does it make? Death?" Herb Myers said to me. He was the head doctor at our health center. He mentioned Betty Anne, an elderly white lady with long greasy hair who inched around our neighborhood on crutches. "She's going on seventy, she's overweight, she's severely diabetic. But Betty Anne's still living. Lem was young. He was sturdy and energetic. And Lem is gone."

Either death was completely arbitrary, or it was a great mystery. Lem's was the first early death of someone close to me, and those are the departures that awaken questions without answers.

All our feuds seemed petty now compared to what I had drawn from Lem's strength and his confidence in me. There were many good reasons, I remembered, that I had asked this man to stand by my side on the most joyous day of my life, when I pledged my life to Donna.

In his proverb Lem left me something to live by. I considered it a great gift that our last significant moment together was that night that he came to make peace with me. I disappointed him, and yet he pursued me.

My lasting memory of him, overwhelming all the others, was of Lem, giver of undeserved gifts.

# *Antioch Family Album*

Perkins family in Mendenhall, Mississippi. Spencer (left), Joanie (next to him), Derek (far right), 1964.

Dad (right) in Hattisburg, Mississippi, for Freedom Summer, 1964.

Chris (with gun), siblings, and Mom with Korean
family friends. Seoul, South Korea, 1967.

Rice family in the mission field in Seoul, South Korea.
Check out Mom's hair! I'm the boy next to her, 1970.

A clipping showing Randy Rice and other missionaries, with nooses around their necks, in a hooded human rights protest. Seoul, South Korea, 1975.

John and Vera Mae Perkins in front of the Mendenhall Bible Church, Mendenhall, Mississippi, 1977. Far right: Spencer. Third from right: Volunteer Phil Reed, who became the Voice of Calvary Church pastor in Jackson two years later.

Voice of Calvary gospel choir in 1979. Many of the people were embroiled in the church's racial crisis in 1983. Second row from the bottom: Gloria (second from right), Donna (third from right); second row from the top: Arthur Phillips, pianist (far left), Lem Tucker (third from left), Derek Perkins (fourth from left).

The Good News Club with Chris and Tressa as leaders, 1981.

Spencer on his Suzuki, wearing a smile that was unfamiliar to me at the time, 1981.

Spencer and Nancy's wedding. Third from left, Joanie; fourth from left, Nancy's sister Dorcas. Next to Spencer are brothers Phillip, Wayne, and Derek, June 1983.

Chris and his rusty Peugeot "hoopty," 1983

Voice of Calvary Church members in front of the Fellowship House, 1986.

Neighborhood houses newly renovated by the Ministries, 1987.

Gloria and Tressa outside the Big House not long after we purchased it, during the heady days when dumpsters seemed like wheelbarrows, 1987.

Lem and Ellie Tucker at Chris's wedding th'ow down, 1987.

Chris and Donna's wedding. From left: Chris's sister Liz, Tressa, Phil Eide, Lem Tucker, Donna's brother Mark, April 1987.

Spencer and baby
Benjamin Rice, 1992.

Cover of the first issue of
*Urban Family* magazine,
Winter 1992.

The Big House on
Robinson Street, 1993.

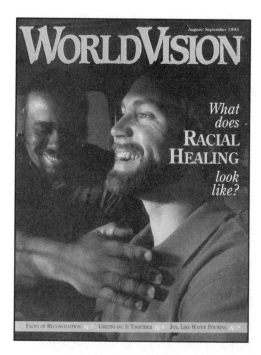

Spencer and Chris on the cover of *World Vision* magazine, 1993.

Spencer and Chris speaking at "Healing the Heart of America" conference, Richmond, Virginia, June 1993. (Photo by Robert Lancaster)

"It's weird here. But it's a good kinda weird." Chris's first white Mississippi friend, Cecil McKinley, 1993.

John (in his famous tie-dyed T-shirt) and Judy Alexander during their first visit to Mississippi, on an Antioch hike with Nancy and baby April, 1993.

*Urban Family* magazine staff. Back row: Chris, Nancy, Spencer. Middle: Christy Haas, Helen Wambari, Elisha Risser, Jennifer Parker. Front: Vera Mae and John Perkins, 1994.

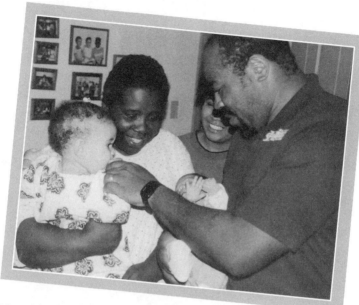

Adopted daughter Talia's Antioch homecoming.
From left, Gloria (holding April Joy Perkins), Jennifer
Parker, and Spencer (holding Talia), 1994.

Donna holding daughter Talia, Joanie with daughter Varah, and Lue holding
newborn Christopher Rice, 1995.

Antioch's expanding urban campus. From right to left: the Duplex, the Office, the Small House, with the Big House on the hill to the left, 1995.

Spencer and Phil Reed preparing a th'ow down on the famous Antioch hot water tank– barbeque grill, 1996.

Spencer hauling Antioch kids and friends on a yard-cleaning day, 1996.

JP in a classic, energetic
pose, 1997.

Antioch community in front of the Big House. Back row: Christopher, Chris, Jason Dewey, Donna, Gloria, Nancy, Spencer, and April. Front row: Benjamin, Johnathan, Jubilee, Lue, Talia, Jon, Joanie, Varah, Ron, 1997.

The Antioch family and friends around the dinner slab, 1997.

"Yokefellows Against the Odds" conference, 1997.

Spencer and Chris giving the closing message at the "College, Ethnicity, and Reconciliation" conference in Jackson. Spencer had collapsed that morning and sat on a stool to save strength. This turned out to be our final time speaking together, 1998.

Chris, Donna, Benjamin, Talia, and Christopher on sabbatical in Oregon, November 1998.

Nancy, Johnathan, April Joy, and Jubilee Perkins, 2001.

# 18

# RELUCTANT PROPHET

$\mathcal{B}$y July, two weeks after Lem's funeral, Spencer and I were spending many hours discussing what should be done.

We feared the Ministries' board of directors might hire a new president from outside our ranks. Our leaders had invariably been home-grown, and Spencer and I saw that as vital to our mission. But we didn't think the management team was acting decisively enough to make sure an insider took Lem's place. We brashly decided to set things right, and I began drafting a proposal from the two of us.

Our first summer internship with five college students was in full swing. I was ecstatic that one of them was my own baby sister, Liz, who had graduated from Middlebury and come to work with Spencer and me for an entire year. On the Fourth of July holiday—simply "the Fohf" in neighborhood vernacular—we had a big crowd over to Antioch for a th'ow down, including Liz and the interns.

Spencer contended with the communal grill underneath the pine trees, flipping chicken leg and thigh pieces, slapping sauce on, barking orders to Kortney and Johnathan. He considered them, at ages five and four, capable of toting utensils and plates of meat back and forth from the Big House. Peals of laughter rang out as barefoot kids ripped across the grass. Antioch was always loud, and holidays were louder. Gloria was inside, doctoring canned baked beans with her secret recipe. "These are the best beans I've ever had," raved a white volunteer as we ate. Gloria nodded her head and broke a sly grin. "If those white folks only knew how much brown sugar and bacon grease I packed in those beans," she said later.

The Fourth's climax, as always, was ice-cold watermelon, cut in thick three- to six-inch slabs, consumed not like an hors d'oeuvre but a second meal. Immediately the judging began as to how sweet it was.

But something was stewing inside of me the entire day. After seven months of sharing an office with Spencer, his hours-long absences during the work day were troubling me. At first I gave him the benefit of the doubt. I thought, *he's probably working on an article. Or he's in a meeting somewhere.*

But the absences became more frequent. He rarely bothered to tell me he was leaving or where he was going. Other staff at the Ministries would call or come looking for him, and I didn't know where he was.

Adding to my frustration was Spencer's failure to initiate and stir things up around the Ministries. This puzzled me. He was so good at spurring growth at Antioch. But he had a lot of homebody in him. He mostly stuck to our little office at the Ministries and spent hours just fiddling around at his desk and allowing himself to be easily interrupted.

Beginning in the spring, however, one urgent affair did get his attention: fishing reports. Arthur Phillips, the church pianist who owned his own plumbing business, dropped in every other week or so, just back from a bluegill expedition. He plopped into Spencer's office, and they would burn up a good half hour swapping their latest fishing stories.

"Spawn-se, I sweah, man, that bass that got away was a six-pounder," Arthur would drawl. "But I got a good twenty-five bluegill out in the cooler. They're big slabs, man. They all 'bout a hand and a half wide. I'm gonna fry those babies up too-night!"

*For heaven's sake,* I thought, *doesn't Spencer realize he's burning up work hours?*

It occurred to me that maybe some of Spencer's absences had something to do with brimming bluegill beds. It also irritated me that Spencer didn't keep an organizer or a date book. "Oh, we got a meeting in ten minutes? Uh, let's see, OK, let me pull somethin' together." Spencer had once told me something he learned during his Thriftco fiasco: "I ain't no great administrator." Was I seeing a snapshot of what Lem knew and I didn't, when I had argued that Spencer was the best athlete in the draft and Lem just stared back at me blankly?

My respect for Spencer's gifts was unwavering. But this irresponsibility was too much. In the days before and after the Fourth he left the office three times. The first was after I confronted him about blaming others for what wasn't happening at the Ministries. I said he ought to be initiating some leadership himself. The next day he left for several hours in the afternoon without bothering to tell Liz or me. Later he called and said he didn't feel well.

Meanwhile I was putting in long hours. It was becoming very difficult for me to see the management team proposal I was writing as ours. It felt like mine.

❖

A couple of days after the Fourth I did something I'd never done before: I confronted Spencer in a blunt letter. I detailed his recent absences, and I told him I was discouraged and embarrassed.

"I know you're struggling to find your niche," I wrote. "You feel you have a legacy to live up to. You know that 'to whom much is given, much is required.' You know you have a gift for leadership, but you feel uncomfortable in public situations. You're shy toward new people. You don't like speaking to an audience. You're not comfortable promoting yourself."

Many of these qualities endeared me to Spencer. There was a humility about him. But I told him I was concerned about his attitude toward his struggles.

"It seems like when you're not feeling motivated by a situation that you just withdraw, retreat, and rationalize your inaction," I said.

I listed his tremendous gifts and the amazing opportunities I saw opening to him. A book publisher had been impressed with his article, "The Pro-Life Credibility Gap," and had approached him about writing a book on racial reconciliation. "Someone needs to speak up for reconciliation in the American church, and you can fill that need. You understand more than anyone what this ministry is all about and what sacrifices are required. You have a prophetic gift for understanding Scripture and articulating it to others. When you talk, people listen."

But I told him I felt like he just sat back and waited for others to push him. I got right into his face, challenging him.

> If you're not willing to put forth more effort and discipline, I don't think you're ready for more responsibility. You'd be setting yourself up for failure. No one's holding you back anymore, now that Lem is gone.
>
> I have a burning desire for the Study Center to make a difference. But I'm like you, Spencer. I'm not motivated to go places on my own. I need to have others on the journey with me for support and motivation. I need to know that you're giving everything you have to the task, because that will help me do the same.
>
> All that holds us back is ourselves. Are you ready? I am! I think you should take this writing thing and pursue it full-speed. I think we should sit down and figure out what you're gong to produce in the book, "The Lamppost," magazine articles. There's a tremendous contribution you can make where you are.

I closed with a plea and a reminder. "If I've made any hasty judgments, forgive me. But I don't want to be untruthful about what I see either. I love you and am committed to you."

My words were pure and unselfish, I was sure. I really did want what was best, both for our mission and for Spencer. I saw a reluctant prophet before me, and I held nothing back to drive him out of complacency, even if it meant him rising higher than me.

The next day I put the letter on Spencer's desk, mumbled a prayer and anxiously awaited his response.

In the afternoon there was a note on my desk. My hands trembled as I opened it and read Spencer's scribbled handwriting.

> Chris, thank you for caring about me. I appreciate you very much. I agree with what you said in the letter. I know I have some weaknesses to overcome. I don't understand all the reasons I do what I do.
>
> But there are no "buts." Maybe we can talk about it sometime but not now. Don't worry, though. I'll come through. It's great to feel secure in the fact that the reason you bother is because you love me. Believe me, that alone is a lot of motivation.
>
> I love you too! The worst part about this whole mess is hurting and disappointing the people I love and that love me. Please don't worry. Your caring helps me put things in a clearer light. Spencer.

I knew black people who could hardly take such criticism without throwing the race card, who would have shot back with, "Listen, Chris, this is a black thing. I knew you wouldn't understand." But Spencer received my words as the words of a friend.

His response reenergized me. I finished the proposal to the management team, and Spencer touched it up, "making it sing," as he liked to say.

Our ideas about picking a three-person team of leaders, with one of them first among equals, sparked a crisis within the management team. The looks on their faces said, Who do Chris and Spencer think they are, stepping in like they got the inside scoop from almighty God?

As intense debates began Spencer left town for a few days. I hardly slept at night. My head throbbed during the day. I took long walks to hold myself together. Donna felt helpless; she wasn't directly involved in the discussions. Once Spencer returned I was like a tag-team wrestler, stretching out my hand in exhaustion, sending my teammate into the fray. "You go get 'em, Spence." And he did. I saw how much I needed him.

Over the next few weeks cards got put on the table, egos and motives were sifted, and positions gradually softened, including Spencer's and mine. The determination to survive Lem's death as an intact family won out for all of us.

Everybody agreed Lawrence was the one to take the helm of the Ministries. He had matured immensely over the last year, and we worked out a plan to surround him with a strong team. At church the next Sunday unity seemed to fill the air, electrifying the claps, singing, and faces of the entire congregation.

Relationships between leaders, I saw, had enormous ripple effects for ill or for good. It was certainly true about Spencer and me. We had survived our first big confrontation with flying colors. At least it seemed that way.

# 19

# "FROM CAIN'T TO CAIN'T"

While peace reigned at the Fellowship House divorce hit the Big House again in August 1989. A letter from Betsy in Donna's and my box confirmed what others at Antioch had already told me.

Part of me was relieved when I read that Betsy felt her medical problems were one reason she and Harold were leaving. Helping her get better often felt like trying to fill a bottomless hole. In spite of countless discussions, Antioch fell short of being the kind of support group Betsy needed. We lacked the patience and vision for letting one person's needs take up so much energy. But as I read about their other reasons, familiar, excruciating emotions clawed their way into my heart.

Betsy said Antioch wasn't moving toward its goal of reconciliation. "I see, and feel, the painful scars of many twisted conversations and events in which I have manipulated or been manipulated."

*That's way off, Betsy, like you were living in a Jim Jones cult or something.*

"At first I thought we needed to just try harder. But I believe this pattern of manipulation goes to the core of our relationships and that we need some distance before we can begin to work on them again."

*Manipulation? Is she living with the same people I am? Puh-lease.* The next part really lit my fuse.

"Harold and I have searched the Scriptures," Betsy wrote, "and we do not see a pattern or call to community in the early church."

*Y'all can't just admit you're not cut out for this, can you? No, you have to question community itself, slap a spiritual veneer on your lack of commitment, declare yourselves clean, and diss Antioch. Is changing your convictions this easy for you? This is nothing more than adjusting the Sermon to justify yourselves. And if you really cared for us, why didn't you give us a chance to hear your concerns before you decided to leave?*

The familiar cycle of hardening hearts was already under way. But over the following days it all moved much faster.

My emotional system shut down into callousness. I became defensive about Antioch's rightness and moved on to wondering how we could survive, feeling betrayed, and squelching my genuine deep affections for them and for little Catrice. *Fine. Go. We don't need you.*

Two weeks after I received Betsy's letter their front room off the main hallway was empty. Like Phil and Tressa, they kept their names on the house note and didn't demand any money back. But Antioch had lost two major incomes, and Joanie was entering law school in just a couple of weeks. Antioch supported Joanie's decision wholeheartedly, and with her keen analytical mind and outspoken personality, we knew she was going to be a great lawyer bringing a good income into our community. But it was a long-term investment. With Gloria doing child care, Antioch was down to four salaries.

Harold and Betsy moved into a house in the neighborhood. I never visited them. They continued worshiping at the church. I avoided them. Just as they had their reasons to justify their departure, I had my reasons to justify squeezing my heart shut.

After three years, with more ex-members than members now, the six of us who remained were well trained in closing ranks, brashly holding onto our vision, ignoring the odds, and marching forward. It still never would have occurred to us to ask if there was any weakness in the way we handled those who left, or whether we needed to examine anything inside of Antioch.

Just because our core members had dwindled didn't mean our ministry had to. Spencer had predicted that when Antioch's tree was strong enough, the birds would come. If only they were all adorable, self-sufficient chickadees. But stretching way back, we had always believed that "good news for the poor" meant making the vulturous "Joyces" of the world truly part of us. Nobody stretched that challenge to its limits more than JJ, Mr. Unimpossible.

JJ had declined a long way from once being Lem's poster boy for "Harvard minds with ghetto opportunities." Between our early days on Valley Street and now, there were years of his trash talk, controversies, and charades, and then his burglaries at the Ministries and break-ins at the homes of church members. Then the forgery had started. That was what landed JJ in prison at age twenty-three. He'd served four years by now.

With JJ's release imminent, Spencer had a plan. Spencer, who never lost hope for anyone's redemption, proposed that JJ come to live with us. I couldn't believe my ears. My old nemesis? A con man who had stolen everything from Ministries' computers to Spencer's cologne and once, nearly, Joanie's entire living room living in our house? I was unimpossibly unexcited.

But I already knew what Antioch would decide. This was JJ. He could be the biggest pain in the neck, but he was still family. Plus, there was Harold and Betsy's empty room to fill. Plus, Spencer said JJ would never do anything really crazy, like do anyone physical harm. Plus, there was living the Sermon, and you never took a break from that. And on and on and on. Living together made the unimpossible possible.

Antioch never made a big move without everybody agreeing. We did, and JJ moved directly from prison into the Big House for the first few weeks after his release, time enough to find a job and get on his feet.

His room soon became an obstacle course of smelly clothes and dirty dinner plates. Then JJ came to me with a request. "Hey, Chris, bruthah, could I borrow your car tonight, man?"

I knew it was coming, but I hadn't manufactured a good excuse. That night I nervously handed my keys to JJ, wondering whether our Chevy Nova was departing for that great car heap in the sky.

The car got home, intact and on time. It did occur to me that there might be a duplicate key in JJ's pocket now. But even though he stirred up more than his share of conflict, JJ genuinely seemed to be pulling his life together. When he departed Antioch after a few weeks, on good terms, the only mess he left behind was a moldy, half-eaten pie under his bed.

Maybe Spencer was right. Maybe there really was a gem inside every rough stone. And I had seen JJ's orneriness unearth depths of patience and loyalty within Spencer that sometimes made me wonder if Spencer's heart was part-Labrador retriever.

Meanwhile, other signs of fresh growth were in the air.

The board had approved Lawrence's appointment to president of the Ministries, and during our staff trip to CCDA's kickoff conference in Chicago, Spencer and I met with an editor from InterVarsity Press, the publisher that had approached Spencer about writing a book on racial reconciliation. Spencer thought the two of us writing would be much more powerful, weaving our black and white perspectives, and the editor agreed. Now a deal looked promising that could elevate our work to a whole new level.

During the staff's packed van ride back to Jackson I announced to claps and cheers that I was going to join the church choir for the first time. I had no idea what a precious gift this experience would bring to my life.

The next Thursday night I sat in the church sanctuary, happy to be beside Lawrence in the tenor section. But even for me, an eight-year veteran of clapping on two and four, what followed was an outright hazing.

When everyone was finally assembled, I thought, *Where's the music?* I was looking for a sheet with notes on it or something in a book.

Soon "the song" was passed out. But this was not music as I knew it. It was just hand-scribbled words, on paper still warm from the copy machine. And it was only a temporary crutch for newcomers who didn't know the words, for gospel music is not read, it is proclaimed, and since singing it is a full-bodied experience, we were going to need both hands to sing.

This exuberant singing, I discovered, did not begin in the mouth but from deep within, in some mysterious place white people like me seemed to have trouble locating. Soon I was gasping for breath. But there was a long way to go yet, because we were not only supposed to clap while we sang, but to perform "the rock"—swaying from side to side, in sync. ("Move your feet, man, move your feet" was one bruthah's advice.) And only one variety of rock, of course, would be uninteresting, so there were several. But how did I know which rock and when to begin the darn thing, not that it mattered? "Keep your eye on Shirlene, man," said the bruthah, pointing to Arthur's wife in the soprano section. "She starts the rock."

At least I could blend in with Lawrence's rich, resounding voice. My confidence was building as we headed into the second stanza. I felt good about my progress.

Then things really fell apart.

Lawrence went solo, and the words he was singing were not on the sheet! A four-alarm bell went off in my well-categorized head. No song books, no music, and now words that aren't even on the sheet? Absent from the author's original writings? OK, maybe black folks call this improvising. But in the white community we call it a copyright violation. The ambiguity was killing me.

"So, Arthur," I asked, "will the song end with Lawrence's solo?" Arthur thought for a second. "More than likely," he finally answered. He was also fond of saying, "If the Spirit leads." Translation: If you don't want to make a fool of yourself, watch Arthur, because only he and almighty God know where this thing is headed.

After my throat moved from intensive care to recovery three days later, I had my big Sunday morning debut. As Arthur played soft prelude music, I shuffled nervously up front with the other choir members and took my spot.

Arthur began to play a song that I swore we hadn't practiced on Thursday night. I was right. What was practiced, it seemed, did not limit "the Spirit." I tried to mumble my way through the words without attracting attention. But I got off beat with the rock, and I began to bump into the two people next to me. A couple of black altos in front of me did not politely ignore my mistake. Several heads and eyes turned. Some seemed to say, You look kinda funny, Chris. Others burned right through me. I finally understood why many pale-faced newcomers swore their skin turned two shades lighter after their first choir song.

But my bumbling was a minor sideshow. When Lawrence went solo he got caught up in the song. Arthur let him go; the practice sheet went out the window; the song went on and on; and in spite of all that had gone wrong for me, I felt an exhilaration I had never experienced before. I couldn't believe I had missed out on this all these years. Singing in the choir every week brought a new dimension of joy to my life, an outlet for pouring out the highs and exorcising the lows that built up within me.

The jolt of freshness I got from being in the choir spilled over into my work at the Ministries with Spencer. In early November we went to Georgia with Lawrence and Phil Reed to lead a conference for the staff of Habitat for Humanity, a national organization that built affordable housing.

Spencer shone during our reconciliation talk. He spoke of his recent trip to South Africa with his parents and Nancy, of the horrors of apartheid and his intense stomach pains the entire four weeks. He told of attending a worship service with six thousand people in an all-white area of Johannesburg, of whites lifting their hands in praise and claiming God as the answer to South Africa's problems. His voice rose with indignation.

"We wouldn't spend ten seconds defendin' a type of Christianity that's been known to oppress people of color around the world! Only hours before, we saw the brutal poverty of an all-black township. And if that was the God they were worshipin', there was no way I could worship that same God.

"Eighty percent of white South Africans claim to be born-again Christians," he said. "As a black person, I have to be glad that we don't have that many white Christians over here." The audience laughed appreciatively.

*I have to hand it to you, bruthah,* I thought. *You got a gift. And I'm proud to see how you bounced back from our confrontation four months ago.*

Only our marriages trumped the relentless daily intimacy that Spencer and I were putting in service of our ideals. As old black folks working cotton fields used to say, we were often together "from cain't to cain't"—from "can't see in the morning because it's too early" until "can't see at night because it's too late." In between before-sunrise Bible studies and late-night meetings, our lives were nearly completely synchronized. Mornings and evenings I knew the sound of Spencer coming down the upstairs hallway by the creak that only his weight made in a soft spot on the floor outside my room.

We shared an office and the nightly dinner slab. Spencer claimed the seat at the end near the living room, and habit-driven homebody that he was, he never left that spot.

I gave his articles order and coherence; he made mine sing. We could finish each other's sentences. By the time we went into a meeting with a hot topic on the agenda, we had already hashed it through and come to one mind. Our strong opinions could get either of us quickly volatile. But usually it didn't happen at the same time, making for an effective "good cop, bad cop" routine.

With only me in charge, we would have been an efficient machine without much soul. With only Spencer in charge, we would have had great heart, but would have lacked the muscle and drive to expand and subdue. My gifts gave our partnership width. His gave us depth.

I was about always improving, never being complacent, staying doggedly focused to see a project through. He counted on me to initiate and design a program and to push him. I counted on him to jump on bad attitudes in a meeting and to speak the truths nobody else dared to touch.

We were having a good time, and he was even beginning to pull me into his "no worries" orbit. At his favorite pond we tugged on cheap cigars as he taught me the secrets of fishing Mississippi waters—different tactics for bluegill, catfish, and bass. "Bass are predators," he would whisper. "You gotta keep the bait movin' to get one. Look for 'em by the banks, around the weeds. Look, see that swirl? He's goin' after my line, Chris. Ou, I got a hit!" When Arthur stopped by with a cooler full of fish, I wasn't so uptight anymore. And talk about miracles. Spencer was toting a leather organizer around, dutifully jotting down to-do lists.

In my first big "Lamppost" article that fall of 1989, I wrote about the journey of whites in the black community. Through intense conversations Spencer helped me hone my ideas, processing my journey from know-it-all "solution," to the painful learning of the Reconciliation Meetings, to the ultimate goal of what I described as blacks and whites "putting our lives into the same boat."

I wanted to give each of these stages memorable names. I called the first one being caseworkers, the second becoming converts, and I scoured the Scriptures to find a compelling metaphor for the final stage of complete mutuality.

A verse in Paul's Letter to the Philippians grabbed my imagination: "Indeed, true comrade, I ask you also to help these women who have shared my struggle in the cause of the gospel."

Comrades. Yes, this was what we were shooting for. Like Paul and his loyal comrade, to shed blood, sweat, and tears together across the most intimate barriers of race. To become a corporate witness that counters the lie that races cannot live together in peace. Comrades. The word was good. It gave me three Cs. Yet it didn't move me.

But another word, a different translation of the Greek, nearly brought me to tears. And it summed up all that Spencer meant to me and I to him.

The two of us had come to find each other indispensable. An existential urgency was driving us toward a truth and a message that we were determined to bring to a wider national circle: Neither black nor white could ever reach their fullness as people in alienation and separation.

The word was *yokefellows*. It was what Spencer and I had become. And if we could become yoked together, in spite of all our inadequacies, even in spite of Antioch's ups and downs and all the forces that had sought to break Voice of Calvary apart or from ever coming together in the first place, then there was hope that black and white in the nation could too.

# 20

# BLIND CURVES

On the bone-chilling Tuesday that followed New Year's Day, 1990, my sister Liz and I drove over to the vacant Study Center building to get it ready for our annual Winterim boot camp.

The rambling two-story house that first assaulted me with neighborhood life hadn't been used for over a month. While I unloaded cleaning supplies, Liz unlocked the door and went in.

She backed out quickly, like she was scared. "Chris, somebody's in there."

I cautiously entered the kitchen and felt a blast of suffocating heat. Gas heaters hissed on full blast from surrounding rooms. On the stove three burners were blazing, and a can of baked beans was bubbling on the fourth. Strung across the kitchen cabinets were drying clothes.

"Who's in here?" I yelled. After a moment of silence a defiant, muffled male voice shot back.

"Who wants to know?" The voice came from down the hallway, from inside the bathroom.

I deepened my voice to add authority. "Who are you?"

"Who are you?" the ornery voice shot back, as if to say, "You got a warrant?"

"I'm the owner," I said. Not exactly, but he'd get the point. "You need to leave."

The voice shot back again, with stunning creativity. "This is a study center ain't it? I'm studyin'!" I glanced in the living room. To my surprise, *The Autobiography of Malcolm X* and other books sat open on a desk.

I tried again. "I'm telling you, you need to leave—now!"

But this guy was good. "Are you black or white?" he demanded. When in doubt, throw the race card.

"My race doesn't matter! You need to leave!"

Now he was insulted. "I'm using the bathroom!" he yelled, as if to say, "Can't a guy take a poop in peace around here?"

"Well, I'm calling the police," I said. Thirty minutes later, Liz and I watched two officers escort a short, heavily bearded black man out of the building. He held his head high like a protester, persecuted for righteousness' sake. A homeless break-in artist was the Study Center's first student of 1990. It just went to prove that you never knew what was coming around the bend at Voice of Calvary. I could never quite get comfortable.

A week later Winterim doubled in size to almost forty students, promising explosive growth for the Study Center. But after four trouble-free months since Lawrence had taken the lead at the Ministries and Harold and Betsy had left Antioch, I already saw smoke.

For one thing, Spencer and I felt that Lawrence was gradually squeezing us out of policy decisions. He had recently hired a new development director, a rugged black activist from Detroit named Rufus Lilly. Lawrence didn't require Rufus to move into the neighborhood or join the church, and Rufus and I had already gotten into an argument over the three Rs. What put Rufus in the catbird seat and us in the doghouse so quickly?

There was trouble brewing in the church too, where three new energetic black couples were pushing for members to raise their hands during worship songs, come to long prayer meetings, and do more evangelistic outreach. All this, the Two-Hands-Up Gang (as I thought of them) insinuated, was a superior spirituality to the three Rs lifestyle.

What showed more trust in the Almighty—singing sugary praises to Jesus from suburban security or Marcia Reed crying out to God for peace and safety after being attacked in bed? What took more faith, not falling asleep during all-night prayer meetings, or blacks and whites enduring through the Reconciliation Meetings? What took greater love, telling a troubled soul "I'll pray for you, friend," or making them your next-door neighbor, or even taking them into your home? To Spencer and me, these were incompatible schools of thought.

To add to these troubles, a couple of sistahs in the church were taking Liz through a personal version of the most mean-spirited aspects of the Reconciliation Meetings, accusing her of outlandish things and hounding her about it. She called me over to her house one day in tears. As I held her, it was so hard to see her being put through this. At least her antagonists were the exception; Spencer had become her trusted guide into racial understanding, just as he was for me.

On top of all this, Donna and I had been trying to have a baby for almost a year. The "negative" pink dots month after month on the tiny, white-papered self-pregnancy tests, the infertility exams, Donna's teary nights—it all added an edge of despair to the atmosphere.

❖

Soon that rope that seemed to keep me constantly tethered to unpredictable "others" dragged me around another corner.

Since he had lived with us the previous fall, JJ had regularly stopped by our office and the Big House, mostly to see Spencer. He was working, he was excited, he was happy. But he was preying on volunteers like Liz too, getting under their skin just as he used to get under mine. JJ could never quite get his behavior onto the right side of the road. He drove his life into oncoming traffic instead, leaving screeches and bangs behind him all the way.

One day in late January JJ stumbled into our office like an escaped convict. He was dripping with stinky sewer water. Between gasping breaths, he said that two policemen came to his apartment to arrest him; he had just escaped through a drainage creek. He didn't know what the charge was, and he was in a panic.

Ever-faithful Spencer took JJ to the Big House, let him shower, got him some fresh clothes. Then he sat JJ down and shot straight: "You got to turn yourself in, man." Reluctantly, JJ agreed. An outstanding forgery charge had fallen through the cracks. JJ was jailed for violation of parole, and a court date was set for March.

When Spencer told me what happened, I blurted out, "What are we going to do, man?"

"We"? Did I just say that? Had even my stubborn heart been penetrated by a genuine affection for JJ, finally conquered by Spencer's dogged perseverance? Many young neighborhood bruthahs were destined to shuttle in and out of prison for the rest of their lives. Maybe we could snatch one friend from that grim destiny.

Spencer and I began crisscrossing the city through a gauntlet of parole officers, lawyers, and judges. They all seemed puzzled by this interracial twosome with no legal case, no political connections, only a wildly absurd request—to give this JJ outlaw mercy. Oh, and would you mind releasing him into the care of our household? We're rather fond of repeat offenders, you know.

❖

Getting JJ's life in order was, at best, a bleak possibility. At least I could channel my creative energy into the Study Center. By the end of February our first Christian Community Development workshop of 1990 was under way. The Fellowship House was packed with forty-eight people, our largest group ever.

Ivory did his black history–kung fu attack; and in the redistribution talk, JP (in from Pasadena again) pooh-poohed the cliché "Give a man a fish, and he'll eat for a day; teach him to fish, and he'll eat for a lifetime." "That's a bunch of junk!" he cried. "I wanna own the pond!"

A dozen joint performances had turned Spencer's and my tag-team reconciliation talk into a solid stump speech. By the time he stood up to speak, we both knew exactly where we were going.

But Spencer's mother, Vera Mae Perkins, had joined JP from Pasadena, and she stopped in to hear her son speak. We hadn't anticipated how Spencer or Mrs. Perkins would react.

I never called her Vera Mae. Calling her Mrs. Perkins was what she expected and deserved, having grown up witnessing the indignity of young whites addressing their black elders by first names. She and Spencer had tender places in their hearts for one another.

He was born during a painful time in her marriage to JP, a fifteen-month separation after he returned from the Korean War in 1953. "I made up my mind," I'd once heard her say. "I didn't need JP." When she came to California to settle up for the impending divorce, it was JP's first time seeing his child. "Spencer went right to him, like he knew who he was," she had said with a chuckle. "He even reached up and tugged at the unlit cigar in JP's mouth, like he was sayin', 'No daddy of mine is gonna smoke cigars.' That baby musta tugged at JP's heartstrings. Later he said that the minute he saw us, he knew more than anything that he wanted us to be a family." During JP's long absences during the civil rights struggles Mrs. Perkins was the anchor at home. Spencer's love for fishing also came from his mother.

She sat across the room now as Spencer began telling the story of sitting in the Brandon jail with her and watching his father walk in. Seeing the bloody shirttail. The bulging eyes. The chilling fear on JP's face.

Spencer's lips started to tremble. A swollen, solitary tear traced a line down his dark cheek. I'd never seen Spencer cry, not telling this story, not ever. I wondered if it was because his mother was here.

"Sorry, y'all," he muttered.

The soothing voice of a black woman answered. "That's all right, Spencer."

"Take your time," said another. *Pain is all right. Don't rush through it. Feel it. Tell it. Take your time with it. Your pain reminds us of our pain, and we must not squeeze it inside where it eats away. We must speak it.*

Someone passed a tissue up to Spencer. He dabbed his eyes. Mrs. Perkins stared at the floor. *This happened twenty years ago,* I thought.

Somehow Spencer limped to a finish. I was filled with emotion as I followed him at the podium and spoke of making commitments to racial reconciliation. I felt a profound admiration for my partner and his parents, for their sacrifice, for their perseverance, for the way they demonstrated how our struggle must be waged. I finished and sat down, and the room was quiet.

Slowly, Mrs. Perkins rose from her chair. Her eyebrows were scrunched together, and she seemed lost in thought. Her large dignified frame was commanding. She clasped her weathered hands above her waist, the hands that taught her son how to tie a fishing hook as they sat by the muddy bluegill beds of his boyhood. She was silent for a few seconds. Then, softly, she started to speak.

"Me and my brothers . . ." She grimaced suddenly, and closed her eyes, as if shutting out a painful image.

"Take your time," said the soothing voice again.

"Yes . . . me and my brothers . . . well, we used to get hauled up to the Mississippi Delta in the back of big trucks—like cattle," she said. "We'd pick cotton on the plantations owned by the white farmers. Every year we missed school in August and September. That way we'd have enough money to get clothes for the rest of the school year. The first thing we did when we got to the farm was clean out the dirty old shack where we slept."

She grimaced again. Two words had pierced me—"like cattle."

"Yes. We sho' did. Then we went out and picked enough cotton to fill a sack. That was our bed for the next two months."

Mrs. Perkins cocked her head slightly forward, pursed her lips, and widened her eyes, letting the story sink in. Then she narrowed her eyes and shook her head slowly. "But I'm not angry anymore."

She let silence speak, and in the silence I heard both a telling of the truth, and a releasing of it, and I heard that we must never let go of either the telling or the forgiving.

"After the second year at the white high school, Spencer and Joanie . . ."

She grimaced again, shutting her eyes. "Spencer and Joanie were the only black kids at that school by then. After a while, the bus stopped pickin' them up. I had to drive them up to that school every day. Every single day a crossing guard stopped the car and asked to see my license."

Again the narrowed eyes, the slow shake of her head. "But I'm not angry anymore." Silence.

"It got to be real hard . . . Yes, it did . . . Phone calls makin' threats. Men guardin' our house with shotguns. Every mornin' before I started up the car, one brave man checked under my hood for bombs.

"But I'm not angry anymore." Silence.

"When JP went up to Brandon to see after those volunteers, well, it got too late at night, and he still wasn't home. The phone rang. I picked it up, and a voice said, 'Have they hung 'em yet?'

"I said, 'Hung who? Who is this?' The next morning we set out for Brandon. I had no idea what I'd find there."

She grimaced and shook her head again. "But I'm not angry anymore."

She gazed intently around the room, letting the truths of telling and forgiving sink in. She sat down.

After a pause a white man rose up on the other side of the room. He was John Anderson, a native Mississippian who had just started attending our church.

John was overcome by emotion. He looked up at the ceiling, as if drawing strength from what he saw there, then turned toward Spencer's mother. "Mrs. Perkins, my grandfather was one of those Delta plantation owners."

He let the words hang vulnerably in the air like a confession, unjustified, undefended. *Like cattle,* I remembered.

"I graduated from Kosciusko High School in 1963. That's only fifty miles from Philadelphia, Mississippi, where the three civil rights workers were killed in 1964. We thought they got what they deserved. We thought they were all troublemakers.

"Two years ago, when I read a book called *Black Like Me,* I finally realized there was something wrong with the way we related to black people. Especially now, because of my relationships in this church, I understand the hurts of that system." John sat down.

"No justice, no peace," it was often said. In the spontaneous liturgy between Spencer, his mother, and John, I witnessed a reversal: truth telling and forgiveness opening the way for confession, making possible a new space of life with one another, a space where sons of Mississippi like John and sons of Mississippi like Spencer could sit at one table and sip from one cup.

How could any of us leave unchanged by this exchange? These were the spaces I wanted to create, this was the work that Spencer and I were called to. To be changed was a continual challenge to open a space for "the other."

✦

Two weeks after the workshop, with the lawyer we'd hired for JJ beside us, Spencer and I sulked outside a dark courtroom in downtown Jackson. The cranky white judge inside had just shooed another repeat offender away to prison for the same violation as JJ's. We had also been informed that JJ's parole officer had changed her mind about supporting our plan.

Our lawyer sighed. "Gentlemen, all you can do is plead for mercy."

In the courtroom filled with Voice of Calvary members, as Spencer and I testified, we each seemed to have just the right words and spirits, even as the prosecuting attorney peppered us with questions. JJ's parole officer recommended sending him back to prison. I couldn't explain it, but that attorney and the turncoat parole officer were strangely meek and uncertain, as if contending with an unfamiliar force. But JJ looked sullen and defeated. And the crusty judge had a no-nonsense look on his face.

After the parole officer's testimony he announced his decision. I braced myself.

"I don't often see a group like this willing to provide an alternative." *OK*, I thought, *here comes the yes-but*. The judge paused.

"I'm going to give it a chance. I'm releasing the defendant on his own recognizance, for a ninety-day test of this plan."

I leaped out of my seat, rushed forward, and embraced JJ like he was a just-released hostage. I saw it as God's victory—showering JJ with undeserved favor, using Spencer and me as vessels, making a way out of no way.

Now it was up to JJ to respond through his life, and we were prepared to walk with him. Back at home that night, his few belongings sat in his old room again. During our spontaneous celebration party, JJ said he had something to say. "I just wanna thank everybody for all y'all did for me. Especially these two bruthahs." He turned to me and Spencer. "I'm not gonna let y'all down this time."

❖

Two months after JJ's release Donna came up into our room after work, took my hand, broke a big smile, and raised up the familiar white paper that had brought so much disappointment to us month after month.

I had almost given up hope for us to have our own child. But there before my eyes were two blue "positive" dots.

"I'm pregnant," she said. "I am absolutely, positively pregnant."

"Yes! Yes! Yes!" I shouted, raising my arms, jumping up and down, and breaking my biggest grin since my beloved Pittsburgh Pirates won game seven of the 1979 World Series, as if to say "We won! We won! The sperm and egg unite!"

"Oh, Donna," I said, pulling her close, "I'm the happiest guy on the face of the earth tonight." Our baby was due February 26.

Telling our big news at choir practice that night, we were assaulted by hand claps and hugs. "You done good, bruthah, you done good," said Arthur. I had to admit: Coming around those blind curves, you just might get surprised by joy too.

# 21

# "A GOOD KINDA WEIRD"

*I*n his fig tree talk years before, Spencer had foreseen the day when Antioch's branches would be sturdy enough to welcome more people into our life. In June JJ was joined by five of our summer Study Center interns, then three of them decided to stay. By summer's end fifteen people crammed the Big House without the foundation crumbling or JJ inciting a riot.

The birds were flocking, Antioch was booming, and growth was coming not by membership but by hospitality. Antioch had two kinds of citizens now: the inner core of six adults and three children, and what we thought of as our "greater metropolitan area." We dubbed them Metro Antioch.

Our Metro Antiochers represented an astonishing range of people, from eager-beaver young folks just out of college, to a pregnant white teenager who worked the welfare system as diligently as some people worked the stock market, to "whatever the need" Bruderhof volunteers with the girls in polka-dot scarves and long dresses and the guys in blue shirts and suspenders. The Metro Antiochers came and went; they didn't share money with us or attend our members-only meetings. Some were a royal pain. Others were a great boost in our work, bringing a freshness and vitality.

One notable example was Collin Phungula, who had met Spencer and Nancy during their South Africa trip a year before. Collin grew up in an all-black segregated area, and when I took him to lunch at a local hole-in-the-wall off Lynch Street, where enormous hamburgers came off an electric hot plate, he exclaimed, "This is just like the township!" His colorful phrases became embedded into Antioch's vocabulary. "Spencer, my friend," he'd say, "would you sponsor me to go to the mall?" Translation: I need some cash, plus a ride. "Chris, I'm thanking you in advance for seeing that I get the bus ticket." Nancy's peach cobbler was a favorite Antioch dessert, and the crust was treasured. "Nancy," said Collin once, passing his plate for more, "just a bit of crust please." Protests erupted, "No way, Collin! No way!"

Our nightly dinners with Metro Antiochers became an informal seminar on race relations and Christian discipleship. We talked about everything from affirmative action to predestination around Antioch's massive new dinner table. Donna and I had built it, and it seated sixteen comfortably. After we had glued the table's pine two-by-sixes together at a nearby vocational-technical center, a puzzled stranger had stopped and asked, "What is that? A boat?"

One night Gloria told us about an incident at Kortney's first-grade class at a local Christian school. "Kortney shook me up, y'all. When he got home, out of the blue he said, 'Momma, I wanna be white.' He said his teacher read that Scripture in Psalms where it says if you confess your sins, God will wash you clean and make you whiter than snow. The teacher told the kids God could wash them whiter than snow too, if they confessed their sins. That's why he wanted to be white.

"It's depressing, y'all. And black kids think this kind of thing all the time."

Meanwhile, as we pushed conversations way beyond Reconciliation 101, JJ was not making good on his promise. He poisoned the atmosphere with gossip, constantly broke community, and squabbled with Metro Antiochers. If he couldn't get attention by making himself useful, he got it by picking a fight. In July I had been appointed to the church's elder board, and now I knew about all the trouble he was stirring up in the church as well. Spencer would confront him about changing his ways, and JJ would refuse to act differently. Antioch wasn't a boarding house. If you weren't willing to keep growing—or at least keep the peace—there was no point in living there.

By September even Spencer had had enough. Just four months after the courtroom miracle, Antioch asked JJ to leave. Phil and Marcia Reed said he could stay with them, and JJ's dark cloud scudded away from the Big House.

---

True to the new Antioch motto—"If a room's empty, fill it"—his old quarters didn't stay unoccupied for long. In November a new tenant showed up who truly tested our principle of welcoming the stranger into our midst.

Ten offenders, none of whom had committed violent crimes, were released from Mississippi prisons for a one-week community service project. They stayed with families, who were assured that their guests were all well-behaved Christian boys. We knew better. A couple of years before, one Voice of Calvary family had really hit it off with an inmate from the same project. After his release a year later they found him a place to live and a job, and even began teaching him to read. When their house was robbed of cash, credit cards, and TV a couple months later, guess who was arrested?

At least we thought we could minimize some potential difficulties. On the Sunday afternoon that Antioch was scheduled to get our inmate, we sent Collin with specific instructions. "Choose a black inmate. He'll probably feel more comfortable in this crazy interracial house."

While he was gone parents gave the children a final pep talk, last touches were made to the guest room, and we all sat in the living room waiting—loose, loud, and eager.

When Collin walked in, behind him came a twenty-something white guy who looked as though he'd just walked off a movie screen full of hooting rednecks in the movie *Mississippi Burning*. What this fellow lacked in height he made up for in width. His ruddy, round, oversized head was like one of those "Have a Nice Day" smiley faces, with a grin just as wide.

"Hey y'aaaaaaall," he said, doing a slow wave to a stilled and shaken room that just saw everything but the KKK hood and sheets come in with him. He took a seat in the rocking chair.

I knew what he was thinking behind that slick con-man smile. "Puh-lease tell me I ain't stuck with a buncha nigras and Yankees for the next week."

"Ahm Seas-ul Mah-Keeen-lee," he drawled. I heard him, and I didn't have a clue what he'd just said.

"Cecil McKinley, huh?" said Spencer, who could translate any Mississippi accent after those two years at the white school. "So, Cecil, where you from?"

"Pineville, Miss-sipi. We got one intersection in town," he said with a wink. "But if ya blink, you'll miss it. Har-har-har!"

My heart skipped a beat. Pineville? *My God, I know Pineville. We all know Pineville. It's a stone's throw from Mendenhall.* Spencer and Joanie's heart rates had to be climbing with bad memories of small Mississippi towns. We always saw JJ as kin, not criminal. But this dude wasn't just an anonymous alien inmate, he was bona fide PWT, three slimy letters that never should have been linked but crawled into my head anyway: poor white trash. Antioch had never had a houseguest like this before.

Later that afternoon I asked Cecil why he was in prison.

"Burglary, Cree-us. Some people put me up to it when I was just a kid. Got kinda addicted to it, I guess. Got a seven-year sentence." It was the "addicted" part, I think, that put me on edge.

But Antioch's children could care less about prison time, Pineville, and PWT. All Kortney, Johnathan, and Jubilee knew was that this jolly man let them pin him and his potbelly in a wrestling match after dinner that night. They loved this guy.

The following night there was the usual animated conversation around the dinner slab. Cecil's eyebrows were permanently raised, hearing us talk so explicitly about race. But he jumped right in with our routines that week, joining Donna and me at choir practice, going out to dinner with Spencer and Nancy, and helping out around the house.

One evening toward the end of the week several of us were talking in the kitchen. Cecil ambled over and started to open up. "Ya know," he said, "I been other places where people are around each other all the time, but they don't like each other. Ya know what I mean?" We nodded our heads.

"But y'all live together, and y'all really like each other." He paused and narrowed his sparkly, marble-sized eyes. "It's weird, what y'all are doin'. . . . But it's a good kinda weird—ya know what I mean?" He broke his broad, smiley-faced grin, and we all doubled over with laughter.

The night before his return to prison Cecil and I were doing dishes together. He looked unusually serious. "Ya know, Cree-us, this has been a straaaange week." I nodded. It was true for both of us, and here we were now, so-called carpetbagger and so-called cracker, inside the Big House's interracial zoo, with a sadness in the air between us, hating that we would part tomorrow.

"I cain't help the way I was raised. There was certain things I was taught. Ya know what I mean?"

I nodded again. It could have been my confession too.

"I cain't change the way other folks think. But I learned somethin' here, and I'm never gonna be the same. I'm never gonna forget this place."

"I'll never forget you either, Cecil."

After we finished the dishes I went to bed, convicted of my arrogance toward Cecil's kinfolk and feeling a strange unfamiliar compassion. Each of us had received grace, it seemed, in the form of a stranger.

The next afternoon was painful as the children gave Cecil their good-bye hugs. "We'll miss you, Cecil," everybody said over and over. All of us fought back tears. For whose sake had this outlaw been sent to us?

# 22

# NEVER FORGET THE SOURCE

*B*y December 1990 Spencer and I were looking back on a very fruitful year at the Study Center. We had doubled workshop attendance, tripled the number of summer interns, and signed up two new schools for the upcoming Winterim. We had done reconciliation talks in Chicago, Atlanta, and Birmingham, and invitations were coming from other cities. Spencer was churning out "Lamppost" articles; several publications were reprinting my "Caseworkers to Comrades" piece where I'd coined the term "yokefellows"; and we had signed a contract with Inter-Varsity Press to write the racial reconciliation book.

But the more success we had, the more opposition we felt from Lawrence. With his approval, we had approached several donors to support the "Lamppost," and raised over $7,000, only to have Lawrence insinuate that we were being selfish and self-promoting. Pay was never important to me. But Rufus and other new project directors came on at higher salaries that trumped my seven years of seniority. And while Spencer and I applauded Lawrence's emphasis on local ministry, he seemed to resist our national focus. CCDA's national membership had doubled after only one year, but Lawrence was filibustering about a major proposal we had made for the Study Center to become CCDA's official training arm.

Why all this friction? A friend had recently made an offhand comment to me. "Y'all are jammin', Chris. The Study Center's better than it's ever been. People are just envious, that's all." *Is that what we're really doing wrong?* I thought. *Being too successful and entrepreneurial under an insecure boss?*

In early December I received a disturbing memo from Lawrence. He insinuated that I had tampered with the Ministries' computer system. It was beyond bizarre. I immediately asked to meet with him.

I took a seat in his office and waved the memo. "You don't really think I did this, do you, Lawrence?"

"I hope you wouldn't."

"Look, Lawrence. I need a yes or no."

"I said I hope you wouldn't do that to the Ministries."

"That's the best you can say, Lawrence? 'I hope you wouldn't'? I can't believe you're saying this."

Across the table he just stared at me, unmoved, unperturbed, unsympathetic.

What poison had defiled our trust? Disagreements were one thing. But betraying the family, the Ministries that raised me? Being accused of deceit by the friend who declared me "one of us"? This made my feuds with Lem seem like the good old days. Lem never, ever questioned my integrity.

Tears of bewilderment welled up and trickled down my face. There was no more to say. I got up and walked out.

Over the next few weeks Spencer and I talked more and more seriously about something we had already started to contemplate: leaving the Ministries. We didn't know what we'd do if we left. We just knew we didn't fit here anymore.

As 1990 turned to 1991 and another Winterim boot camp began, our turmoil with Lawrence had Spencer and me spending many hours wrestling with a question that Voice of Calvary never took lightly: When was it OK to leave a situation?

A bedrock belief for us, even when we failed at it, was fidelity to a people and a place. After the Reconciliation Meetings, with battle smoke still settling and wounds still raw, we who remained had crawled into worship together, Sunday after Sunday, to keep professing our belief in a God who reconciles. I was accustomed to uncomfortable seasons of disharmony—after Antioch's "divorces," during the tough times with Lem. Hanging on to each other in times of strife meant staying at the table, being patient with tension, and waiting for breakthroughs—and sometimes that meant many months. Maybe that was the essence of reconciliation itself.

Spencer and I left no stone unturned.

Was parting ways with Lawrence giving up on reconciliation?

Was leaving the Ministries a surrender to ego?

By staying, were we stifling both Lawrence's gifts and our own, smothering both his vision for the local and our vision for the national?

Were we willing to release the momentum and success of the Study Center, without knowing what came next?

Was shutting up an option?

Not exactly. Spencer and I were too hardheaded, too entrepreneurial, too confident of our ideas. Had we labored to come to a common mind with Lawrence? Yes, for months now, only entrenching our differences. Could we counter the sneaky winds of suspicion against us? No, they were too elusive. Had we hashed the pros and cons over with Nancy and Donna and Antioch? Ad nauseam. And Phil Reed, our die-hard pastor and fellow elder? He was understanding of our dilemma, grudgingly, reluctantly, reservedly. His attitude was, "It's tough for you guys? Join the club. Try shepherding these ornery sheep every day like I do. But I can't just walk away." And he never had.

Yet our choice, we now believed, boiled down to either submitting to Lawrence or leaving with integrity.

What finally gave us permission to leave was seeing our church, and not the Ministries, as our basic commitment. Leaving the church over such tensions was like deserting your family. But leaving the Ministries was simply moving to another part of the vast vineyard of human need. Our fundamental relationship with Lawrence was as brother, not boss or coworker. We would still be worshiping with him every week, still knocking heads as elders over the relocation issue, still hitting the field every spring on the church's softball team, with Spencer roaming left, me right, and Lawrence on the pitcher's mound. Even though it was awkward right now, I'd still be singing, rocking, and clapping beside him in the tenor section every week. There was space in the church to work out any healing between us.

In early February Spencer and I made the painful decision to resign, unsure of what we would do next. We immediately got pulled into the fast lane of an autobahn that seemed to have no speed limit.

When Spencer called JP about our decision he shifted into high gear. "Spencer, look man, here's what we need to do," said JP excitedly. "Let's open up a Mississippi office for the Foundation. You and Chris head it up. I've got big plans and y'all can help me."

With JP's California office and staff as partners, CCDA on the rise, JP as its apostle and chairman, and us by his side, there would be no stopping us now. Being JP's writers and program developers would give our ambitions and dreams all the room they needed.

But when I sat down to draft my resignation letter to Lawrence, I was overcome with anger and loss. I ripped off a litany of reasons why Spencer and I felt suffocated. Oh, venting felt good! Oh, I couldn't wait for Law-rence to read this and seethe!

That night Donna helped me to see all that was wrong with that approach. "Put it behind you, Chris," was her gentle advice.

Some people thought Donna was cowardly when it came to con-frontation, and sometimes she was. But the flip side of that was an enor-mous gift—her patience with tension and her ability to pick her battles well, to internally work things out while others stabbed and stirred up more trouble, and to transcend conflict and care deeply in spite of it. Some-times she saw ahead to how relationships might get better on their own, made possible because she gave people the benefit of the doubt. It had always stuck with me how gracefully she had accepted her demotion after the Reconciliation Meetings and how she had kept a good relationship with Lem. There was a time to confront, and there was a time to let it go.

The next day, the wiser for Donna's good advice, I wrote a different let-ter, one that was conciliatory, grateful, and encouraging.

"There's an old Chinese proverb," I told Lawrence. "It says, 'When drinking water, don't forget the source.'" I was so thankful, I said, to have sipped from the springs of the Ministries. It was my first job. It was where I had been given good work, in a great mission. "Yet our church," I wrote, "is a tie that transcends our labors and truly makes us 'family.' There is much work for all of us to do, Lawrence. Let's get to it and get behind each other." It was time to make the best of things and move on.

The week after Spencer and I left the Ministries was one of our happi-est ever. It was typical late-February Mississippi, warm and sunny, with golden daffodils bursting out over the Antioch property. Our baby was due any day, and Spencer and I repaired the Big House's side porch together, dreaming of wider arenas for our reconciliation work.

On March's first morning our son arrived. Since birth can never be called "easy," especially by the father, it could only be said that Donna's experience inspired envy in many other mothers. We left for the hospital at 1:00 A.M., and three hours later, after twenty minutes of pushing, Donna gave birth to Benjamin Richard.

Benjamin entered Antioch's paradise for children, and soon Spencer's tummy blows would have him giggling with glee. Watching Benjamin eat, Gloria dubbed him Fat Daddy. Donna and I moved a crib next to our bed, and Spencer and I set up our new office in the Small House's back room, with its view of Antioch's tree-filled back property. We had no idea where our work was headed, but we knew we were going side by side.

## PART FOUR

# *Demons Rising*

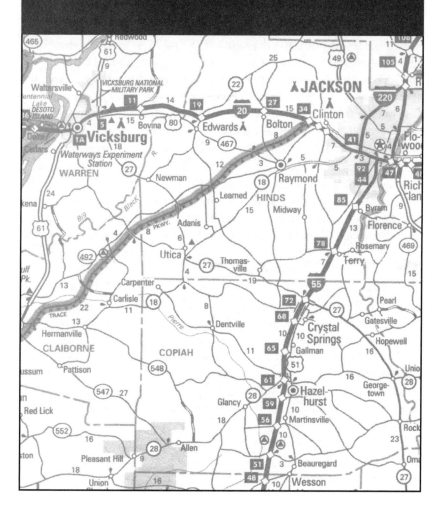

# 23

# MY DIRTY LITTLE SECRET

*A*pril 1991 found Spencer and me sitting in a brightly lit conference room in northwest Pasadena, the heart of Perkins territory. We were there for our first Foundation board meeting as new staff members, and we were thrilled to be presenting our proposal for a Mississippi office. Next door was the home of JP and Mrs. Perkins, where drug dealers—seeking to drive them out of the neighborhood—had tossed a firebomb on the roof right after they moved into this inner-city area ten years earlier.

I was happy to see Derek Perkins, back helping his parents again in their local youth development work, at the table, together with twenty-odd members of JP's national board. Spencer, who had served as a board member, knew them much better than I did. They included the president of a California publishing company, a Denver neurosurgeon, a San Francisco venture capitalist, and a renowned urban ministry guru from Chicago. Two were community activists from Los Angeles—one Latino, the other from a booming black church. I couldn't believe the bashful guy in the rumpled khaki pants was one of California's wealthiest philanthropists.

Since drafting plans was more my gift than Spencer's, I had done most of the work on the proposal. But we decided that he was going to do most of the talking. JP and Mrs. Perkins beamed as Spencer kicked off our presentation, speaking from the heart.

"I remember years ago, first in Mendenhall, then in Jackson, me watchin' how the work developed, then seein' my parents move out here to California. I can remember not thinkin' long term. Not really havin' much concern about the future of the ministry or what legacy my father was goin' to leave."

*Why,* I wondered, *was Spencer talking about "I," as in "I remember . . ."?* I felt a strange and not very pleasant fluttering feeling in my chest as I listened, but I wasn't sure why.

"Over the last three or four years, as I'm growin' older and my parents are growin' older, I've been startin' to think about that." *Hmmm, he's still saying "I" a lot.* "Within a few years—Derek and his family, Chris and his family, and my family—we'll be in a better situation to fill my parents' shoes. This proposal is a beginning of us thinkin' in the long range."

Now, that was better. He was mentioning my name. It seemed only right to me. The iciness in my chest was replaced by a reassuring warmth.

Hours later, after Spencer sketched the proposal and I the budget, after the board enthusiastically approved it, after watching the love-in between Spencer and his pleased parents and the room full of high-powered Perkins admirers, only as I lay in bed, having considerable trouble falling asleep, only then did I name my feelings during our meeting.

Good fluttering feeling—glory and credit to me.

Bad fluttering feeling—glory and credit to Spencer.

As I replayed the meeting in my mind it seemed as if a dove had descended from on high and hovered over Spencer's head, and JP's voice had declared, "This is my beloved son, in whom I am well pleased." Spencer was now the Anointed One. But if Spencer had been baptized into his rightful inheritance, coming along his father's side in public ministry, I felt demoted from yokefellow to "the white budget guy."

I really wanted these feelings and flutterings to go away. But they didn't.

In the weeks after the board meeting, when JP wasn't satisfied with the ghostwriting on his latest book, *Beyond Charity,* he asked Spencer and me to do a major overhaul. Plans were cooking with CCDA for Spencer and me to organize regional training centers. It was all so exhilarating and promising, and JP called Mississippi frequently to talk vision and plans.

But he wanted to speak to Spencer, not me. I knew that it was not that JP didn't like me or respect me. But I wasn't the Anointed One.

Why did this matter so much to me? I told myself, *So what if I get treated like the lesser partner?* After all, I had invited Spencer's rise—in pushing Lem to hire him and even make him Study Center director over me, in my willingness to give up my management team seat to him, and by exhorting him to step forward, to give his all to opportunities I did not have, to use his Perkins legacy for good. Yes, I had proven myself willing to push Spencer into the spotlight.

Part of me was probably adjusting to what Spencer had gained and I had given up in our change of venues. In the Foundation circles Spencer was a celebrity. I, however, had given up the Study Center director title, the management team seat, and the liaison role with Lawrence. Spencer had taken a backseat to me in prestige; now it was my turn, as he became the point person with JP and the Foundation board.

But two years of working together had complicated things. Spencer's weaknesses were familiar to me now, especially his laid-back approach to office life. I not only felt that I initiated more but that he couldn't go far without my gifts. I was pulling twice as much weight but getting only a fraction of the attention. I felt the unfairness of it keenly. With our boss a thousand miles away in Pasadena, I was the only one who knew about these work dynamics, and Spencer was back into his irregular work hours. It was spring, after all, bluegill-bedding season.

Still, I kept reminding myself that my bad feelings were not Spencer's fault. He didn't have some secret agenda to shove me aside. I told myself that it made perfect sense for Spencer to be point person now. And I knew how much he valued me and depended on me.

Back in Jackson my days were taken up with work with Spencer, followed in the evenings by community dinners, frequent elder and Antioch and Metro Antioch meetings, and care for my own little baby, Benjamin. Much as I struggled, though, the bad feelings continued to simmer underneath the rhythms of our lives.

✧

In small stretches of time Spencer and I could steal from our other work we labored away on our book. In late April we hibernated at a state park cabin to churn out chapters. A fishing lake nearby, of course, was a necessity for the week.

I cooked the dinners, Spencer did dishes. I relaxed with my pipe, he with his fishing rod. I edited his chapters, he edited mine, sharpening each other's metaphors and concepts. We read each other our best stuff, standing and strutting at the best lines.

> Listen to this, Chris: "Blacks blame the whites, and whites blame the blacks. The integrationists have preached their last sermons, and some blacks are now talking about separating from whites altogether—turning the energy they had spent on trying to be accepted by white society into building up black society. Everyone who can afford it, whether black or white, is moving out of the inner city into the suburbs.
>
> "Even after all the progress of the past three decades, both blacks and whites feel that things are getting worse between us. Our tired, embattled relationship has reached an impasse, and we are all suffering from"—get this, Chris—"race fatigue."

"Ooooo-we, 'race fatigue'! That'll fly, man!" I said, slapping Spencer a high five.

"Okay, I got one for you. Brace yourself, Spence.

"'Four hundred years of slavery, forced segregation, and discrimination have left a stubborn residue within us all. For blacks, the residue is anger, bitterness, and blame. For whites, the residue is . . .'—drum roll please—'racial blinders.'"

"Go, man, go!"

I kept reading. "If you drink polluted water, you'll probably catch hepatitis; if you were born white in America, as I was, chances are you're wearing racial blinders."

Writing created precious space to reflect on two decades of interracial life at Voice of Calvary. We wrote as witnesses, not experts, as actors in the larger drama of our church. We wrote to fellow Christians, to those who claimed allegiance to a Lord who said, "By this everyone will know that you are my disciples, if you have love for one another." White Christians had been mostly silent or on the wrong side of the civil rights movement. It was time to get our house in order, because Christianity labored under the burden of a great historical contradiction, that it was possible to be reconciled to God without loving your neighbor. And we believed that whenever Christians had made peace with that fallacy, from slavery to the Holocaust to apartheid, it had spelled disaster for the world.

How could we distill our church's story of racial transformation into a journey for others? We hammered out a three-part framework for the book: admit, submit, and commit.

Part one would be about admitting: understanding what's going on with race by ending polite conversation, telling the truth, seeing how we are all tainted by race's history—by privilege and denial, by anger and lack of forgiveness—and owning up to the power of race to determine our lives.

Part two in the journey, submitting, began with owning that we cannot, as individuals, extricate ourselves from race's power over us. To be freed required submitting ourselves to truthful relationships across racial lines and to crying out for help from God.

The last part of the journey was committing, giving ourselves to a life of going out of our way to cross the racial divide and to forming interracial mission, especially among the poor and in the dismantling of racism. Here we drew on the yokefellow metaphor.

We decided to make the book read like one of our reconciliation talks, a chapter from Spencer, a chapter from me, back and forth, offering our distinct voices, experiences, and perspectives. Some chapters focused on story, some on biblical argument, some on down-and-dirty nitty-gritty topics like dismantling black self-doubt and white fear.

Besides finding enough time to fish, our biggest struggle of the week was whether to address the subject of interracial marriage in the book.

Spencer and Nancy were True Soul Mates, with capital letters. They were best friends, equals as deep thinkers and analyzers, and from doing yard work to having long, intense conversations, they never seemed to tire of each other's company. Spencer had a huge impact on Nancy's family and their racial understanding; one of Nancy's sisters and her husband had adopted a black daughter and relied heavily on the two of them for advice. Nancy had won the deep respect of Spencer's family as well, and his younger sisters especially looked to her for wisdom and counsel. At Spencer's big family reunions Nancy was the lone white person, darting around asking questions of the older folks and writing up family trees. But outside their family circles, the rest of the world couldn't get beyond a basic fact: the mixture of blackness and whiteness into a marriage, into "one flesh."

"I'm still afraid people will write me off if they know I'm married to a white woman," Spencer sighed one night. "Especially black folks."

I tugged on my pipe and pulled the steaks off the grill. "I hear you, Spence. But if interracial marriage is the ultimate racial fear, how can we avoid it?"

"Well, is this a good start?" Spencer began to read what he'd written about a conversation he'd once had with Lem Tucker.

> We'd talked for hours about the vanishing black male role model and the importance of strong black families. We'd agreed that we black men needed to marry black women in order to build healthy black Christian families. Many interracial couples, we noted, are lured by the social taboo and consequently build their relationship on a shallow, sick physical attraction.
>
> Now I realized that if I pursued my relationship with Nancy, I would become a black man who was not doing his part for my race. Why would God do this to me? Why did the woman who was "the one" have to be white?

"That's the direction I'm goin', Chris. What you do think?"

"That's just what we need to do, man. Hit it head-on. Be honest. Lay out your dilemmas, the tensions between your competing ideals. And then raise the standard at the end."

"Yeah, I can't see us promotin' interracial marriage, like it's better or somethin'. It's not. But I can't see not addressin' it either. Let's go for it. I'm ready to eat. I wanna hit the lake once more before dark."

Book-wise and bass-wise it was a productive week, our days full of laughter and hearty discussions. When we were alone, I had no doubts about our interdependence. But public settings were different. There the comparisons I made between his glory and mine were becoming more distressing.

---

Two weeks after our week of writing and fishing, at a CCDA board meeting in Chicago, my fluttering bad feelings turned into full-blown gnawings. *Why,* I wondered incessantly, *does Spencer seem to get so much more credit and attention than me?*

Spencer shone in these board meetings—his charisma, his wordplay, his bold opinions. He was an official CCDA board member; I was not. Nobody would miss me if I wasn't there. He was the apostle's eldest son; I felt like the white administrator. People wanted to be near him. They were always looking for a single bottom line in our partnership, and they chose him over me.

After the Chicago board meeting I was not just wishing for those fluttering feelings to cease, I was begging for it. I'd rise early, walk over to the office, read "Why, God?" psalms of anguish, and pray for the bad feelings to be removed, or destroyed, or handled in whatever way God did pest control. Maybe being perfect was shooting too high. But I was used to solving my problems by trying harder, by disciplining myself more.

My cravings for glory and credit were far bigger than I ever imagined, going all the way back to my Middlebury days and the pain that had come with giving up that diploma. Until this I had felt such purity in relationship to Spencer, cheering him on. Now I saw a troubling side to this friendship, how increasing closeness with Spencer was revealing more and more a side of me that I would have preferred not to know.

It had been hard enough confessing this dirty little secret to myself. What I decided to do next was much harder. To tell my secret to a real person—even my biggest fan on earth—seemed like admitting to humiliating failure. But I also was in such agony I couldn't keep the truth inside.

After Donna and I climbed into bed one night, I said I needed to talk.

"What about?"

"It's embarrassing, Donna. I'm not sure how to say it. But here goes." My wife was about to learn that she had married a fake, an impostor, a man who could turn into a monster. From innocent beginning to ugly end, I traced the growth of my nagging internal struggle.

Lightning didn't strike. The curtains didn't flutter. Haunting organ music didn't play. Donna didn't bolt out of the bed shrieking. So I really wasn't morphing into something hideous before her eyes? Why was it so difficult for me to do this?

"The bottom line is, Donna, this yokefellow idea is a joke. Spencer's Batman, I'm Robin. That's how this thing makes me feel. I hate these thoughts. I hate them so much. The envy and jealousy—it just eats away at me. It's like . . . a demon."

I gave the agonizing truth about myself a name, envy and jealousy, and it was not hard for me to think of it as a force that possessed me in spite of my attempts to defeat it.

"It hurts," said Donna, "seeing you feel so bad about yourself. I think you underestimate what you bring to Spencer—and your own character. You're not Robin. You're not just a sidekick."

I stared at the ceiling, feeling hopeless. Donna put her arm around me.

"You're too hard on yourself, Chris. Of course, the thoughts you're feeling aren't good. On the other hand, you are struggling with them. You're not content just to adjust to your weakness."

We talked for a long time that night. Donna had a question at the end. "Do you think it would help to talk to Spencer about it?"

"Oh, Lord. That would not be easy."

"Well, think about it. It might be best."

Spencer was right down the hallway as we spoke. He and I were busy pulling our plow through the fields of the Foundation, Antioch, neighborhood, and church, and he didn't have a clue what was stirring inside of me.

The next morning, as I sat in my office and prayed, I felt a ruffle of courage, as if seeing my enemy clearly, naming it out loud, and pointing to it in Donna's presence gave it a clarity, a shape that could be attacked and defeated. I longed for that, but I knew that such a victory was not going to come quickly.

24

# INTO URBAN AMERICA

---

*I*n July, two months after I had confessed my failings to Donna, a fax from JP rolled off the machine between Spencer's desk and mine, bearing a startling vision that would challenge us even more. The fax outlined JP's most ambitious and costly project in thirty years of public service: a national magazine, aimed primarily at African American Christians, to inspire hope and solutions for the nation's urban communities. As I read JP's vision I thought, *Sounds like he's talking about the woes of west Jackson.*

"America's cities are in trouble," he said, "and something needs to be done. Something has to be done to change the minds of our people. We, as blacks, have to take a leadership role. Violence, drugs, family break-ups, crime, school dropouts, and AIDS plague our urban communities. There is a need for a moral voice, a voice of personal responsibility, a voice of hope and solutions."

Spencer and I believed the nation was ripe for such a message.

In 1991 six of every ten black children had no father present in the home; black-on-black murders approached five thousand a year; one of every four black men was incarcerated, on parole, or had a criminal record—and the nation didn't blink an eye. A prison boom was building more holding pens; urban schools were police states; criminologists gave apocalyptic warnings about new "urban predators"—as if assigning them to a subhuman species; and gated communities were flourishing. Some aging leaders from the civil rights movement seemed obsessed with the action in Washington, D.C., which felt inconsequential in thousands of deteriorating neighborhoods like ours.

The depth of urban problems defied political solutions alone, nor could racism by itself account for their complexity. Twenty-three years after Dr. King's murder the clear black and white of the 1960s had faded into the grays of the 1990s.

Many voices contended for the hearts and minds of black Americans.

Nearly every day on Robinson Street, I passed the intersection where bow-tied Black Muslims hawked hundreds of *Final Call* newspapers to passing cars, with Louis Farrakhan's face beaming on the front page and a message of self-help and racial paranoia inside.

Jehovah's Witnesses in snappy suits and dresses regularly showed up at the Big House on their door-to-door forays, pushing glossy literature and warning that only 144,000 would get to heaven, so we'd better get on board.

*Ebony* magazine's glitz, fashion, and celebrity profiles said that if you could just be as healthy, wealthy, and wisely educated as white folks were—throwing in a pinch of black pride—everything would be all right. While the message sold like hotcakes, it was a far cry from the sacrificial call of Dr. King.

Where were the stories of urban hope, offering a different alternative? Spencer and I knew that for every so-called urban predator there were fifty families working, struggling to pay bills, trying to keep their children safe, in school, and right with God and others. As church members, parents, and neighbors, they wanted to know "What can I do?" They would be our primary audience: black, urban, self-confessing Christians, numbering in the millions.

But we would be David in a world of magazine Goliaths.

There was no newsstand-magazine experience on our editorial team of Spencer, me, and two Pasadena staff—Rudolpho "Rudy" Carrasco, a Latino Los Angeles native and recent Stanford graduate, and Pat Warren, a streetwise black journalist.

Our marketing prowess was also questionable. JP, always the outsider, had high standing in the renegade CCDA world, but a weak network among traditional black denominations. Spencer and I loved writing, but we hated selling. The grunt work of marketing, advertising, and selling subscriptions felt overwhelming. Yet even if we reached only a few thousand urban pastors and community activists, we believed this magazine's influence could be significant.

But there were two daunting realities—only one magazine out of a hundred survived three years, and you needed bags of cash just to get that far. Our best immunity against failure was Roland Hinz, a former Foundation board member who owned a line of popular magazines like *Dirt Bike* and *Mountain Bike Action.* Roland was kicking in his hefty wallet and invaluable know-how. Decisions moved along quickly.

The magazine was named *Urban Family,* with a slogan of "the magazine of hope and progress." We decided to start off quarterly, with a voice that would be politically independent, rallying readers onto a common turf of personal responsibility, interracial cooperation, and moral solutions at the grass roots.

Articles, said Roland, should focus on "how you can do this in your own community" and "shouldn't be any longer than what can be read on the toilet."

Making *Urban Family* successful would demand a total commitment, but it was all very exhilarating. Everybody at Antioch anticipated the first issue as though a new baby were coming, still six months away. After feeling confined like animals in a zoo under Lawrence at the Ministries Spencer and I were roaming vast plains, guided by JP's boundless vision and energy.

So here I was, fired up and set free by JP, yet I was still haunted by how others were doing around me. I hated the way my unruly emotions kept dragging me down, but dividing up responsibilities and titles seemed to fuel my envy and jealousy.

JP would be at the top of the masthead as publisher. How should the rest of us be lined up underneath?

Of course, I knew what was best: Spencer should be right under JP as editor-in-chief. He had the right stuff, the editorial and leadership gifts. He was black, a Perkins, the Anointed One. His daddy wanted him there. Made perfect sense.

It was best for Rudy to be listed next as managing editor. He was in Pasadena with JP and Roland, he could organize people, he got the work done.

But underneath Rudy came a senior editor, a part-time consultant. A rung below her—miles below Spencer, it seemed—were two associate editors, Pat Warren and me.

Behind the scenes Spencer and I would work on *Urban Family* as we had always handled everything, leaning on each other's gifts, constantly aware that one plus one equaled more than two. Titles didn't tell the truth.

But it hurt. Me the associate, him the chief. Pat had already made that his nickname. I felt like a royal loser.

A conviction grew within me that Donna was right, that I needed to tell Spencer about my struggle. On too many days I felt unclean in his presence. Maybe I was giving my envy-jealousy demon too much darkness to hide in. Maybe the brighter the light, the further away it would move. And maybe the most intense light of all, a confession to the very object of my comparisons, would scatter my bad feelings like cockroaches.

But then I worried—what if knowing the truth about me alienated Spencer forever? I shouldn't burden him with this, should I? Several times I worked up the courage and backed off. But I knew there was too much at stake not to step forward.

Finally, I invited Spencer out to breakfast one morning. I was glad to have strangers around. Spencer was mixing his eggs and grits, and he might hesitate before rubbing his plate into my face.

"So, Chris, what's up?"

It was difficult enough knowing this truth about myself. But telling Spencer was downright humiliating. My voice faltered and cracked. Then I told him the same sordid story I had told Donna two months before.

Again there was no lightning, no flickering lights, no organ music, no look of disgust on my confessor's face. I finished.

After a long silence, Spencer spoke. "You know, Chris, it doesn't surprise me when I'm bad. But it seems like it really bothers you when you're bad." It was the most precise diagnosis that had ever been made of my unforgiving, unrelenting pursuit of perfection.

We bared our souls for the next hour, flooding light into the dark interior of weakness. Spencer said he didn't wish to be other than who he was, but he dreaded what lay ahead. He feared letting his father down, not having his daddy's gifts, not warming up quickly to strangers. He didn't like the idea of traveling and being in public more. I owned my fears about not getting the credit I deserved, about my ambition being stunted, about constantly operating in the shadow of a Perkins.

"Spencer, it's strange. It's like for you, the doors are opening too fast, and for me, they're opening too slow."

He chuckled. "Yeah. Like it or not, our commitment to each other is puttin' us both face to face with our weaknesses. I suppose that means we're right where we need to be."

I nodded my head slowly. I didn't like it, I would never have invited it, but where I found myself in relationship to Spencer had a sobering ring of counterintuitive truth to it. It was not a gift I would have chosen, but maybe it was the gift that I needed.

"You know," said Spencer, "God sure is a genius. Seems like he's got our sanctification well in hand."

When we pulled up into the driveway back home, before we stepped out of the car, Spencer turned to me. "Hey, about this Batman and Robin thing. Don't worry, man. I got your back." It felt very good, having Spencer extend the embrace of our neighborhood outlaws to me.

✦

As peace settled into my heart, at least for the time being, Antioch gave thanks for five years in community, over a weekend retreat at a state park in November. We sang, we prayed, we ate well and played well. We took drastic corporate measures to counter health problems in the group—swearing off pork, agreeing to buy nonfat milk, and teaming up in exercise groups.

Mostly we dreamed, asking, What should Antioch look like ten years from now?

We pictured our six acres, bustling with *Urban Family*'s headquarters, maybe a school tapping Gloria's gifts as a teacher, or a hospice tapping Donna's as a nurse, and Joanie's future law office (after she graduated the following year). We saw a neighborhood park filled with children, a path running around the perimeter filled with bikers and walkers, and the surrounding blocks, scattered with Voice of Calvary families of all races and classes.

We also sketched plans for a churchwide, adults-only, New Year's Eve extravaganza. Why not offer Antioch's th'ow down gift to the whole Voice of Calvary family?

Our holiday rituals carried us through the year.

At Thanksgiving thirty-plus people tackled a feast that included two mandatory turkeys with dressing: Donna's with white bread and Gloria's with cornbread.

December's annual cookie baking day left a new record of fifteen hundred–plus on the dining room slab.

At our gift exchange two weeks later, as always, Gloria was responsible for a disproportionate share of the foot-deep gift wrap. Antioch was Gloria's family, and she found as much delight in giving to Johnathan, Jubilee, and Benjamin as she did to her son, Kortney.

The theme for our big New Year's party was "Celebrating the '70s," the beloved decade of adolescence for most of us. We cleared the dining room floor for dancing, set up an ancient record player, and tracked down albums from Motown to the Rolling Stones. There'd never been a churchwide party quite like this before.

A standing-room-only crowd showed up. Church members decked in bell bottoms, platform shoes, and miniskirts strode up the Big House's candlelit sidewalk and passed through a haze of burning incense and a curtain of beads into a living room pulsating with music, dimly lit with green and yellow lightbulbs. Signs covered the walls—"Right On, Brother," "Far Out," "Give Me Five."

Lue walked in, and we hugged. She was a mother by adoption now, with an eighteen-month-old son named Jon, and she had stayed in close touch with many Antioch members.

I was overjoyed to see Phil and Tressa. Four long years after their departure from Antioch, we were slowly becoming friends again.

I missed seeing Harold and Betsy. They had left the church, and I wondered how they were doing.

But the Two-Hands-Up Gang, as I still called them in my own mind, came, and Lawrence too. The gang had won my respect by now, with them adopting more of the three Rs commitments and the rest of us letting worship services become a bit more lively. And without the Ministries to fight about, it was easier to be friends with Lawrence, even if my relationship with him seemed shallower.

Everybody hit the food bar and played Twister and Name That Tune with 1970s television show themes. A few minutes before midnight I stood on a chair and reviewed Voice of Calvary's 1991 family album—our births, adoptions, and marriages, the joys and difficulties we had all shared.

Afterward we circled together, wrapping arms into an unbroken chain. Midnight struck, and fifty members of the ever-resilient Voice of Calvary family closed 1991 by singing an old Motown hit, "It's So Hard to Say Good-bye to Yesterday."

A few minutes later the real party started. Black folks were teaching white folks the steps to the Electric Slide. Everybody from smooth-moving Arthur and Lawrence to prancing Phil Eide were doing freelance dances down a spontaneously formed Soul Train line of cheering friends.

I couldn't help but remember that these were the same people who had been torn up by the Reconciliation Meetings seven years before. Most of us shared at least a decade in one church and neighborhood. Maybe it was only a drop in the bucket, but to me it was interracial life at its fullest and finest.

# 25

# OUR SIX-RING CIRCUS

hen thirty thousand copies of *Urban Family* rolled off the presses in late January 1992, we were mighty proud of our new baby. The glossy cover boomed "Who Speaks for the Black Community?" amidst a medley of famous black faces: W.E.B. DuBois facing down Booker T. Washington, Dr. King eyeing Malcolm X, Jesse Jackson leering at Clarence Thomas. "There can be no substitute for personal involvement and responsibility," wrote JP, calling for massive sacrificial investment in urban America. Articles ran from building positive self-esteem in black boys to starting Good News Clubs modeled on ours at the Ministries, and Chief Spencer wrote a feature story called, "Can Blacks and Whites Be Neighbors?"

In putting out the magazine we had to master a dizzying new body of knowledge: cover lines and bluelines, pull quotes and endnotes, renewals and list rentals. Until then, I'd thought "four-color separation" referred to racial division between blacks, whites, Asians, and Latinos—not a printing technique. It was all a bit overwhelming. "This feels like when me and my brother started up the Battery Clinic," Spencer told me with a chuckle one day. "We had no idea what we were doin', man. It's easy to be afraid of somethin' you've never done before. We'll get used to it."

Six months after I'd confessed to Spencer over eggs and grits, the bad feelings had still not been exorcised. When I turned to *Urban Family's* credit box on page two and saw my name next to "Associate Editor," three long lines under Spencer, I flinched. But I thought I could grit my teeth and think and work my way out of these feelings. And there was work to do, and it pressed in upon us. Plus JP was coming to town.

He came in February for an *Urban Family* promotion week, pushing subscriptions to a hotel banquet room packed with pastors and business leaders. I felt good in his presence. When it came to strategizing, JP valued my gifts. But on the day when he and Spencer drove around town to hit radio stations and media interviews, I sulked at the office. Why did Spencer get more of the fun and glory? When our local newspaper, the *Clarion-Ledger*, wrote a story about the magazine a few days later, it was great publicity. But I flinched again. "Perkins serves as publisher," it said, "his son, Spencer, as editor-in-chief." My name was nowhere.

There was little time to lose on self-pity. The next two issues were in the works, and in the spring we moved our offices into the Duplex for more space, with red-headed soccer-lover Anne Berry as our assistant. Anne had grown up in a Christian community, and as replacement for my sister, the way she shared Liz's desire to please and do things just right was proving just as indispensable to Spencer and me.

Spencer's desk and mine were only a few feet apart, and most of our days were full of satisfying work. We made decisions using Antioch's traditional combination of persuading and relenting. We knew each other so well we usually resolved things quickly.

But some days the relenting part got tiring—very tiring. One week I was giving in on everything. At least I thought so. I felt like Anne was at Spencer's beck and call, paying little attention to my desires and direction. It felt too much again like Batman and Robin. And Spencer had claimed he was going to look out for me—he "had my back," right? But it didn't feel like it.

Later in the week he and I happened to find ourselves in the yard between the Big House and the Small House. I decided to bring up how I saw things. I ran off my list of how I was giving in. "Spence, I wonder, how do you see things?"

He chuckled. "You don't really want to know, do you?"

He proceeded to run off his own list—a long one—of all the ways he had given in to me the previous few days, including how Anne responded more to my needs than his. It never occurred to me there might be more than one way of interpreting our daily life and partnership.

I started to laugh. "All this time, I'm thinking I'm submitting to you, and you're thinking you're submitting to me. Spence, this is crazy. It's like our relationship is about constantly submitting."

"You right, man. 'Constantly submitting.' That sums up how I feel most of the time."

"It ain't easy, is it?"

He grinned and shook his head. "Nope. Sho' nuff ain't for me. You either."

"You know, we need to keep talkin' about this stuff."

"Agreed."

But we didn't talk about it nearly enough. Call it part inertia, part not wanting to hash through every little imagined slight, part unconsciously justifying my resentments and not wanting to be shown where I was wrong. There was a certain weariness about the constant communication our partnership seemed to require. It wasn't hard for little reservoirs of unfairness to keep building up, to keep spilling over.

---

And there was so much to do.

We faced the daunting challenge of getting a national magazine off the ground.

Spencer and I were getting more and more requests to do reconciliation workshops.

JP, as the joke went, was nearing "retirement age," as if that was even a category for him. But he was talking to Spencer about putting *Urban Family* into our hands in three years, with headquarters moving to the Antioch campus. In the meantime, working under JP meant following up on his gushing fountain of ideas.

All this had Spencer and me slated to take at least twenty road trips away from Jackson over the next ten months, and that was sure to multiply when our book was released the following year. Voice of Calvary folk knew better than to swoon at our every word, but outsiders were looking to us for hope and guidance, putting us on a pedestal, and pressing high expectations on our relationship.

Then a scream for help erupted from the heart of the nation itself, from Los Angeles, to be exact.

In the fall of 1991 police officers had been captured on videotape, beating a black motorist named Rodney King. Now, in May, two weeks after they were declared not guilty by a suburban jury with no blacks on it, a vast segment of Los Angeles lay in ruins: forty-eight dead, five thousand fires, millions of dollars of goods looted, people pulled out of their cars and beaten, and the race picture considerably muddled beyond the black-white paradigm that had dominated the national consciousness. Latinos were implicated in much of the looting, and Korean American businesses were heavily targeted for destruction. This wasn't 1968 Detroit or Watts or Newark. It was the most prosperous nation in history at the crest of the twenty-first century, and it blew the lid off the idea that the nation had "arrived" when it came to race and class.

If the demand for our stories of racial and urban hope had already been increasing, the Los Angeles tragedy seemed sure to tax our supply. Spencer and I now faced a dilemma, one that we had begun to discuss.

How did we carry light to others without diminishing the flame we already had? How did we respond to swelling public demand without pushing energy away from the very kind of local, day-to-day commitments that made our story possible in the first place?

Spencer and I knew that our life was our message. Just our showing up together, a black man and a white man who cared for one another, who stuck it out, who had been brought together through a very messy story and who kept together through a community of friends—that was our greatest witness. We embodied our most important message before we even uttered a word.

But growing public demands for the message led to a subtle temptation, one that my desire for glory found attractive: favoring the glamorous public work over the tedious local labors. For Spencer public work was more the duty, and community was more the pleasure. For me community was more the duty, and work was more the pleasure. I enjoyed traveling while Spencer mostly just put up with it.

But for both of us public work offered much more immediate gratification. It seemed to touch more people, and thus it seemed more relevant. A slick national magazine pieced together in a few weeks garnered far more social praise than all the years we had invested in Antioch, and Spencer's profile was rising as editor-in-chief. What credit did anybody give you for living peacefully—unless you told a crowd about it? There was a danger of self-deception. Public efforts could easily woo more and more of our energy, making us think we were more and more successful, while growth in our relationships became more and more stagnant. Spencer and I were becoming a twosome writing and talking big public noise about reconciliation, but how could we and Antioch keep from going at each other's throats back home and not face more "divorces"? Doing a talk with Spencer in Chicago was the easy work. The real job was taming my envy-jealousy demon.

As we rushed a special insert addressing the Los Angeles riots into the next *Urban Family* and started preparing a special issue on race, the complexity of life at Antioch continued to intensify. Metro Antiochers filled the Big House with unlikely housemates. A friend of Gloria's lost everything in a house burglary, and the community took her and her five-year-old in for a few months.

In the summer Cecil McKinley, the white inmate who'd lived with us for a week two years before, was coming directly from prison to Antioch as a free man. Fifty kids were signed up for Gloria's first-ever summer program in the Small House, and her new after-school program would start up in the Big House in the fall. Volunteer groups were coming to help in our work, and they needed to be housed, fed, taught, and acculturated.

Donna and I, at least, were able to leave Benjamin in Spencer and Nancy's care and escape for a week in May, courtesy of her brother, Mark, who worked for a cruise line. Was it wasteful, amid all the pressing needs of the world, to celebrate our fifth anniversary on a Caribbean cruise? I had always been able to work hard for long periods and play hard for short ones. Over five-course dinners, we unwound.

One night, as we held hands and walked around the deck, Donna opened up about some of her frustrations. She'd been working for over a year doing home-health nursing. She requested west Jackson patients—the so-called dangerous terrain—and loved the work. She was so matter-of-fact about it all, like the time she came into a helpless, bed-bound patient's room, found a fire burning, calmly put it out, called 911, and moved on to the next visit.

For Donna part of the sacrifice of living in community was having to work outside the home full-time. But what about Benjamin, our one-year-old?

"I just wish I could spend more time with Benjamin," she said. "Sometimes I feel like all Antioch's interested in is my income. I know it's not completely true, but community's monetary needs outweigh my desire to work fewer hours."

It was not something we had voiced to community, and Donna put a high premium on conflict avoidance. Sometimes that was wise; sometimes it wasn't. Her guilt over falling short as a mother in this case just kept simmering in the background. After a week of rest so relaxing it felt surreal, we plunged back into west Jackson.

Then, to heap more stress on top of intense pressure, in May Spencer approached me about having Nancy join the *Urban Family* staff. Whatever he was thinking, this suggestion felt immediately threatening to me.

When it came to visibility, Donna was quiet and content to be in the background, whereas Nancy was outspoken and comfortable being out front. Not only that but Spencer and Nancy's union as both True Soul Mates and Mendenhall-Mennonites made great copy. What would keep their white-black story from supplanting mine with Spencer? Donna and

I had gotten on each other's last nerves when we'd tried to work together; we didn't mind a little space in the relationship. Spencer and Nancy would have been happy being together 24–7. To me, while Nancy's high loyalty to Spencer was admirable, it could take on a knee-jerk quality at times, and it was very rare for her to disagree with him publicly. And although Donna had enjoyed a close relationship with Spencer for many years, Nancy and I only became friends once Antioch started. I knew that Donna's affection for Spencer helped check me from descending too far into negative critique of him. I wasn't at all confident that Nancy would keep Spencer from critiquing me. I feared losing my special partnership with Spencer and the authority that came with it.

It didn't matter whether I was right or wrong about all these observations; what mattered was that they ignited a truckload of conflicting emotions within me. All this aside, the bottom line was that they were husband and wife. How was the pillow talk dynamic going to affect my work with Spencer?

But I was too chicken to tell Spencer what I should have said. What I should have said, with gentleness and truthfulness, was this:

> Listen, Spencer, please. I'm all in favor of Nancy joining our team. She's an awesome administrator, she's got great gifts of wisdom and articulation to nurture the new people we bring on. She respects me. I respect her. I know how much peace and joy she brings you.
>
> But the sweet soul mate you sleep with, the mother of your children, cannot be objective about you. And you cannot be objective about her. What will that bring into the office and our work? How might it affect our relationship as yokefellows? Nancy's not a mild-mannered volunteer—she's bold and opinionated. How do we avoid having her taking your side when disagreements come up? How is our work not going to become more "Spencer and Nancy" instead of "Spencer and Chris"? How's this going to feed my little demon? How might this even cause you not to grow in ways you would grow otherwise?
>
> Look, let's get some nonpartisan outside advice on this. Let's ask somebody to gauge if we're getting too high on the stress charts, to help us minimize the potential problems. Let's get to the bottom of how this is—and isn't—a good idea and how we can turn it all to the good. Whatever motives I have for resisting this, it's just as important for you to see—and me to know—all your motives for pushing it. Let's go into this with our eyes wide open.

But I didn't say any of that. Spencer and I constantly communicated about things that deeply mattered, but not nearly enough about the most tender, most difficult dilemmas of our own relationship.

It was hard to keep exposing my weaknesses. I feared him saying, "Suck it up, Chris." To shed too much on this whole subject was to risk a certain loss of relationship. It just seemed easier to do what I imagined Spencer would tell me, to suck it up. I relied on my own powers, and pillow talk with Donna, to wrestle with my dilemmas. And who could we go to for help? We had never invited anyone else into the difficulties of our relationship. We had never felt the need for it.

But more and more, a problem was lurking under our life on Robinson Street, a problem that we didn't have the resources to see or to solve.

All the richness of our crazy life within the Big House was why we had moved into community in the first place. Only by daring to plunge in over our heads had we learned that human beings were capable of far more than we usually imagined. But now there was a real danger of not recognizing our limits, of not ever being able to see the gradual effects of mounting pressures upon us all.

The tiny mustard seed of our little fellowship had become the hectic activity of a six-ring circus, with each of us scurrying, juggling all kinds of balls in the air, from one ring of busyness to the next between individual pursuits, family lives, Metro Antiochers, the church, neighborhood involvements, jobs, and the public ministry that affected us all.

How many more acts could the six of us add before we fell into a heap of exhaustion in the middle of a performance? How much more could we handle before this frenzy squeezed the life out of the relationships that held the whole show together? Maybe if I had known the real Nancy, I wouldn't have felt so threatened. But with six rings and counting, frantic activity could cover up all kinds of things.

But, hey, Chris Rice could handle it. Add more rings! Give me more balls to juggle! Turn up the intensity, baby! I was all about trying harder, doing more. It was Antioch's motto. And given the disproportionate influence of our tiny circle of six members, arguing with it was awfully hard.

# 26

# THE MAN IN THE
# TIE-DYED T-SHIRT

n June the Antioch members and our children piled into two
vans and headed out to Los Angeles for a week of vacation
wrapped around a speaking event for Spencer and me. It was an
unusual conference called "Wineskins," attended by only a couple dozen
people and sponsored by a network of West Coast congregations that
lived communally.

These folks seemed a bit strange, the kind of funky white folks Joanie
dreaded being associated with back when we first debated the community idea.

Their uppity attitude toward people who didn't "do church" exactly
as they did troubled me. In a "get to know you" time with a group of
their leaders they pumped Spencer with questions about why Antioch had
not split off from Voice of Calvary church yet to form our own separate
congregation. During our reconciliation talk one guy ripped into us about
the irrelevance of the race issue for Christians. Nancy—who could get
fiery—couldn't contain herself, and I was glad she didn't. She blasted him
as a racist in front of the whole assembly. Meeting in endless small groups,
we answered a long, nauseating list of questions I had no desire to discuss
with strangers, like "What was your most embarrassing life moment?"
One of their most irritating habits was giving each other foot massages.
Whenever I saw Joanie she was rolling her eyes, as if to say "When it this
ordeal gonna be over?"

Yet through all the weirdness, I kept my eye on one person who didn't
press us with self-righteous questions, act like race was beneath him, or
tickle anybody's toes.

At age fifty John Alexander looked like a relic from the 1960s with his
fluffy salt-and-pepper beard and rainbow-colored tie-dyed T-shirt. I knew
Alexander as a celebrity from the who's who of Christian social activists,
as an author, and as the former editor of an influential magazine. But
something was strange.

Nearly a decade before, this guy had disappeared from the national radar screen. Now here he was at this conference, in his new identity as a pastor in an obscure little house church in San Francisco.

At dinner the first night John plopped himself down at my table and started pumping me with questions. But his interest was in us and our life. He was fascinated by our interracial membership. "Listen, Chris," he said. "I've never seen a community with black and white people. I've wanted to see this happen for years."

I was also captivated by him. And what I found most fascinating was John's gradual descent into anonymity.

After studying on a prestigious scholarship at Oxford University, he had launched a promising academic career teaching philosophy. In 1965 he left academia to found a magazine, *The Other Side,* with his father. The magazine's influence in bringing together faithful Christianity and social justice was enormous. John had served as editor and primary spokesperson for nearly twenty years, and helped start an array of other projects, including a fund for third-world development and a business that supported indigenous artisans. Over these decades John had gained a wide national platform, speaking all over the country.

But while Spencer and I were on the rise, John had self-consciously stepped away from the spotlight. He still did some writing. But most of his energy was devoted to pastoring San Francisco's tiny Church of the Sojourners and its twenty members living among a low-income population and to being a kind of itinerant peacemaker for struggling Christian communities. While we were becoming more and more national, John was becoming more and more local.

John's story of maturing downward, his years of experience, and his listening presence and articulate voice captivated me. I sensed his life had something to say to mine.

His wife, Judy, was also at the conference. She was warmer where John was more cerebral, but both were full of good humor and simply did not take themselves as seriously as the rest of the Wineskins crew.

During Antioch's long drive back to Jackson we spent the first five hours swapping Wineskins stories on CB radios we'd hooked up. Those vans had to be rocking side to side with the laughter inside. Everybody was fighting for the microphones, trying to get in their favorite "Can you buh-lieve this?" episode about a particular foot rubbing, outrageous comment, or weird personality.

But John's letter to Antioch a couple of weeks later proved that there was a strong mutual attraction going on. John said Church of the Sojourners wanted to send a group from San Francisco to visit us. They wanted to know what our needs were. Did the house need painting? Did we need help tutoring kids? They wanted to put Antioch in their budget. I'd never seen—and Antioch had never received—a letter quite like this before, a kind of blank check of voluntary service. This Oxford-trained philosopher didn't want to come lecture to us. He wanted to wash our dishes for a week. I was impressed. We began to work with John on a visit for the following year.

Meanwhile Antioch's six-ring circus kept buzzing.

Cecil and his humble, ornery soul had wiggled back into our life after his June prison release. He lived in the Duplex and worked a handyman job. What made us such suckers for charismatic ex-cons? After all of JJ's mess, when he still visited from time to time, Spencer would amble outside to see him and share some laughs. And even after we lost touch with JJ for good, even after we heard he was dealing drugs again, Spencer's soft spot for him never hardened. For JJ Spencer had a very high—and puzzling—kind of persevering affection.

I found myself in a similar situation with Cecil. Over that summer we patched the roof of the Duplex, fished together, and had long conversations about prison life, about how, exactly, one got addicted to burglary and about the ways of rural Mississippi white folk. Every week I had to push and prod Cecil not to quit the truck-driving classes he had signed up for. When Donna and I drove down to a country church for his sister's funeral after her death in a car crash, Cecil was very thankful.

In spite of my unspoken reservations, Nancy and I got off to a very good start after she joined the *Urban Family* staff at the end of the month. She was "awesome," as Spencer liked to say of the gifts of those who worked with us. Nancy bent over backward to show no partiality. *Maybe,* I thought, *she's anticipating potential difficulties.* Still, it was hard not to imagine more and more of Spencer's energy being directed toward her, and less toward me.

In July a sobering concern entered Spencer's life when he was diagnosed with diabetes. The doctor ordered him onto a strict regimen of healthy diet and regular exercise. I knew the latter was going to be a lot easier for Spencer than giving up high-fat rib tips from E&L's hole-in-the-wall barbecue shop. But our continuing witness depended on his continuing good health, and I was happy to see him take up power walking with Nancy.

Gloria's summer program at the Small House was a big hit, and as fall came, her after-school efforts brought fifteen kids to the Big House every day. The downstairs hallway bathroom should have had a warning sign: "Enter at Your Own Risk. Used up to 1,000 Times per Week by Daycare and After-School Children." Sometimes after a tiring day at the office, I didn't want to navigate a maze of wired kids to get to my bedroom. But I was grateful that Gloria was extending her gifts and that Benjamin was in her caring hands all day.

✤

Attendance at the annual CCDA conference in October 1992 doubled, drawing over seven hundred urban activists to Detroit. Jackson was chosen as the site for the 1993 conference, with Spencer and me slated to be among the speakers.

In November we worked out a three-year plan with JP to move the entire *Urban Family* operation to Jackson.

By the end of the year Spencer and I had spent seventy-five days on the road.

When Antioch ended 1992 with our second churchwide New Year's Eve bash, Cecil was out somewhere else that night. Maybe living at Antioch had gotten to be too much like prison for him—too confining, too many boundaries, too many people in his business. Many episodes of irresponsibility had led him and me into more shouting matches.

By the end of January, after five months with us, everybody was ready to see Cecil go. I was happy that he made the decision to leave himself, that we didn't have to boot him out like JJ. He moved back to his hometown, found a decent job, and stayed out of trouble. With ex-offenders, that was often the most you could hope for.

A couple of weeks after he left, someone told me Cecil was outside. He had come unannounced.

I caught myself mimicking Spencer with JJ—ambling outside, smiling at the sight of my old friend, listening to him go on and on, laughing at his jokes and language, losing track of the time, and being very glad to be with him again. Our verbal scuffles of the past few months never even occurred to me.

"Remember, Cecil," I said, as he finally climbed back into his beat-up car. "There's always room for one more person at the Antioch dinner table."

"I know it, Cree-us. I shor 'preciate it."

# 27

# ROAD SHOW

*I*n the fourth month of 1993 the birth of Spencer and Nancy's third child led them to an inspired name: April Joy. Other ecstasies were in the air too. Spencer's and my book was finally published. Our two faces grinned from the cover under the title, *More Than Equals: Racial Healing for the Sake of the Gospel.* Benjamin affectionately dubbed the new baby "A-po," and Spencer and I ramped up our road show. And Joanie was in love.

Joanie had met Ron Potter at a conference of black Christians held in Jackson a month earlier and had brought him over to Antioch. Ron's jolly laugh and easygoing manner won me over. Ron, who taught at an urban seminary in Philadelphia, described himself as a professor and theologian. His great big vocabulary, endless stream of knowledge, and ample belly proved that he spent a lot of time in books. He had strong intellectual gifts to offer community, and it was a joy to see how happy he and Joanie were together.

Sensing that the publication of *More Than Equals* was about to change our lives, Donna and I got away for a weekend. One of our activities that weekend was to fill out paperwork to begin the process of adopting a baby. We'd always planned on adopting, and after more unsuccessful months trying to get pregnant, now seemed a good time. We applied for a Korean baby, and also locally, and were told the wait could be two to three years.

Meanwhile Spencer and I anticipated the months ahead filled with the pleasing, starry-eyed request that can become a dangerous measure of one's significance: "Could you please autograph my copy of your book?"

Spencer and I were quickly brought down to earth.

Although we were not on the program, at our own expense, expecting a windfall of book sales, we flew to a reconciliation conference held at a huge downtown arena in Norfolk, Virginia. We got a hotel room, had books rushed from the publisher, set up a massive book table near an arena exit, planted our huge poster of the book cover on it, and readied our credit-card machine. After the first night's session ended hundreds of people poured out of the arena while we stood behind the table like eager-beaver cashiers ready for Disneyland rush hour.

We sold five books. Maybe. The second night, maybe three more. By the third night, we had that giant poster of our grinning faces stashed under the table. We didn't want anybody to mistake us for the guys on the cover. Back at the hotel room each night we laughed until our sides ached.

But at a nearby speaking engagement to twenty pastors, the book sold out. Rule number one in the education of two public relations bumpkins: If you ain't speakin', you ain't sellin'. And as speaking requests poured in, it looked like it would be a while before we paid for another plane ticket or hotel room.

Wherever we spoke during May and June, from Dallas to Chicago and Richmond to St. Louis, we found far more urgency since the Los Angeles verdict and riots of the year before. It was easier to get people, as we called it, to "admit."

On planes headed to speaking events, with no busyness to interrupt us, Spencer and I had some of our best conversations, ranging from *Urban Family* shoptalk, to dissecting racial issues with reckless abandon, to the sports world, to discerning how Antioch people were doing and furthering all our growth. Eyes turned when we broke into raucous laughing. The plane would pull up to the gate, and Spencer would take a deep breath and mutter, "Time to put on the game face."

Spencer and I had taken up a new teaching method, a physical symbol of our life and message. Instead of one sitting while the other spoke, we stood together the entire time. It was very effective. I could tell people were more attracted to our message because of it.

We could prepare for a talk in minutes now, referring to "the short version" (fifteen minutes), "the medium" (forty-five minutes), and "the long" (ninety minutes). We often shared a hotel room and ate meals as just the two of us, which gave us more time for debating, laughing, and eye turning.

"You know," I'd tell our audiences, "Spencer and I are often together in airplanes, airports, hotels, restaurants. And we get a lot of strange looks. Like 'Who are these guys? A black guy and a white guy who seem at ease with each other, talking about deep issues?' Sometimes we have fun trying to imagine who people think we are.

"'I know, maybe they're professional athletes!'" Laughs erupt from the audience. "That's not funny," I'd deadpan.

Oh, maybe they're FBI agents! Or military guys! Or maybe they're gay! That's when they see us walking into a hotel room together. Are they rock musicians? You see a lot of integrated bands these days.

But you know what, y'all? It doesn't even occur to them that we might be together because we're followers of Christ. All those lifestyles I just mentioned offer far more demonstrations of interracial trust and common cause than Christian churches do.

What if Christians were to become known as people who refused to be determined by the idolatry of race? What if America looked at this agonizing race problem and said, "But, you know, there is a people among us who live differently, who haven't given in to the normal ways we operate as races. They go out of their way for the sake of the other—even when it's uncomfortable, costly, and inconvenient."

If Christians were to become those kind of people, the world would have to take notice.

Audience members swarmed up afterward to ask questions and have books signed. It was exhilarating to see our light touch them with hope and point toward a pathway forward.

Then it was back on the plane to reality, back to our light source, back to Joanie's taco salad, to dishes that needed doing and souls that needed guiding, to sharing a refrigerator with the people who kept our feet firmly planted on the ground, to the cultural blending that had made my two-year-old Benjamin's favorite songs the *Barney* show theme song ("I love you, you love me, we're a happy fam-i-ly") and a popular rap tune called "Whoop, There It Is," which he would sing to squeals of laughter from Johnathan, Jubilee, and Kortney.

Even now, though, I still fretted almost constantly over Spencer's higher status.

After we spoke, why was the line of people waiting to talk to him always longer than the ones seeking me? The white "ga-ga" factor really got under my skin. At my worst moments, I felt like Spencer could say "blah-blah, blah-blah-blah, blah-blah-blah-blah," and this was assumed to be a profound statement. I knew white folk needed their black high priests to give them absolution. Many of them had never talked about race with a black person, and Spencer was their big opportunity. I felt like Spencer didn't need my presence to legitimize his words, but I needed his blackness to legitimate mine. My authority on race came from Spencer; his authority came from his blackness.

But what if his line was longer because he had better things to say than I did? Spencer was a gifted confessor. He listened patiently; he offered choice words and wise advice. He was bold, direct, and compassionate. Yet he didn't overexplain. He left people with puzzles to figure out, to wrestle with. Was his gift of language the public one and my gift of organizing the private one? If so, I wanted his gifts, not mine. I wallowed in obsessive analysis and comparisons and the unfairness of it all.

Returning to Jackson threw me back into the intensity of the Big House, the office, and constantly submitting, with Nancy's presence reminding me that Spencer's soul mate, not mine, worked with us, with JP's calls reminding me that Spencer was the Anointed One and not me, with Pat's faxes to "Chief," not me. More and more frequently, all this left me feeling inferior. I began to doubt that I really had much to say, that I was insightful, or that I could write well. *Maybe*, I thought, *we should just stop pretending and admit there aren't two equal partners here, just one top dog.*

The odd thing was that even as these internal battles raged, my conscience was clear as we proclaimed reconciliation side by side.

Spencer and I were bound by a mission that was far bigger than us— and I believed that great causes always came with great struggles. I also knew I wasn't running from my dilemmas. Through many conflicts over my Mississippi years, I had learned how dogged fidelity to a particular place and people created a possibility for eventual transformation and peace, and I had developed a high tolerance for tension. When Spencer and I spoke, my weakness was ever before me, and this, I felt, kept me humble. I also refused to follow my envious thoughts where they could have led, to actively undermining Spencer, cutting him down behind his back, and cutting off his opportunities. Donna was the only person I confided in, and not very often. She listened. She hurt for me. But she genuinely loved Spencer, and she didn't fuel my comparisons. Mostly I wrestled in private, in agonized early morning prayers.

But my thoughts were becoming more and more toxic. They couldn't help but poison my behavior. Sometimes they left me cold and distant in Spencer's presence, not even wanting him near me. It didn't occur to me that I was as powerless as an alcoholic without a support group. I didn't realize how much help I needed, and I wouldn't have known who to turn to if I had.

---

In July the much-scorned Wineskins conference of the year before finally bore good fruit when John and Judy Alexander and three other Church of the Sojourners members drove forty hours from San Francisco to Mississippi. And what was the point of this singular investment of five lives over two full weeks at Antioch?

They bought ribs from E&L Barbecue for our whole house one night. Painted our foyer, at their expense. Cooked with us. Washed our dishes. Took some of us out to a movie. Organized activities for our children.

John, in another one of his kooky shirts, wearing discount purple Birkenstocks he tried to dye black, helped out with baby A-po.

It was as if they had invested time and care meditating on how to bring Antioch joy and rest. What was in it for them, giving up all these days to serve little old us? It seemed so wasteful. It was as if they had come to slow down our life for a week. They weren't in a rush to save the whole world. It was enough to serve someone and to take the time to do it well.

When we asked John to do a teaching, he taught from Paul's Letter to the Ephesians, using a captivating phrase. The purpose of the church, he said, was "growing each other up." The phrase seized my attention, pointing to a different challenge than constant doing. I still couldn't get over how he traded a national platform for the comparable obscurity of their little church. As far as success was defined, John had chosen to make himself irrelevant. I was captivated again by his wisdom and witness, and while San Francisco was a long way from Mississippi, I wondered if John was someone in whom I could eventually confide.

Something special was starting between our two groups. Antioch thought we had chosen to go to Wineskins to school those white folks in racial reconciliation. But maybe we had been taken there in order to receive a gift. Maybe the truth was, John and Judy and their church had something we needed.

After the Sojourners folks left, Spencer and I bounced back into the fast lane, responding to ever more urgent calls for racial reconciliation, both nationally and locally.

In a Boulder, Colorado, stadium later in July Spencer and I sat with JP in a strange sea of forty thousand mostly white, suburban, Republican men who were caught up in an exploding Christian movement called Promise Keepers. On the stage below, University of Colorado football coach and Promise Keepers founder Bill McCartney called for faithfulness to marriage, children, and church. Wild cheers followed each pledge. But the crowd grew eerily silent and still when McCartney began outlining a commitment to racial reconciliation, using a word rarely uttered from white evangelical lips—*racism*. At our *Urban Family* booth we had intense conversations with dozens of men. The experience convinced Spencer and me that the definition of *reconciliation* was up for grabs, whether it ended with hugs and tears in a stadium, or led into the trenches of the inner city. We strategized about using the influence we had through the magazine and our speaking engagements to ensure that "reconciliation" didn't become a cheap cliché or a passing fad.

Meanwhile, in Jackson, a new interracial coalition called Mission Mississippi was being birthed. What these black and white leaders did together—meet, eat, pray, and worship together—might have once resulted in a Klan firebombing. Some of the white pastors were with congregations that had turned away black worshipers in the 1960s. The danger was sugarcoating racial inequalities, wounds, and distrust with sweet talk and syrupy prayers, never getting to honest conversation in mixed racial company. But if extended over time and accompanied by truth telling, their actions together had the possibility of binding and transforming lives. Spencer and I determined to join the budding network and labor behind the scenes to see that the truth-telling element didn't get lost.

But the irony was that I didn't know how to tell Spencer the whole truth about my struggles in our relationship. It was an increasing theme of our partnership—our life put pressure on our message, our message put pressure on our life.

In August Joanie and Ron got married after five months of courtship. Joanie was the first Perkins daughter to get married, and JP was so joyful that somebody said the emotional ceremony was the first time they'd ever seen JP speechless. As Joanie and Ron headed up to Philadelphia so that Ron could finish his teaching duties and return to Jackson in a year, Antioch's hustle and bustle accelerated, and pressures mounted.

We hired another staffer at *Urban Family*: Jennifer Parker, a black Mississippi native and Harvard graduate moved into the Big House with us. The annual CCDA conference was coming to Jackson in three months, with Spencer and me speaking one night, and much of the organizing was on the shoulders of our staff.

Late in August, while Nancy was running errands during a magazine deadline frenzy, her van was broadsided by a Mack truck. The car was totaled, but somehow Nancy survived with only bruises and glass cuts. In what Spencer called "an ironic twist of fate," the policeman said that if Nancy's seat belt had been buckled, she would have been killed. Instead, she was thrown to the passenger side of the van. All of us were shook up, and Spencer seemed continually on the verge of tears.

When I told my mom and dad how overwhelmed we were feeling, they came down from Vermont (where they had moved in 1989) in September as full-time volunteers for ten weeks, to help with the CCDA conference. Dad was so pumped up, like he was back in his missionary days in Korea. He even joined the choir, singing next to me and taking on rocking, singing, and clapping with great enthusiasm, though not quite in sync.

If we were stressed out, at least we didn't have the immense grunt work of the magazine. That was still Pasadena's responsibility. All of a sudden even that changed in October. True to form, JP followed his instincts, ditched the previous three-year transition plan, and declared that it was time to put the magazine into Spencer's and my hands—within two months.

Maybe Nancy's accident was the wake-up call. Maybe it was the dawning realization of what it meant to have *Urban Family* heading our way. When the Antioch members went on a weekend retreat at a cabin in early October, shortly after JP's startling announcement, we talked seriously about the chokehold that our busyness was putting on us.

Why were we all so tired? Why had we failed to follow through on commitments we knew were important—spiritual, family, fitness, health? Was obsessive doing overwhelming the "growing each other up" that John Alexander had called us to? Could *Urban Family* eventually erode our life together? How many times was too many times for Spencer and me to travel?

They were the right questions. But Spencer and Nancy, Gloria, and Donna and I needed rest that weekend too and time for play, and by the time we checked in on how everybody was doing and hashed through the endless nitty-gritty issues of household management, there wasn't enough time to take the bigger questions very far.

We were both overextended and at the height of public success. *More Than Equals* was creating an audience that far exceeded our expectations. After six months it had sold out of its first print run of eight thousand copies, and a second printing was under way.

But as our name recognition climbed, so did my obsessions about Spencer.

One of his *More Than Equals* chapters had been reprinted in *Christianity Today* in September. Its 150,000 Christian readers saw Spencer's picture smack dab on the cover's upper corner. Inside, he was named as a new contributing editor.

Then, two weeks later, Phil Reed unknowingly rubbed it all in my face. In his Sunday sermon he spoke proudly of "Spencer's book" and his *Christianity Today* honor, and how Spencer's growing national voice made the whole church shine.

Of course, Phil didn't know how much thought, initiative, and work I'd put into getting the exposure in *Christianity Today*. Yet didn't he notice the other name and face on that book cover?

But I blamed Spencer, not Phil. Why didn't Spencer go out of his way more to affirm me? I wished he was the one to say something when I didn't get equal recognition. To myself, I thought, *at least come to me, say you noticed the slight and that you felt for me*. Instead of cheering for Spencer's success, I constantly resented it, and this was toxic indeed. The haunting comparisons between him and me, the pain of constant submitting were never far from my consciousness.

My love for Spencer ran deep, but now it was deeply conflicted. Loving him was more and more painful to me—to my ego, to my self-understanding, to my self-sufficiency. Being around him magnified my dark side. On many days it made me sick of myself. Sometimes it made me sick of him. But my pain was not inflicted by the nails of outsiders. My enemy was inside of me. This had become an insidious sickness, and I counted it all part of my cross to bear. And by God, I was going to bear it to the end.

As much as I believed in what Spencer and I preached about racial reconciliation, as well as I could articulate the truths of cost and sacrifice, of "denying yourself" and "picking up your cross daily," I found it harder and harder for one simple word to fall off my lips when I described my life with Spencer: joy. What I did not yet grasp was what the New Testament passage from Hebrews 12:2 witnessed to be the very thing that drove the Son of God to the pain of shame and humiliation: "who for the joy set before him endured the cross."

If I couldn't eventually find a way to joy, to internalize it, to testify to it, to make it just as much a part of my life as bearing crosses was, what was I doing here? What was I passing on to my son? And what did I really have to say to the world?

# 28

# COMBUSTIBLE KNOWLEDGE

inally, in October it all came to a head. I started a long letter to Spencer. I thought I was heading off one of Antioch's nagging afflictions.

Each announcement of Antioch's "divorces" had come to us as a shock. Why had nobody realized how serious the problems had become with Lue in 1986, with Phil and Tressa in 1987, and with Betsy and Harold in 1989? These were people we lived with. Yet there had not been truthful communication. And if others knew of their grievances, nobody had sought to intervene. The lack of honest airing of tension, whether through self-disclosure or confrontation, had allowed inevitable conflicts to fester into such acute antagonisms that were long past resolving.

To grow in virtue required facing the truth about your desires, and one of the strengths of our life's intensity was exposing how conflicted our desires really were. Telling the truth *to* each other required knowing the truth *about* each other, and our lives were accessible to each other in a way that made this more possible. But such intimate knowledge of one another was dangerous. It could be used to build us all up toward purer desires and greater growth, or it could explode us from within. The question was how to use greater exposure of vices and weaknesses in a way that built up rather than destroyed our friendships, to bring them into the light without the glare becoming unbearable.

After seven years in community, we could make detailed lists of each other's crap—the stuff that pushed your worst buttons. Who seemed goody-two-shoes or know-it-all. Who had perks you didn't have. People who it seemed you could never satisfy, who would automatically say no if you said yes. Who was judgmental. Opinionated. Quick-tempered. Didn't pull their weight. Got on your last nerve. Was easily irritated. Couldn't take criticism. Was inhospitable to houseguests. Was too tight with money. Was too loose with money. And so much more than this had been exposed over the years. Everybody had their dark sides—and we knew them very well.

Antioch had always been exquisitely clear with people like JJ and Cecil about where they needed work. There was less at stake with those we were "helping." If they refused to grow and left Antioch, it hurt. But it felt nothing like a divorce.

So much more was at stake between Antioch members, and we had mostly come to an unspoken, "don't ask, don't tell" agreement regarding vice and weakness: "You know my crap, I know yours. I won't bring up yours, if you won't bring up mine." The problem was that vice, resentment, grievance, and disordered desire could get toxic. And I wasn't aware of any as serious as mine.

In my eyes, writing a blunt letter to Spencer was going to my friend and putting the toxin in the open before it became too destructive. I sincerely wanted Spencer and me to be more transparent in our relationship, and I felt I needed more of his help to become free. But any letter I wrote to Spencer now would be very different from my pure-hearted missive of four years before, the one designed to inspire the reluctant prophet.

Back then I cheered for his success. Now I would have been happy to see this prophet reined in. I was less and less able to sort through the complexity of what was churning inside of me.

We were very busy, and it took me days to get the two and a half pages right. If I had understood how treacherous some of my statements were, I might have shown the letter to somebody besides Donna. How could she be objective, being my wife? But outside of Donna and Nancy, nobody had ever been invited into my relationship with Spencer.

Donna read my letter and sighed. "I feel torn, Chris. Spencer and I have been friends a long time. It's so hard, thinking of the conflict getting worse between you two."

Donna never fueled my demons. I knew she kept me from the worst. Stuff she sucked up and dealt with internally, I found unbearable to keep inside. She avoided conflict, and this was inviting it. Donna helped me make some minor changes, but I was determined to go forward. I doubt that she slept well that night. I certainly didn't.

The next day I put the letter on Spencer's desk and held my breath.

I hoped Spencer would respond with the grace with which he received my earlier letter and my "Batman and Robin" confession. But two intense years had passed since then.

I could imagine his eyes rolling and his face puckering up when he opened the letter and started to read.

"Dear Spencer, I've been trying hard to pinpoint the source of some deep discouragement. It's rooted in a continuing struggle related to you and a dilemma over our relationship and partnership."

I imagined Spencer muttering. "What's Chris layin' on me this time? Sometimes this bruthah is too much for me."

"I confess this struggle leaves me miserable, in retreat from you, and generally cold and distant. Sometimes I find myself not cheering for you, wishing you wouldn't get all the opportunities you get, or gain more motivation. Imagine how much further behind that would put me! Sometimes it's even hard being in the same room. These are deep, recurring negative thoughts and attitudes."

The intensifying toxic effects were new information to him. And with one subtle sentence—"Sometimes it's even hard being in the same room"—I had made a new move: I gave his weaknesses equal blame for my misery. Being so tightly attached to Spencer and around him so much was making me feel so miserable so often, I reckoned that there had to be something miserable about him. I pressed the theme.

"I know how being jealous and resentful of you can consume my time—how feeling undervalued can turn into a self-pity that disables me from thinking deeply—how your weaknesses can sometimes grate on me to the point of not even speaking to you—how hypersensitive and touchy I can get until I find a reason to resent your every action and word. How I need to repent! But I'm at a loss to know how to make a turnaround."

"Grate on me," "not even speaking to you," "resent your every action"— if only I had eaten those volatile words! Writing lacked tone of voice. If I had spoken those words to Spencer's face, at least he might have understood my intention as confession, not accusation. But was I unconsciously somehow trying to make him feel as miserable as I felt? To say you can't stand to be in somebody's presence is an awful burden. I never considered how such words would have wounded me if Spencer had written them to me.

Why didn't I remember my disgust at how the Reconciliation Meetings handled dangerous truth with such carelessness? That truth telling is as much about how and when you speak as what you say? All along, as incidents between Spencer and me happened, I should have followed the apostle Paul's simple but profound exhortation: "Do not let the sun go down on your anger." Or as Harold had once put it, "Settle any misunderstandings or hurt feelings before CNN news night at eleven." I had not developed the skill of doing that, and I should have at least apologized for that. And yet what was my alternative? To say nothing? To continue to keep it inside?

I stumbled forward in the letter, laying out the raw truth, ticking off a list of Spencer's weaknesses, the stuff that grated on me. It felt good, getting it off my chest.

I named his not doing enough to counter the Batman-Robin dynamic, not going out of his way to affirm me and share more of the credit. I asked why he said nothing after Phil's sermon and told him how that hurt. "Sometimes I wonder if you would serve our partnership under the circumstances that I have. If it was me getting the credit and the opportunities, would you struggle through it and hang with me?"

I named his blunt, suffocating, opinionated style that made it seem like there was only his way of seeing things. I remembered a comment I had filed away, one that Lawrence made to Spencer several years ago in an elders' meeting. "Why you always got to run things, man? Act like you know it all? Why you think you always got to tell folk what to do?" Exactly.

I named his inability to say "I'm sorry" and my growing conviction that he couldn't stand to be corrected or to apologize. He was good at confrontation. When someone was bold enough to tell someone else in Antioch about their bad attitude, it was invariably Spencer. But he was poor at confession.

I named his contentedness with his weaknesses, how his mantra about "I know I'm bad" became complacency.

There was no telling how Spencer was reacting now. This crap list was the riskiest part of the letter. Then I raised another new question: Were my expectations for our relationship too high?

"Maybe I am called to be Robin to your Batman. There's a certain peace in that—you accept that Batman gets most of the credit, that you're the loyal follower, that your job is to make him look good."

But being yokefellows was a different vision, as I wrote in the letter, one "of interdependent equals, fighting through decisions to the point of unity, different gifts equally valued, mutually respecting, submitting, serving and honoring one another. I know we agree this is what we've been shooting for. But it's the hardest mission I've ever undertaken." For how could we ever be true equals, given who he was and I wasn't?

"You are John Perkins's firstborn son, his named heir apparent, and a leader fit to follow him (I don't add that lightly)." As a result, I said, credit flowed to his feet, doors whooshed open, and people automatically gave more weight to his words than mine. "I often feel like the dispensable partner—my side of this partnership could be filled by any organized white guy who stuck around for a few years.

"But these are unchangeable facts of life. Why can't I accept the realities, and be thankful for what God has chosen to do through me? How could I possibly say—even with all the trials—that I'm not where God wants me to be? How many others get the chances I have? Why can't I just let God get out the pruning shears and go after me? After all, this is basically a big ego problem."

I went on: "What I do know is this: I need help—from you. I must begin to work through more things with you, on a deeper level. I think there's a higher cost than I thought to the kind of relationship we've been striving for."

I knew he was right when he said my expectations for myself were too high. But Donna had helped me see there was a strength in this too. "I'm not content saying 'I might as well adjust to my weakness'—and forget everybody who suffers the consequences." Was that a subtle dig at Spencer, at what he said about not being surprised by his badness? Probably, given how I concluded my truth telling.

> Until now, Spencer, I thought I was the whole problem. Now I think there are also things you do, or don't do, that add to my difficulties. I realize I'm inviting a lot of pain by being so honest. But I'm ready to move to another level. I'm willing to risk being taken to the cleaners. I'm sorry that I haven't been more forthright before—knowing my weaknesses doesn't make it easy to pick on yours.
>
> This is as honest as I've ever been about my agonies. I'm scared to talk about them. I'd rather not face them. But I'll be restless until I do.

I signed the letter "Still your yokefellow."

In the days that followed I was meek and mild around Spencer. I couldn't read him. I hoped he would ignore my letter's flaws and read it as a plea for help. We had learned to keep moving when our relationship was under stress, and the atmosphere demanded it. With the CCDA conference just over a week away, we were all drowning in logistical details.

Four days before CCDA, Mission Mississippi held its first big public event. In downtown Memorial Stadium, where, in 1962, former Governor Ross Barnett had whipped up a cheering University of Mississippi football crowd against opening the school to James Meredith, its first black student (a riot followed on campus the next day, countered by federal troops), fifty black and white pastors raised a huge cross to launch a rally for racial reconciliation. I marveled at the hundreds of black and white Mississippians around us. At stake in my partnership with Spencer was a chance to influence them, to show them how far they could go in trust and common cause.

Two days later Spencer summoned me to his bedroom, down the upstairs hallway from mine. We were alone. Our CCDA talk was just two nights away.

Spencer had done a masterful job of hiding his emotions over the past nine days. Now I saw how angry he was. "You know, Chris, I'm tryin' to be patient with your problem. But projectin' stuff back on me? That's pretty rough, man."

"Well, maybe it's time you took a look at your problems too, Spencer."

"Just cause you strugglin' with stuff doesn't have to make my struggles like yours. I can't get why you'd even think of tryin' to link 'em together like that."

His voice was already rising. So was mine as I protested.

"All I'm sayin' is that I need more help from you. See, that's just the problem, Spencer. You're too content with your weaknesses, and . . ."

"No, I ain't! You're not hearin' what I'm sayin'. I'm sayin' your problem and my weaknesses are separate issues. I can't change who I am. All that stuff that gets on your nerves? That makes you feel less valued? I'm lookin' out for you all the time, makin' sure you get pulled into stuff!"

"Puh-lease, Spencer. Spare me. See? You can't even squeeze out a simple 'I'm sorry' for not sayin' nothin' after Phil's sermon. I mean, what went through your mind when you heard that? That you wrote the book yourself? That our work is just about you?"

"Well, if you think your problem depends on me fixin' it, that's messed up!"

The argument went on and on. We were shouting, accusing, pointing fingers. I brought specific things up from the letter, and Spencer shot back. He brought up specific things, and I shot back. Neither of us was giving ground, and I was getting fed up.

"Spencer, don't you even care . . ."

"I do care! Why you think I'm even up here talkin' to you right now with all the stuff we got to do? Why do you think I bother to put up with all it takes for you and me to do everything we do together? Constantly submitting? Havin' to run everything past each other? Don't you know how much I value you? I know where I'd be without you. I know who I'd be without you."

Those words jarred me. They were words I longed to hear. I needed to know what I meant to Spencer, that my life and presence was a gift

to him, that he needed me not just to get work done, not just to carry a
message, but because our friendship mattered. Suddenly the room was
silent. I had been broken. My grievance list seemed unimportant.

"Well, I wouldn't be nothin' without you either," I muttered.

We both stared at the floor.

It would have been nice to go on, to tell each other what we respected
and admired about the other. We didn't do that kind of tender thing very
well. But the good memories inspired by silence seemed enough.

We rose without speaking, crossed the room, and embraced. And in a
choked-up voice Spencer whispered the highest compliment he'd ever paid
me. "Chris, I love you like one of my own brothers."

That night we didn't nearly get to the bottom of the toxic buildup in
our relationship. But for now it didn't seem so overwhelming. Spencer and
I had revealed our best desires to each other. And seeing what those were
made all the difference in my hope, that somehow we could find a way to
a deeper peace.

Two nights later, at a downtown Jackson hotel, Spencer and I climbed up
behind a podium to the generous applause of a record CCDA crowd of
twelve hundred urban Christian activists. They were our most loyal *Urban
Family* readers, and many had devoured our book. Some put us on a
pedestal. Many of them worked in interracial teams and partnerships, and
a good number were probably facing conflicts. They had to know it was
normal. That they could endure. That there was much at stake in enduring. And they needed to know Spencer and I weren't all we were cracked
up to be.

We stood side by side, Spencer to the audience's right, me to its left. As
always Spencer lightened things up.

"I'm, ah, Chris Rice, and this," he said, pointing to me, "is Spencer
Perkins." Wild laughter broke out. "Switch that."

We had been asked to tell our story, and Spencer launched into the
short version of growing up on the other side of the tracks in Mendenhall, the white school, JP's Brandon beating, the struggle to forgive. "I
knew exactly what the Good Samaritan story meant for me," he said,
wrapping up his first part. "It meant your neighbor is a white person. And
God's sayin' if you're gonna love me, you got to learn how to love white
people."

Spencer glanced at me. I leaned into the microphone. "I'm the white
guy Spencer's supposed to love," I said. Laughter again.

All my old lines got huge laughs. This activist crowd identified with my journey in the urban 'hood—coming to Mississippi as "the solution," my first memory of Spencer and his question, and how he didn't get it from *How to Win Friends and Influence People*. I talked about the Reconciliation Meetings and being tempted to leave. "Hey, I didn't need to put up with these angry black folks . . . like Spencer." I turned my head and glared at him to more wild laughter.

I spoke of the "great white temptation" of walking away when things got hot. "When that time comes—and I promise you it will—are we going to embrace the pain and work through it?"

As I thought of how our trials had led me to the man beside me, my emotions rose inside me. "I came to realize that I couldn't name a single black person who trusted me and I trusted them. This was a mission that was too big for me alone. A new type of relationship had to come into existence in my life.

"But some fields, like the difficult fields we work in . . ." My voice cracked. The past few months and days of struggle swept over me.

> Some fields . . . are difficult to bring to fruition. The ground is rocky. It gets rough. It gets muddy. Sometimes you have to pull your plow uphill.
>
> When a farmer has a job that's too big for one animal, he takes something called a yoke to harness two together and hook them to the plow. The toughest jobs require teams of yokefellows. The more difficult the field, the stronger the team has to be, the more it has to work in tandem, the more different gifts are required. It takes a certain heart, a certain courage, to go into those fields.
>
> To pull the plow into the new territory of reconciliation, I needed to be yoked to someone. To go into a territory of racial healing that I never had experienced before—I needed Spencer.

As Spencer did his final section, among the words he spoke were ones that rushed over me with a cleansing, freeing power.

"Often Chris and I talk about what our lives would be like if God hadn't brought us together. For me half the things I've done, that I do, that I'm involved in now, probably wouldn't be possible.

"Our lives complement each other. When somebody comes up to me to give us a task to do—one that might require some organizational skills? I tell 'em, 'You talkin' to the wrong half of this team.'"

More laughter.

Whatever Spencer detested in my letter, tonight he pushed it aside.

"Chris believes in me," he said, his voice rising with conviction. "And there's a security that comes in that. He doesn't mind pushin' me. And I can take it from him because I know he has my best interests at heart. If we ever separated, not only would I not be able to do half of what I do, I would be a much weaker person."

*How strange,* I thought, *that Spencer told even more about what I meant to him at this podium than he had in his upstairs bedroom.*

It was up to me to finish things up.

> You know, people look at me and Spencer, and they often say, "What a wonderful relationship! What a miracle it is that you're together!" They see our partnership at *Urban Family.* Our families in the same house together. Our children like sisters and brothers. So many times people call him "Chris" and me "Spencer," and it's pretty hard to confuse us.
>
> But what they often don't understand is what's behind this relationship. What those people don't see is the times we've wept together in our office because of how we've fallen short with each other. They weren't there two nights ago, when we put some stuff on the table and dealt with it together.
>
> When you're plowing difficult terrain, thoughts will enter your head that will make you want to give up. You can begin to distrust your yokefellow. You see, any bond that is significant to God's kingdom is going to be attacked. There are going to be moments when you are tempted to break the yoke.
>
> But if the yoke is broken, the mission is compromised. Each of you loses half your strength, half the gifts needed to realize the goal.
>
> Thirty years ago the task in America was social equality, and much work remains to be done. But the calling upon us is to become more than equals. It is to show that our lives can be shared across racial lines, in common mission. CCDA is in a point position to seize this new territory. But it's going to require us to team up together, to hook up the yoke.

I turned to my friend. To the one who brought out both the best and the worst in me. Who had stayed faithful in the sight of both. The one who had been given to me, to take me far further than I ever would have chosen to go on my own.

"Thank you, Spencer, for trusting me. For bearing with me. Not only in health, but in sickness. Not only in the rich times, but in the poor. Thank you for loving me like a brother."

We embraced, to wild applause.

# 29

# TEXAS TIME BOMB

$A$t Christmas Gloria handed out the most presents again, and two-year-old Benjamin tore his open with great anticipation. When he saw clothes inside, he tossed the box aside. Donna scolded him. "Benjamin! You go tell Miss Gloria thank you!" He walked over obediently. "Thank you, Miss Gloria. Don't want dat," he said, dropping the clothes in her lap and shooting back over to his next present. Gloria reared back with laughter. "That's the last time I get that boy somethin' he doesn't like!"

Such light moments interrupted the still-growing intensity of our life. Twenty different Metro Antiochers had shared the Big House with us for a week or more in 1993; Spencer and I were on the road more and more; and the administrative monster called *Urban Family* was in our hands. We were the bottom line for almost everything now—editorial, production, advertising, bookkeeping, and servicing thirteen thousand subscribers. I had taken over the managing editor post from Rudy Carrasco, who had done a fine job. Now, at least, I had a title and position closer to the reality of my partnership with Spencer. The only major responsibility we didn't have was fundraising. JP and the foundation board were doing that, and *Urban Family* was still under their umbrella.

In February we hit Chicago for six days, speaking at three colleges, a seminary, a multicultural student conference, and to a coalition of Latino, black, and other inner-city churches.

A week later Donna and I got a huge Valentine's Day surprise. I received a phone call from the head of the adoption agency we had been working with for nine months.

"Chris, are you sitting down?"

"Uh, yeah."

"We have a child we think you and Donna would be perfect parents for. She's a healthy, two-week-old baby girl." A little girl for Daddy? My heart swelled with joy. But her next words numbed me.

"She's biracial. A black birth father and white birth mother. I know this might seem rushed, but you and Donna need to make a decision within the next two weeks."

That night Donna and I tingled with a confusing mixture of shock and delight. We knew that black and biracial babies rarely got placed with white parents. And we knew what kinds of emotions and issues were triggered when they did.

But Antioch was very supportive. "Whatever y'all decide. We're behind you," they said. That weekend Donna and I went away camping to make our decision.

Favorite camping spots and long drives along the ambling, deeply forested Natchez Trace Parkway had become our getaway from our life's intensity. We set Benjamin loose on a playground with other children and sat down on a bench.

"Donna, can't you imagine all these other parents staring at us right now? Our brown daughter and white son running hand in hand?"

"You know, I can handle stares and snide comments from white folks. It's so much harder coping with what black folks might be thinking."

A close black friend, a single mother, had told us about seeing a white family with a black child at the local mall. "When I saw that, it made me feel like I could do a better job of raising that child by myself than they can as two parents." Even Donna and I cringed, meeting white parents who seemed to think adopting a black child was like adding a cute new color to the family portrait. They raised the kids in an all-white universe and didn't expand their own world to black friends or greater racial understanding. They didn't even bother to learn how to care for a black child's hair.

But were we ready to accept what transracial adoption would bring to our family? Could we raise this little baby girl to embrace the black part of her heritage? How could we train her to dissect and cope with hurts and stings of racism that we had never experienced? Were we dealing her a hand she would later decide she would have never chosen for herself?

The funny thing was that while we weren't a biracial family yet, we were already a bicultural family who lived in a deeply interracial world. Any children we ever had would be touched by that experience and by friends and mentors of different races.

There was something else too, something Spencer and I had noticed on our speaking trips. Often the college students most passionate about racial understanding were biracial, with a white and a black parent. They said they didn't want to have to choose between their mother's culture and their father's, and they were also more honest critics of each culture. Just as interracial couples often developed a passion for racial reconciliation, white parents of black children often developed a similar concern, eventually putting themselves in mixed neighborhoods and churches and schools, places they wouldn't have otherwise considered. Such families became powerful allies in the struggle for racial understanding and justice.

Despite the inadequacies we felt, Donna and I came to believe that this baby was meant to be our daughter. At least we would always be aware that we needed help.

In early March, as soon as I saw that brown-skinned, curly black-haired girl, I felt she was my own, and she immediately had me wrapped around her little finger. Benjamin held her with such wonder in his eyes. It was very strange, walking into an office as three Rices and driving away as four. Everybody at Antioch bent over backward to help, and Gloria was thrilled to have another baby girl in the house, with more dresses to buy and hair to fuss with.

Our daughter's name embraced her rich maternal heritage. Talia, Hebrew, meaning "gentle dew from heaven," honoring Donna's mother Thale (pronounced "Tolly"). Renee, "born again," the name given by Talia's birth mother. Suzanne, to honor my mother, who was the only person to send Talia a card with all three of her names on it.

We'd had so little warning of this arrival. And so what? On our doorstep had come gentle dew from heaven, refreshing, rearranging, and bringing a new happiness to our lives.

Our public work continued bearing good fruit.

Over the spring *More Than Equals* moved toward sales of fifteen thousand copies in its first year, and our *Urban Family* staff grew to five (including a Kenyan member of our church, Hellen Wambari). On speaking trips like the one to a citywide conference in Raleigh, North Carolina, Spencer and I raised the bar for reconciliation.

During the question-and-answer time, a frustrated older white man posed what was probably on the minds of half the white folks in the room. "It's OK to talk about white racism and white responsibility, but why isn't it OK to talk about conditions in the urban black community?" He pressed forward. "Why is the crime rate so high? Why are so many women on welfare? Why don't the men take care of their families? What about all of those junk cars? But even to ask these questions, I come off like a racist and a bigot."

I charitably deferred the hot potato to Spencer. This guy needed to hear from a bruthah.

"Y'all," said Spencer, "it's gotta be safe to ask these questions when you're tryin' to get at the truth. Just make sure your motives for asking are pure."

He paused, looking at the white man. Long ago Spencer and I had chosen to assume that, for people like this, only their willingness to be honest, and ours, could convert them.

"Some uncomfortable truth has to be faced, and it's painful for us black folks to hear it. Black folks like talkin' about racism, because that's the white folks. And there's still a ton of it out there. But if we're talkin' about reconciliation, we gotta get at all the things that separate us." I flinched. Telling the truth about blacks in mixed company didn't score any points with the bruthahs and sistahs.

"A lot of what used to be racism has become fear. To black people it feels just like the old racism did. When I'm in my car, and I pull up beside a white lady, and she reaches over and locks her door, the first thing that comes to my mind is, 'This is an old racist white lady!'"

Spencer chuckled. "But it's not so simple anymore. Some of our own black women are afraid to see a black man comin' now!" he said, his voice rising. He ran off statistics of disproportionate violence by black men. "As black men, we have to own up to some of the responsibility for this fear. We have to deal with both racism and fear, because both of them are causing a separation." He paused.

"But white folks—y'all approach most of us black men like we're all criminals, and nine out of ten of us are the good guys. Plus, most of those crimes I talked about are black on black." He chuckled again. "So when it comes right down to it, y'all have very little to fear."

It was gratifying, hearing later how the Raleigh folks continued honest conversation and formed interracial supper clubs that alternated between black and white homes.

I wish that I could say that my problems with Spencer had gone away, but they hadn't. Unknown to him, I had set a goal for 1994: "Have an honest, open, committed, and loving relationship with Spencer." Our embrace in his room in October had been a moment of great joy, but not a permanent breakthrough. We stumbled forward, not quite knowing how to keep "growing each other up," as John Alexander would have put it.

Had I weighed him down with my letter, with having to worry constantly about me? Anytime I looked "cold and distant" now, why wouldn't he think that I felt he was the cause of it? How would he know my skin

wasn't crawling, being near him, or that my silence at a particular moment wasn't silence at all, but an indication that his weaknesses were
"grating on me to the point of not even speaking"? That, right then, I was
"resenting his every action and word"? I hated it, but as so many times
in the past, the bad feelings escalated.

In early June the Antioch member families and a few Metro Antiochers
loaded into a fifteen-passenger van and headed to Colorado for our annual community vacation. We invited Danny Hill along, a teenager from
the neighborhood who had been a weekly dinner guest for six years now
and was like a son to Donna and me and the rest of Antioch. Also joining us was a newly arrived Bruderhof volunteer named Elisha Risser, who
had gotten attached to Talia. Donna and I were happy for her and
Danny's help.

I enjoyed the company of my Antioch comrades—individually. But thirteen people in a van for twenty-plus hours wasn't at the top of my list for
a restful trip. I was beginning to have my doubts about communal vacations. I needed a vacation *from* Spencer, not with him. The incessant
group thing was wearing on me.

But I hadn't spoken up, and now there I was, feeling like I was constantly submitting to Spencer, this time in a claustrophobic bubble. Stupid stuff that didn't matter got on my nerves. He wanted to stop for ice
cream. I wanted to keep moving. He probably knew I was stewing, but
I'm sure he didn't have a clue what he'd done wrong. I admonished myself
about just letting go. Imagine the thousands of people who had bought
our high-minded book on reconciliation hearing that one of the authors
was a guy who got all wigged out about ice cream stops?

With a whole retreat center in Steamboat Springs to ourselves, the best
two moments of the week summed up my conflicting desires: the first was
trout fishing with Spencer and a CCDA friend from Denver, in a mountain
valley straight off a postcard; and the second was taking an exhilarating
hike through an alpine forest to get as far from Spencer as I could, fed up,
feeling like Antioch was only doing things that Spencer wanted to do.

But all the minor irritations throughout the week were merely symptoms of something smoldering in me that only needed the right match to
burst into flame. On the way back to Jackson it struck.

A young white Coloradoan named David Howard was coming to
volunteer with us for the summer, and he followed the van in his own car.

At one point Donna and I rode with him. We left Talia with Elisha and Danny in the van, thankful for a baby break. It had been a long day.

At night, somewhere in Texas, we all stopped at a restaurant to eat. As I climbed out of David's car Elisha strode over from the van and said Gloria and Nancy had told her to give Talia back to Donna.

Hearing that, somehow all I heard was "Nancy." I marched right over to Nancy in the parking lot and lit into her in front of everybody. "Who are you, telling us what to do with our daughter?"

"She's been crying Chris, for a long time. Talia needs to be with y'all."

I might have gotten it wrong, but her voice sounded snappy to me, high and mighty, and I didn't appreciate it. And so much was already roiling within me. I went from zero to sixty in two seconds flat. "I've had it with this Perkins know-it-all stuff! Are you the parent here?"

"Don't you realize that crying is getting on everybody's nerves in our van?"

"Nancy, you act like you got the inside knowledge on everything! Like you and Spencer wrote the book on parenting. Like you . . ."

This was so, so bad. I was screaming, eyes wild, and there were the Antioch kids standing still on the pavement around me, staring at Uncle Chris and Aunt Nancy, hearing this poison spew out of my mouth. But I could not stop myself.

"I'm sick of this! Sick of it. Sick of it. Don't worry, Nancy, you won't have to put up with our baby the rest of the way." I stomped into the restaurant. Our family ate at a table by ourselves, exactly the way I wanted it.

When we left the restaurant Donna probably wished she could just disappear and return when the situation was all cleaned up and her husband returned to sanity. Our family piled into David's car, and we followed the van. I was seething. A couple of hours later we stopped at a hotel and went to our rooms. The phone rang. It was Spencer.

"Uh, I'm thinkin' the Antioch adults need to meet tomorrow mornin' to talk. How 'bout eight o'clock, in our room?"

"Fine. See you then." I struggled to fall asleep.

The next morning the Metro Antiochers took the kids, and Gloria, Spencer and Nancy, and Donna and I gathered. Too much had been exposed last night. I couldn't pretend it was just a passing moment. I let two years' worth of my frustrations out—things I'd told Spencer in my letter, dynamics at the office, stuff in the Big House, the whole mess.

Nancy ventured a diagnosis, and I did not receive it as an accusation. "You're jealous of Spencer," she said, almost marveling, like suddenly all the puzzle pieces of my behavior had come together for her.

For the first time my jealousy-envy demon stood in the Antioch spotlight, in the middle of the room. "Yes, that is my problem," I said, "and I do not know what to do about it." I felt naked, ashamed, and broken, completely broken. And just like when this dark side was exposed to Donna, then to Spencer the first time, no lightning flashed, the lights didn't flicker, no organ music played. Instead, something completely unexpected happened.

I started sobbing and heaving, and Gloria came over, wrapped her arms around me and let me cry like a baby.

Why had it taken me so long to get into the arms of my friends? By the end of the meeting we were all in tears, asking forgiveness of one another for this crap, for that crap. Spontaneous confessions went on and on. But I didn't feel that anything was as damaging to community as mine.

After we prayed through many tears we gathered ourselves and ushered all the children and the Metro Antiochers into the room.

"Yesterday," I said, "you saw me say some very mean things to Nancy. What I said was very wrong. I've asked Nancy to forgive me. I also want to ask you kids to forgive me." Others made confessions too. Then we all held hands, and sealed our peace with a prayer of thanksgiving to God.

---

The day after we got back to Jackson, a Monday, the Antioch members met in Donna's and my room. I'd never seen Spencer look so worn down.

"Nancy and I talked a long time last night," he said. There was a bleakness in his eyes, a hopelessness in his voice. "We're thinkin' of goin' to Pasadena for a few weeks. We could keep workin' on the magazine from there. We feel like we need some distance, some space to think. Maybe we need to make some changes around here. I don't know how to move forward, y'all."

We had done what we could in the hotel, confessing, asking for and granting forgiveness. But for the first time, it seemed, everybody knew there was a deep pain in our midst, pain that was beyond our ability to resolve.

"I don't know, Spence," I said. "I'm afraid that things will get worse, not better, if you and Nancy leave right now." He nodded his head.

Suddenly, Nancy got an inspiration. "What about calling John and Judy? Why don't we ask them to come for a few days and counsel with us?"

Spencer nodded, and the proposal immediately sounded right to all of us. The Alexanders were an older wiser couple whom both Spencer and

I respected, who knew so much more about "growing each other up." Spencer said he would give them a call.

"But, Chris," he said, "what about that talk we're supposed to give to the Ministries' summer interns this afternoon? I ain't in no mood to do that. Can we back out of that?"

I thought for a second. "I just think we've got to grit our teeth and do it, Spence. Stand together and testify, even in the midst of all our difficulties. Sometimes it's what reconciliation is all about. Not having things resolved, but moving forward anyway, putting our hope in God's faithfulness."

"I suppose you're right. But it's the last thing I wanna do right now."

"Me too."

That afternoon, we did speak, saying what we always said. But I felt the pressure of life upon the message as never before. Those interns had no idea how desperate Spencer and I felt inside.

For the first time Antioch looked outside of itself, outside of Voice of Calvary, outside of our years of Mississippi experience, for a way forward. We dialed 911 to San Francisco. Three days later, on Thursday, John and Judy were on a plane to Jackson. From witnessing foot rubs together at Wineskins two years ago to treating us like royalty a year ago, they were about to see the real us.

# 30

# RESCUE ATTEMPT

*T*here was a great calm about John and Judy as they navigated the Robinson Street property on Friday, moving between one-on-one meetings with Donna and me, Spencer and Nancy, and Gloria who were laying heaps of raw feelings and unresolved dilemmas at their feet.

With their thirty years of experience with friendship, church, and community, John and Judy were two master artisans who could shape us into a body capable of ascending to a new plateau. Their presence was a great relief to me, even as Spencer's comment about getting away to Pasadena haunted me.

That first afternoon John and I sat down alone at a downtown coffee shop. His thin frame was adorned, as usual, with blue jeans and colored T-shirt. As he listened to my sordid story for the first time, he stroked his salt-and-pepper beard. He gave no hint of shock or surprise. He grinned knowingly a couple of times. And when he started talking, I understood why: My road was so similar to his.

He reminded me of his rise in academia, his books, journalism, social justice work, and his early years in an inner-city neighborhood.

"But you know what, Chris?" he said in his gravelly voice. "All those years, there was a huge missing piece. Sure, we were serving the poor and oppressed more than other Christians. But I finally realized our lives were just as troubled as theirs. I'd try to make peace at work, and I'd throw a tantrum. I'd try to be a good husband with Judy, and I'd neglect to be home for my son's birthday party. Old community conflicts weren't being resolved, and trying harder wasn't helping. I couldn't make my life work—in the big things or the little things."

Change the details, and it was all me. I was entranced.

"There I was," he said, laughing, "after nineteen intense years of all this ministry, and I couldn't make myself grow enough spiritually to make life livable for me or for those around me. I knew I was going to keep making terrible messes my whole life long. And I broke."

"How did you keep going, feeling like such a mess?"

"Some days I was in despair. But mostly I was relieved. I didn't have to run around fixing things anymore. Believe me, others were relieved too."

I laughed. How peaceful would the Colorado trip have been, if not for me?

"I realized it wasn't my job to fix the universe, and I started telling myself that ten times a day. Somehow, that slowed life down. I could get hold of pieces I could do something about."

That was when he and Judy left Philadelphia to move between communities, looking for deeper answers. They finally settled in a small church in Los Angeles that, John said, had a different approach.

"Before we got there, I'd concluded Christians didn't really change and grow. Maybe they quit drinking and smoking. But their character didn't change, in the basic kinds of ways the New Testament seems to assume— becoming deeper in love, joy, peace, et cetera."

"That's exactly what I long for, John."

He gave me an intense look. "Well, there's a lot of work ahead for you then." John wasn't going to baby me. But I heard no scolding in his voice.

Driving back home, he said one more thing that stuck with me. "You know, Chris, I probably needed to fail spectacularly, in order to be saved from myself."

The next day, on Saturday, we met again, with Judy also present. They had talked to everybody and come to some conclusions. They seemed to be preparing me for their big talk tomorrow to the whole group.

"Chris, I don't knooooow. I'm not clear we've got all this right. But here goes." I was learning these were John's trademark self-effacing opening statements. First he took the edge off, then he shot straight to the heart of the matter.

John said most of the blame for my troubles with Spencer was mine. I was lost in jealousy and envy of Spencer. Of course, I was disappointed to hear this. This was the risk of inviting them in—that Spencer and Nancy's view of our conflict might get validated. But what I didn't understand was how unimportant my failure was.

"Still, Chris, your failure isn't even interesting," said John matter-of-factly.

*Huh? Say what?*

"That's what we're going to talk about tomorrow. How your failure isn't a big deal, once we understand what forgiveness is all about." I was about to be introduced, it seemed, to a puzzling new paradigm for moving Antioch to a new plateau.

---

On Sunday afternoon Antioch gathered with John and Judy in the *Urban Family* office at the Duplex. It was only a week since my meltdown in Texas, and this was our first meeting since last Monday in our room. Emotions were still tender, and everybody looked anxious.

John told us to get comfortable, because he had a lot to say. There was a great affection in his voice.

"We really want you all to last. Not just because we love you and like you, but because the world, and other Christians, need your witness—the witness that people can live together in reconciliation. Especially people who are not the same race." Even after seeing all our doo-doo, how were John and Judy still so attracted to us, so hopeful about our future? I was amazed.

His next affirmation startled me. "Judy and I are not concerned about your ability to survive. You're mature people who asked for help before this conflict got out of hand. You can manage it. But there is a price." He paused, scanning our faces.

John then named our biggest challenge: how to bring vice, weakness, and failure into the light in a way that built up rather than tore down the group. It was his alternative to Antioch's "don't ask, don't tell" policy, the "you don't bring up my junk, I won't bring up yours" approach.

"One of the foundations of community is knowing that you will sin and be sinned against. It needs to be our daily expectation. But there also needs to be an expectation of forgiving others their sins and being forgiven. For some of us 'being forgiven' is harder, because we want not to sin."

That last part nailed me to the wall. Then John put my failure front and center. "We need to create a culture that expects people to sin, and also expects them to be forgiven. Then, if someone loses it without much observable cause, like Chris did, or if deep-seated jealousy pops up—like Chris has confessed—it's no big deal."

He had shoved my sin into the spotlight, then pulled it right back out. I was starting to get what he meant when he said that my failure wasn't even interesting.

"We know sin's going to happen, we deal with it when it does, but we don't feel destroyed or shocked by it. Actually," John added, "we like Spencer's phrase that it doesn't surprise him when he's bad."

*OK, and what about complacency,* I thought. John beat me to it.

"But if you can't expect people to change, it gets discouraging." *Amen.* I had no clue how to change myself anymore or how to get Spencer to make changes. It was so painful to both of us.

But again John emphasized the normality of all this. "Jesus told us to forgive not seven times, but seventy times seven. And in community," he drawled in his deadpan way, "you can exceed that amount in one week."

Everybody laughed. "I know that's right," said Gloria.

"So expecting ourselves to be bad can't be an excuse not to change and grow. If that were true, community would be unbearable."

John had gotten to the heart of my dilemma, the unbearable feeling of not knowing how to change and grow in relationship to Spencer. But John was also saying that growing and changing weren't just my issues.

"All communities reach plateaus," he said, "a point where if they're going to survive they need to reach a higher level, to make a commitment to grow."

One step toward growth was being open about our failure and sin, learning to confess it to each other. "The way Chris has done," said John. "Chris needs to tell you whenever his jealousy and envy becomes a big struggle."

Another key to change was being open with others about their sins. "You need to learn to confront openly and without apology. But also without dogma, without anger.

"Above all, it means bearing the burden with the person confessing, as it sounds like Gloria did. If the person feels judgment, they'll shrivel up and die inside. But if they can tell you're really feeling the pain with them, they're enabled to change." I smiled inside at the memory of Gloria's hug at the hotel on that awful morning.

"You have to know you can't make these changes on your own," exhorted John. "You have to want help."

The further John went, the more I realized that his solution was not the answer I had hoped for. I was ready to be more open with Spencer, but I resisted relying more on the whole group. Maybe it was my tendency to be judgmental, to focus more on people's weaknesses than their strengths. If so, everything John was saying hung together. I had to learn how to make sin and weakness—mine and everybody else's—not such a big deal. And that meant learning how to be less demanding and more forgiving.

John went further, with words that got right in the middle of my not cheering for Spencer. The big paradigm shift in community, he said, was coming to see things as they affected the group, rather than just you.

"Becoming a contributing editor at *Christianity Today* may be nonsense, just harmful status. Only one honor really counts: helping the body grow into greater love. Of course, an article in a big magazine isn't unimportant. But it will help if everyone realizes that's a meaningless sort of success. Chris isn't the only one who needs to learn this. You all do.

"Public success is a detail. What really counts is being a reconciled, multiracial community."

I didn't like being reminded of that. Public success was so much easier, compared to taming my ego or serving someone I didn't feel served me very well.

"My gifts aren't for my own edification," said John, "they're for others. Take Spencer's bluntness. It's merely a pain if he uses it just for himself. But it's a gift if Spencer uses it to see that other people get what they want. The same for everybody's idiosyncrasies. Serving others takes on a whole new appearance when we make the shift from how things affect me to how they affect the whole body. It's not me helping another individual— it's me helping my own body."

While John was the philosopher, Judy's great gift was bringing his ideas down to earth. She was blunt. "You have to put more energy into community. If you don't, Antioch won't survive."

She talked about practical steps: In every meeting we needed to have far more positive affirmation than negative confrontation. We should give each other lists of how people could make you happy by serving you. We could talk in our meetings about how we saw God at work in each other. We could list other people's irritating habits, choose a few you'd never tell that person, and ask them to give one of them up for you.

"But be careful not to overwhelm anyone," Judy said.

My letter to Spencer last October was just the opposite, so carefully targeted with how he bugged and irritated me. I wished I could rip it from his memory and start all over.

When John and Judy finished, the five of us started to talk.

We affirmed that what got us through eight years would not get us through another eight and that we needed to put more time and energy into "growing each other up." But that meant something had to give in Antioch's six-ring circus.

Drop the summer program that had thirty kids in the Big House all day, Monday to Friday? Fewer Metro Antiochers? Decreasing *Urban Family* responsibilities or eliminate some of our speaking trips? Having Donna and others work fewer hours?

The details weren't clear. But as we talked, I sensed spirits lifting. There was hope in the room that hadn't been there an hour before. That old "vision thing" was gearing back up. With vision, all the questions did not have to be answered before you undertook the quest.

For me the road ahead seemed as daunting as choosing Mississippi over Middlebury, enduring the Reconciliation Meetings, and making the climb with Antioch to become a community. Until the last three years with Spencer and what they revealed about myself, I never would have imagined that perfectionists like me who were so obsessive about goodness could be just as lost as rebellious prodigal sons who ran with the pigs. My question now was simple: Did God just tinker with you, or did God do overhauls?

John and Judy had handed us a map for a new climb: creating a daily atmosphere of forgiveness with one another. Admitting that it wasn't a big deal to be weak and in the grip of great powers. Telling your friends when things got hard, so very difficult for such a disciplined person like me who had never met a problem I couldn't solve—or ignore.

It was all very scary. But together, Antioch had taken a huge step. We had expanded the story that we lived by—beyond the three Rs, beyond the Voice of Calvary experience, beyond endless activism. We had allowed a crisis to expand our circle of friends, welcoming new mentors into our midst. Desperate, we kept our hands open and received a wonderful gift. Just as I needed friends who were close, I also needed friends who were at a distance.

I was grateful, scared out of my wits, ready to climb—all at once.

# 31

# SETBACKS AND GIFTS

*J*udy Alexander had warned us to invest more energy into community—or else. But old habits die hard. A couple of weeks after she and John left, at the end of June, Spencer and I added another ring to the circus.

At a weekend with an interracial pastors' group in a Midwestern city, their simmering tensions bubbled into the open. "I've given up," sighed one black minister. "White folks aren't ever gonna change." A nervous white pastor admitted he'd kept his mouth shut in the past, not telling the group what he really thought. Another pastor summed up the skepticism that Spencer and I were hearing all over the country from African Americans. "Look, I hear the word *reconciliation* more and more from white folks, and what I hear is cheap grace on white terms—on your turf, with your music, under your control."

Afterward the pastors stood in a circle, asking forgiveness for not being honest before and pledging to make truthful relationships as high a priority as their urban partnership.

Flying back to Jackson, Spencer and I became convinced that we needed a new persuasive tool to tell stories like this, connect like-minded people, and spell out authentic reconciliation in an ongoing way. We sketched the vision for a quarterly publication we would call *The Reconciler*—just twelve pages an issue, produced as cheaply as possible and mailed to anybody who requested it. Somehow we'd scratch the funds together.

---

Back at the Big House, while Gloria and Danny ran the summer program inside, volunteers built an expansive screened-in porch and open deck off the left side, funded by our book royalties. With three new people coming into the household—a new baby and Lue Shelby and her son—we needed all the space we could get.

After Donna had told me she was pregnant in July, I wished I had a dollar for every person who chuckled, "That always happens right after people adopt!" Once we got over the shock, our hearts opened with anticipation.

In another surprising but entirely pleasant development, there were no *I told you so*s when Lue started talking to us about rejoining Antioch after leaving eight years before.

She had thought she could do better financially outside of community, but she hadn't. She thought she could raise her four-year-old son, Jon, on her own, and she was struggling. Lue had no illusions this time. She wanted to come back, she said, because she needed our close friendships to be a faithful disciple, and she knew it wouldn't be any easier than before. I did have a minor concern that I didn't voice. Since Lue was Mrs. Perkins's half-sister, this meant adding another Perkins family member to Antioch's core. Whenever Joanie and Ron returned, that would be two more. To me there was a real weakness to Antioch, being dominated by so many Perkinses. But I was not ready to raise this touchy issue. Lue agreed to move in for a one-year period of "seeking membership" status. After that she, and we, would decide together if it seemed right to bring her into the long-term core group.

By September Lue's slow steps were shuffling through the Big House; her greens were cooking in the kitchen again; and Jon was beside himself with a huge house and yard to roam and our raucous children as his constant playmates.

Fourteen years after I had left Middlebury Spencer and I accepted an invitation to speak there in October. Mom and Dad lived only thirty minutes away, and they insisted that we bring nine-month-old Talia with us.

Spencer and I found ourselves in the Boston airport, one of us toting a diaper bag, the other the brown-skinned baby girl I nicknamed Big Hair, chuckling at the turning heads from startled passersby. When we sat down all eyes and ears were upon us.

"Chris, why don't you take a break, man? I'll take Tali-Wali," says linebacker-looking black man.

"Oh, that sounds perfect," says placekicker-looking white man, who hands the brown baby over, followed by a bottle. "Here, she probably wants this about now."

"OK, got ya covered."

"I'm outta here."

On campus it was gratifying to see what Mississippi had to say to Middlebury. A dialogue with a group of skeptical black students started with the question: "When I heard you were going to be Christian speakers, I thought, 'Oh, no, some religious garbage.' I mean, what do Christians have to say with their record on racial justice?" The question gave us a chance to distinguish the grave historical sins of Christians from the gospel's true message and to point to Christian-inspired movements like the abolitionists and even CCDA. "So the best stories of racial justice," I argued, "are also being done by Christians. Go figure."

"Are you saying you have to be Christian to do this?" one black student challenged.

"All I know is," said Spencer, "I sho'nuff wouldn't be doin' it if I wasn't a Christian. Chris and I would have given up on each other a long time ago."

I had been eager to introduce Spencer to a Vermont fall, so with our obligations finished, we canoed out onto a windswept lake to fish, surrounded by the fiery red and yellow woods sweeping up the mountains around us. Spencer couldn't stand that canoe. Whenever he shifted his weight, it felt like we might tip over. But we hauled in four big-mouthed bass—him catching more, as always.

Our work together was shifting into a higher gear.

The first issue of *The Reconciler* was mailed to three thousand people; *Urban Family* was getting rave reviews from readers; and we were ramping up outrageous plans for 1995: growing from quarterly to bimonthly, getting a hundred thousand copies into black congregations, and hiring several new staff to do it. This meant a lot more money, and who was going to see to that? We counted on JP and the Foundation board, of course, who were still our organizational sugar daddies.

But unknown to us, they had begun behind-the-scenes discussions about spinning off *Urban Family* completely into our hands, including the financial part.

❖

Meanwhile, as 1995 opened, I privately vowed to look for ways to empower Spencer, even when it was painful to me.

And it was. When Spencer approached me in early February about Nancy becoming his personal assistant, I got agitated. Why, I asked, did he need someone at his beck and call? This had to make the pillow talk dynamic even harder. What I didn't say out loud was, How is this not going to make the True Soul Mates the new yokefellows of *Urban Family?*

I was supposed to be leaving the next day on a spiritual retreat with Donna, and Spencer and Nancy had graciously offered to take care of Benjamin and Talia. I was irritated that we had to have this latest conflict before we left.

The next morning Spencer slipped me a letter, a precious gift.

> I hope that getaways like this will help you in the struggle of our life together. I know you sincerely want this whole thing to go away and are doing all you can to deal with it. As the song goes, "I don't know which way the wind will blow, but I know that this too shall pass," and that God will eventually get the glory out of it. I am as committed as ever to our relationship and to our partnership. Whichever direction the specifics of our working relationship goes, I will be happy as long as you are fulfilled and content and that both of us can grow and reach our potential. Have a good time.
>
> And don't worry about the kids. We love them.

He signed the letter, "Yokefellows forever."

With a burden lifted, at least for now, Donna and I drove three hours to a rural retreat center in northeast Mississippi run by three Franciscan sisters, called the Dwelling Place. There was a strange but comforting sense of permission about it all.

"Do what you need to do," said one sister when we arrived. "Catch up on sleep, read, come to meals and prayer times—or skip them. If you need someone to talk to, let us know."

Donna and I had our own little cottage, and in the solitude of that stark, flat landscape, I noticed things within myself I had not noticed before.

There was a profound hunger within me not just to work for God, but to be with God. On our trips Spencer always said that the way we showed our love for God was by loving our neighbor. "You can't give God a great big hug," he'd say. But as I meditated on the two great commandments of Scripture—to love God and to love your neighbor—I was struck, for the first time, by the order. I desired to learn more about that first commandment. What did it mean? Why was the order significant?

The sisters offered to pray over each of us in their tiny chapel. Donna went first, and she came back to the cottage with a glowing smile on her face. Whatever they were handing out in that chapel, I wanted it.

But when the sisters laid hands on my shoulders and started to pray, they said things like, "Oh, God, I sense . . . confusion," and "Things are not clear." No one blurted out, "This guy's in a mess! Only you, omnipotent God, can straighten him out!" But that was what it sounded like to me.

I told Donna what they had said. "What happened when they prayed over you?" I asked. She hesitated, like she didn't want to make me feel bad. "C'mon, Donna. Tell me."

"Well, it was wonderful, actually. They said . . . well, they said they sensed light flowing out from me."

There was a reason why Donna's home health patients adored her and why her bosses gave her the toughest cases. There was a genuineness and authenticity about her that could touch difficult people. She was so much more pure-hearted than me. She worked long hours and longed to be at home more with Benjamin and Talia, but she rarely complained about it. And without her good humor and hopeful spirit, without her objectivity and care for others in the face of conflict, not only would my struggles with Spencer have been far worse, but so would the entire atmosphere of community. Mrs. Light and Mr. Confusion—it wasn't a bad description of the difference between us.

But I was being hard on myself, as usual. I didn't give myself credit for being on this retreat in the first place. For the first time in fourteen intense years of Mississippi activism I had opened my hand to the gift of stillness, which offered me a view of my life that I could not see in the blur of my usual busyness. I also did not recognize that I had looked outside of Voice of Calvary to find this treasure. Stillness was not a concept in our world. It was unproductive, and there was too much need in the world to ever move in slow motion. After baring my soul about my struggles with Spencer to one of the sisters, she left me with encouraging words: "God would not give you this kind of understanding, then leave you alone."

Donna and I returned to Jackson, she to spread light, me to reveal my continually confused desires.

In late February, at Amherst College in Massachusetts, Spencer and I spoke to several hundred people in their chapel, then held a successful workshop the next day for about forty students. But on the way home, in an office meeting the next day, and at an Antioch meeting the day after, I stewed over some silly, stupid things related to Spencer—just symptoms, symptoms, symptoms. Spencer could tell that I was stewing.

A couple of days later he left me another letter, this one not a gift the way the last one had been. He was having more difficulty sleeping, he said, unable to cope with the stress in his life. He said some of it was his own fault, some was mine, and he was holding in too much. He had made a new year's resolution that he wasn't going to let my attitudes affect his well-being. "Well, so far, I have already failed on that one," the letter said. He cited instances of my attitudes over the last few days. "When I feel that there is a cloud of negative vibes (real or perceived), then I feel that the spirit of God cannot operate among us."

What could I say in response?

Spencer was right about every single one of my attitudes, and there were no grounds for any of them. I had hoped he wouldn't notice my stewing. Or maybe I hadn't. Was I still trying to control him through the only power I felt I had? The good thing was that Spencer had confronted me quickly and without much anger. We talked, I apologized, we moved on. John and Judy would have been proud. But I also sensed that my problem was becoming increasingly wearisome to him.

A month later, in April, Donna gave birth to Christopher Ransom, and Gloria dubbed him Doughboy. But the joy of our third child's arrival was short-lived. A sudden series of setbacks hit *Urban Family*, beginning at the Foundation board meeting in Pasadena.

After seeing the magazine through its first three years, the board was ready to be free of its financial burden. JP, of course, always handed off his projects to new leadership—whether they felt ready or not. But this was moving much too fast. The board did commit resources to the transition, and JP would continue to be involved in significant ways. But *Urban Family* was our baby now, plus we were putting out *The Reconciler,* and finances were already tight.

We immediately cut salaries and expenses. A couple of weeks later, our consultant for the so-called big marketing campaign admitted that he had failed to secure the promised advertising. We lost $16,000, with nothing to show for it. A week later a bookkeeping error revealed that we were $10,000 short of what we thought we had.

Spencer, Nancy, and I were in the dumps, at wit's end, angry with the board and JP for sending us into waters we weren't ready for.

But our able staff associate Jennifer launched into a pep talk like a coach looking at a bunch of losers at halftime. "I'm not ready to give up," she declared. Jennifer shocked us into a complete reversal: Hey, this magazine is ours, by golly, to stand or fall by our leadership alone. We retooled our marketing campaign and adopted a new slogan—"Hope is believing in spite of the evidence and watching the evidence change."

We seized room to grow. With JP's help we purchased the Corner House to the left of the Big House, and with a bank loan, *Urban Family* purchased new space for our offices—the huge, two-story fourplex between the Small House and the Duplex. Our five-house urban campus now stretched from the Corner House to the Duplex, and we hired three new staff members, including one to assist Spencer and me in producing a new book. She was Alexis Spencer-Byers, an Amherst graduate who had organized the conference there, one of those biracial students passionate about racial reconciliation.

Spencer and I were eager to write a sequel to *More Than Equals,* to take our reconciliation ideas to a new level. But the book idea quickly got tabled.

Our marketing drive floundered, and by early July we owed creditors over $57,000. Spencer and I couldn't possibly raise the $250,000 a year that the magazine required.

"Look, Spence," I told him one day. "We got to decide who we are and what we're most passionate about. What mission are we willing to pick up a cross for?"

The solution to our survival, we decided, was to find an organizational partner with both the money and marketing muscle to make our publications grow.

In July Spencer and I headed to Denver, to the sprawling annual convention of the Christian Booksellers Association. Frequent flyer miles procured our plane tickets, and I slept on the floor while we holed up in JP's hotel room for free. We had meetings with magazine publishers, all the while doing what JP would have called "taking responsibility," which was probably what he had calculated we would do all along.

A month later we sat in a cushy conference room in suburban Chicago, moving toward a deal with heavy hitters in suits who would have looked like alien invaders in west Jackson. Christianity Today Incorporated (CTI) owned nine successful magazines and was strong where we were weak. They had already named Spencer a contributing editor to their flagship magazine, and while they knew we were business bumpkins, they admired our vision, passion, and grit. "It's amazing that you've gotten this far," said one executive. The meeting ended in victory: We tentatively agreed on a one-year partnership to move *Urban Family* and *The Reconciler* to a new level of growth.

Back home real shouts of joy met the announcement that CTI would soon be sending a check for $10,000.

⊹

At dinnertime now more than twenty-five people usually surrounded the dinner slab and an attached folding table. Nineteen people—an all-time record—lived in the Big House, including Ron and Joanie, who had moved back in August with their newly adopted, seven-month-old daughter, Varah. Ron—who joined Lue in "seeking membership" status—was starting a book on black theology, and I learned that his idea of a bookshelf was putting one book on the floor and laying two dozen more on top. He opened books tenderly, with his fingertips, as if each one was a treasured volume from an ancient monastic library. Varah had a wide, winsome grin and big legs, and Gloria created another memorable nickname—Thunder Thighs.

Spencer and I finalized the partnership with CTI in October, and with the infusion of support for *Urban Family,* spirits lifted across our five-house campus. Morale was high when Antioch went to a cabin for a November planning weekend.

The eight of us shot through an endless list of issues and problems to be solved. Gloria offered to care for Jon in the evenings during Lue's evening shifts in a new job. Ron asked for help in his book project and Joanie for help in studying for the bar exam. But from cleaning schedules to Christmas plans to Metro Antioch comings and goings, as deeply connected and accessible as our lives were to each other, we still were still keeping too much inside.

"I'm concerned, y'all," I said after a while. "We rarely share our inner lives with each other, or pray together like we used to. Why?"

Heads nodded. There were so many needs, we said—our children, our jobs, the magazine and *The Reconciler,* our inclination to take on more and more.

On top of all this, JP and Mrs. Perkins had turned over the Pasadena ministry to new leadership and were moving back to their beloved Mississippi—to Jackson, into the Corner House, to be precise, about twenty yards away. Antioch had discussed this at length, and we were unanimous in our support. But we had both eyes open: JP wasn't coming to play tiddlywinks. The pressures stood to increase astronomically.

If John and Judy had been there, they probably would have given us a D in moving toward a new plateau. A year and a half after their rescue attempt, "doing" was still winning far more of our energy than "growing each other up."

## PART FIVE

# Breakthrough to Grace

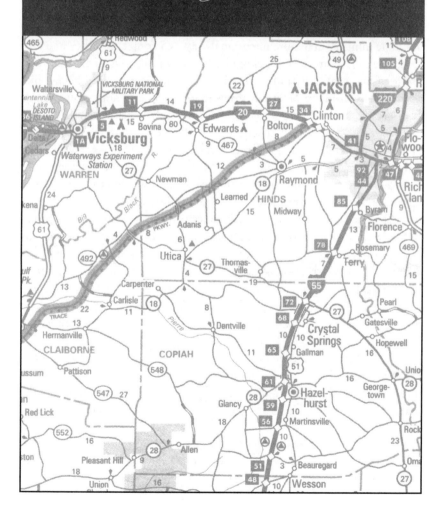

# 32

# PARADIGM SHIFTS

*O*n a chilly Wednesday morning in early January 1996 I found my-self sitting in an Antioch meeting, listening to Spencer and Nancy tell us about a decision they had come to during a weekend away in New Orleans. During their time together they had talked about working in public ministry in a more intentional way as a couple. But they had also faced the great impact that being in a black-white marriage had on their life together, especially in the way it caused Spencer to hold back—like feeling awkward with Nancy in front of audiences and not holding hands in public, as if there were something wrong in their being together.

"What message does that send to our children," said Spencer, "when in fact Nancy and I have no regrets and such a good marriage? Why is in-terracial marriage such a big obstacle for blacks and whites? Nancy and I have learned a lot about this over the years—and we think we could be a help to others. We want to write a book about interracial marriage, and we want to do it right away so that we have a first draft by the end of the year."

My mouth didn't drop open, but it very well could have. Spencer was going to write this book now, on office time, taking hundreds of hours away from the work we had to do together? I couldn't figure out what he was he thinking. What about the new book he and I had planned to start, which we had tabled during last summer's magazine crisis? And I was hurt that he seemed to be bypassing me, going straight to Antioch for approval.

As Spencer continued, I was seething.

"I've never wanted to be known as the black man who promotes inter-racial marriage. But as we encourage racial reconciliation, more and more interracial marriages are gonna happen. We want to help eliminate the fear, to shift the focus to strong Christian marriage, where race is sec-ondary."

I felt like I was watching the "Spencer and Nancy Show," and Nancy was not just a supporting player. My worst nightmares going all the way back to Nancy coming on staff seemed to be unfolding before my eyes. I wanted to know what this was going to do to me.

Nobody else seemed to share any such concerns. They—even Donna, it seemed—all thought it would be a great idea for Spencer and Nancy to write such a book. Finally, I'd heard enough. "Well, Spencer hasn't said a word about this to me," I snapped. "I mean, *Urban Family*'s got financial problems, we've already got way more work than we can handle, and now this? Without even consulting me? This really hurts."

A long discussion ensued. I felt like whatever valid concerns I had were so tainted by "my problem" that the others easily dismissed them. I felt completely outnumbered—how could I get a fair hearing from a room full of Perkinses? The others gave the go-ahead on the book. As for me, I was just going to act as if Spencer and Nancy's book didn't exist. And it looked like Spencer was going to push forward with it in spite of what I might think or feel.

It wasn't that I didn't think that interracial marriage was an important topic. Resistance to it was a more insidious problem than Spencer had ever imagined. Thinking through our adoption of Talia and listening to the college-aged biracial children that Spencer and I had met had also brought the topic even more to the fore.

Other developments in our work were also widening our racial understanding far beyond the binary, Mississippi-dominated, black-white paradigm.

Many of the college students we met were Asian Americans. Spencer told me about what he was learning from his conversations with them, how they experienced being both "oppressed" and "oppressor" ("How come y'all intermarry with whites," Spencer had asked, "but not blacks?"), and how they might have a crucial role to play as "bridge people" between blacks and whites.

Another trend had surfaced nearly a year before when a federal building in Oklahoma City had been bombed. The prime suspect was a clean-cut white American named Timothy McVeigh, honorably discharged from the army. McVeigh was no isolated nutcase. From out of nowhere, it seemed, a militia movement had appeared: angry, white, and well-armed middle-Americans in the thousands, linked by a common ideology. Favorite reading for McVeigh and militia members was *The Turner Diaries*, a novel about a white hero who starts a race war.

We broached another very different dynamic in February's issue of *The Reconciler*: Spencer and I had come to believe that the language of racial critique for blacks was inadequate. My editorial, "A New Racial Virus," dissected one obstacle that we often encountered in our black audiences, what we called *racialism*—an obsessive loyalty to one's ethnic group, even when it meant ignoring the truth. Later that month we saw the virus creep into the packed auditorium of a Christian college in the Midwest.

After Spencer and I spoke at a Black History Month celebration, three white students took the stage and sang a moving a cappella rendition of "Lift Every Voice and Sing"—the "black national anthem" in our neck of the woods. Spencer leaned over and whispered, "These white girls can sing, man."

But moments later, with obvious disgust, several black students stomped out of the auditorium.

Back at the hotel we dissected their protest. To us the white students had made a well-intended public gesture of reconciliation. But the black protest seemed to say, "That song is a 'black thing,' and whi'folk can't never understand." Maybe not, but shouldn't they be affirmed for an attempt at empathy? Actions like the walkout sent confusing signals, forcing white folks into a no-win, darned-if-you-do, darned-if-you-don't dilemma.

But there was no place where these complex issues were honestly talked about. We wanted to push the dialogue into new territory, and we launched a new forum using the exploding popularity of the Internet. By March our Web site, "Race & Reconciliation On-Line," was getting rave reviews, including our weekly editorial, "Reconciliation Wednesday."

Meanwhile I was finding more clarity with "my problem." My new Franciscan friends at the Dwelling Place had pointed me to a local workshop on prayer, and the teacher's words of hope seemed spoken directly to me.

"As divine action reaches deeper, more is exposed. . . . Each time one goes to another level, a crisis of faith arises, and God appears to disappear. This leads to depressed feelings that something has been lost. But mourning is a gift that God alone can satisfy. . . . You thought you could find happiness in the affections of others and in power over others. Now you know none of this will work. . . . Rejoice! You are getting to the bottom of the pile. God has been urging you to come there."

*Is this true, God?* I thought. *That somehow You have been constantly faithful to me, wooing me, at work within me in spite of myself?* I so much wanted it to be so.

I wasn't the only one at Antioch needing a boost. We had begun to meet every Wednesday morning, everybody sacrificing several work hours to give prime time to "growing each other up." But after one long discussion in March, Gloria summed up our spiritual state. "We've been in a stalemate for a while now, y'all. We're drownin'."

"Our circle of life has gotten bigger and bigger," said Spencer. "We've gotten stretched beyond what we can do. The CTI folks warned us too. They said if they get behind *Urban Family,* it'll grow fast, and there'll be ten times as many people who want to come to Antioch."

✤

A couple of weeks later, with Antioch talking seriously about setting boundaries and priorities for the first time, John and Judy arrived for a long-scheduled and serendipitous visit.

By now, Benjamin never referred to them as John or Judy, but always JohnanJudy, like they were joined at the hip. They supplied us all with E&L rib tips, cooked dinners, helped with the dishes and the kids—the simple kindnesses by which they always wiggled into our affections.

I poured my heart out to John over lunch one day. My old list still haunted me, intensely at times, but I didn't have to dump it all on Spencer anymore. John was a trusted outsider, with nothing to gain or lose, who loved us both, and who had become an ongoing gift in my life. I was very thankful for such a confessor, who helped me sort out my problems and concerns—certainly all very serious, he said, but not even interesting, after all, if I was learning how to be forgiven.

John and Judy served, listened, and counseled for a couple of days. Then, meeting with Antioch at the Corner House, John dropped another earthshaking idea on us.

"I don't knoooow. I'm still working it all out. But I think I want to say something like this to all of you. A couple of years ago I tried to settle a long-standing dilemma of mine: What's more important, loving God or loving your neighbor?"

These two commandments were at the heart of our reconciliation teaching and Antioch's life together, and separating them had been the bane of Christians from German Lutherans and Nazism to the U.S. church and slavery. While Antioch was all about the "neighbor" part, I'd been thinking more and more about the "loving God" part, convinced the sequence was important. *Aha,* I thought, *John is going to affirm my direction.*

"To answer my question," John said, "anal person that I am, I did an exhaustive search of the Scriptures, from Genesis to Revelation, listing verses in the category of either 'loving God' or 'loving neighbor.' And I came to an astounding conclusion.

"More than either one of these categories, I found that Scripture's biggest theme by far is God's love for us."

I was stunned. Stopped in my tracks.

"I think the big paradigm shift is understanding that there is only one detail that matters: God loves you. Unless we are gripped by that fact, it's too dangerous to do anything. It's about God's action among you, or it's nothing. The most important person in a community is not others, it's not me. It's Jesus. The more we understand who God is, the more we are changed."

A heavenly spotlight might as well have been shining on John now, pointing to a messenger sent with good news that trumped our constant doing, that freed us of an immense burden.

From the hard-nosed three Rs, to enduring the Reconciliation Meetings, to enacting the Sermon on the Mount and forming Antioch, to toughing out ten years on Robinson Street, to struggling to purify my heart toward Spencer, it never occurred to me that the point of it all wasn't what I—or we—did for God. Faithfulness to God, John was saying, was unintelligible apart from God's faithfulness to us. *Good grief,* I thought, *for me even loving God had become another item on my obsessive to-do list.* Our gospel was too much about our actions. But after so many years of trying, I couldn't even save myself from the powers that gripped me, much less the world. I felt like an intolerable weight had just been budged inside me, the weight that had "Try Harder, Do More" written all over it.

I wasn't the only one sensing a breakthrough. After the talk the eight of us gathered with John and Judy in a circle to pray. Our many years of wrestling with Scripture together had never led us to John's simple insight. As Spencer said later, "When you understand that God loves you, you are so grateful that you want to do something in response to that love. But you know you can't—so you just cry." And many of us did.

✤

Slowly a new truth began to reshape our lives and our work. We were going to need it, it seemed, because *Urban Family* was on the rocks again.

In April CTI told us that making *Urban Family*'s readership broad enough to be self-supporting was "not viable"; it would require at least half a million dollars, with little chance of success.

But they claimed there was good news. There were eight thousand loyal subscribers to *Urban Family* and *The Reconciler,* a racially mixed group, and most received both publications, meaning they cared about both rebuilding broken communities and racial healing. Our readers were leaders who influenced others, at all levels of society.

"You still have an incredible opportunity," said one CTI executive. "We recommend that you combine your two publications into one, invest more resources into a broader mission, and build your support base on one of your strengths: donors who believe in John Perkins, Spencer and Chris, and racial reconciliation."

Gradually, as disappointed as we were, Spencer and I began to recognize the wisdom in CTI's advice. For five years we'd brought readers stories overlooked both in the mainstream and in the Christian media. But *Urban Family* was becoming too unlike us, with too much infrastructure and too much "What a Man Wants in a Woman, and a Woman Wants in a Man" kind of material. Somebody needed to do a popular magazine for the average person in the urban pew, but it wasn't us.

Was giving up our dream for *Urban Family* a failure or a victory? We chose to see it as a victory. A year after taking over the magazine Spencer and I were learning to lead an organization on our own for the first time, and through failures and disappointments we had discovered, and fully embraced, our true passion: fostering racial conversion and moving the Christian church toward authentic reconciliation.

CTI had promised to help *Urban Family* into its next chapter, and they delivered. They made available to us a consultant named Clive Stapleton, a nonprofit veteran. Tall, white, in his late fifties, and completely bald, with a well-trimmed beard, always wearing a snappy suit with a red handkerchief in the pocket, Clive was the organization man next to John Alexander's Jerry Garcia.

Clive immediately became indispensable to Spencer and me, with his keen insight into leadership issues. With his help, we soon made three major decisions.

First, we would combine our two publications into a full-color, sixteen-page magazine called *Reconcilers,* a voice for both racial healing and urban rebuilding.

Second, we chose four thrusts: publications, books and resources, speaking and networking, and a major new effort—a training center on the Antioch campus. Spencer and I had enough national credibility now to woo people to Jackson, and strategic events here would give us a way to move people—and the race dialogue—to a new level of maturity.

The final major decision we made was a new name for our organization, one that described the people we saw as agents of reconciliation and justice as well as our hope of knitting them into a united force for social healing: Reconcilers Fellowship (RF). It was all very exciting.

By May of 1996, with our makeover as RF under way, and Antioch approaching ten years in community, there were signs of great change on Robinson Street.

After a year of "seeking" status, Ron and Lue were officially brought into core membership, Antioch-style: a short, memorable, and emotional ceremony, followed by a long and lively th'o down.

That month, Antioch finally spread our living quarters into two houses, with Spencer's family moving to the Duplex, and mine staying in the Big House. Personally, I was relieved. Nineteen people—between Metro Antiochers, members, and children—in one house had come to feel more like a dormitory than a home to me. Even with the gradual progress in our weekly meetings, I was beginning to think Antioch's members were often more living together than growing together. And more and more, I was reaching for vitality outside of Antioch and in friendship with people like John Alexander and Clive Stapleton and in the gradual rebirth of Donna's and my relationship with Phil and Tressa.

Clive spent many hours with Spencer and me, together and separately. He began to gently press us about our partnership.

"The two of you are a remarkable team," he said at one point. "But this would be a good time to clarify your roles." I filed the thought away, not sure what Clive was getting at. But as I found out later, Spencer had spent the entire month wrestling privately with an ominous decision about our relationship.

# 33

# FIFTEEN-ROUNDER

*A*t the end of May 1996 Spencer and I had a long meeting—a good one, I felt—to finalize our plans for the transition to RF. Later that day he left a letter in my box. As I read it my heart filled with dread.

During all our organizational changes over the past month, the letter said, something had been nagging at Spencer: We were "holding each other back from maturing and developing as wholly as we can," and it was time for us to talk more candidly about our roles.

He made a diagnosis. "Because I haven't been aggressive about growing as a leader, but basically passive, this has hurt me, you, and our entire ministry." He pointed to today's meeting. "The way things usually go is Chris puts time and thought into a plan, then we meet, tweak it, and go with it. Emotionally, I would love for this style to continue. But I'm not sure it's best for our ministry.

"On those rare occasions when I want to improve, I am hampered because I don't want to hurt you in any way. This helps to justify my lack of aggressiveness and almost gives it a hint of nobility: 'I'm being passive for someone else's sake.' Consequently, neither of us grows."

His last words in the letter drew a line in the sand. "For me this needs to be hammered out before I can get excited about our future."

When we met in his office the next day I could tell Spencer was determined to make a decisive change. He said Reconcilers Fellowship needed a single, bottom-line leader, with the title of president, that it needed to be him. "I think you need to be the executive director, under me," said Spencer, with steel in his voice. "You should run the Training Center, too."

I couldn't believe what I was hearing. To me this was not just a big promotion for him and a big demotion for me, it was earthshaking heresy, a violation of everything our relationship stood for—the yokefellow vision, mutual submission, a leadership team of equals.

But Spencer dug in his heels. "I need you to make a response—within two weeks." Why was he being so dogged about this?

Spencer's obstinacy and our argument left me so depressed I could barely get myself out of bed the next few mornings. At least I had an outside sounding board now. I wrote to John and Judy, pleading for advice. I was desperate. I told them maybe my temperament was under too much stress, and I couldn't handle it. Maybe I needed a sabbatical, to get away for a while. Maybe I even needed to be free of this partnership, to find another job. I was so devastated, for the first time I put another option squarely on the table—leaving Jackson. "Pro:" I wrote. "Maybe it's the only way for me to free Spencer up and to have personal peace. Con: Maybe I'm running from God."

✧

A few days after the fateful meeting with Spencer, Clive Stapleton made another visit. After a month of consultations and hours alone with each of us Clive was siding with Spencer, agreeing that a bottom-line leader was needed now, one chief public spokesman, one chief leader for donors to relate to.

Alone with Clive at a Chinese restaurant, I pleaded my case.

A big part of Clive's gift to me was that he had felt what I now felt. He had helped launch a prominent nonprofit organization, working in partnership with the famous founder, had struggled with getting far less of the glory and credit, and had eventually left the organization feeling pushed out.

"Why would Spencer and I make such a big change now?" I said. "I mean, look at all the fruit our yokefellow relationship is bearing. If it ain't broke, don't fix it."

"Your work with Spencer has prospered, yes. But, Chris, success can become your worst enemy. Because what brought success in the past might not do so in the future. Your work is changing and maturing, and your and Spencer's partnership needs to change and grow with it. One of the results of your partnership is that Spencer has stepped out of JP's shadow—and he likes it. Plus JP's moving back to town. Spencer is ready to step into his legacy. He respects you and depends upon you enormously. But I think he's ready both to prove himself to his father and to take on more responsibility." He paused, taking a hard look at me.

"Look, either you or Spencer could be president. You both have the gifts to do it. But Spencer is the best choice at this time. Reconcilers

Fellowship will have more credibility if an African American is at the helm. Plus Spencer is John's son. John's entering the final chapter of his work, and his national relationships can be passed on to Spencer."

"Well, where does that put me? I mean, I see how Spencer gets fulfilled out of this."

Clive peered into my eyes like he understood. He referred to the difficulty he'd faced in submitting to his famous founder. "Chris, one of the questions I was faced with was this: Am I still committed to the mission, even when public recognition decreases?"

"Oh, Lord," I chuckled. "Now you're gonna try to make me a real Christian or somethin', huh?"

He laughed. "Well, I think there is a paradigm shift for you to make here. You see, there's a difference between control and influence. You don't have to control things to have an enormous influence. You don't have to be visible to have enormous leverage. What's most important is keeping the mission in front of you—always. Focus on the mission, not recognition."

Maybe I could take this advice from Clive because I knew he was just as passionate about empowering me as he was about empowering Spencer. Messages have everything to do with their messengers, and Clive had given me something he'd had to find out for himself, a new way of measuring effectiveness. I had not invited it, yet somehow this messenger had appeared exactly when I needed him.

I felt a freeing within me after Clive's visit. *I can do this,* I thought. I can make this shift. Things started clicking in my mind. Instead of Spencer's president-executive director proposal, which sounded too much like him "over" me, I envisioned Spencer as chief executive officer (CEO) and myself as chief operating officer (COO), both of us "chiefs," but him first among equals, the bottom line. Nancy would be executive director, running the shop and reporting to me, because I had the stronger administrative skills. But I questioned whether she could be loyal to me. It was a huge issue.

A couple of days before Spencer's two-week deadline I called John for his advice about my counterproposal.

"I don't knooooow, Chris. I think I want to say that I was around evangelical leaders for years, and it didn't seem like they ever dealt with their egos. I think you and Spencer have a shot at it.

"I do think your relationship has been a saving grace for both of you. With this new direction? I worry about Spencer's soul, not Chris's. At our church here we expect our primary leader to be our primary servant. Corporate-type structures don't do that very well."

John had some final advice. "If Nancy's meant to be your right arm and she's married to Spencer, she's Spencer's right arm. Just lay out your honest fears with them. If they come unglued, find out now."

✥

On the day of my meeting with Spencer I took Nancy to lunch. I was nervous. We'd never talked alone and this frankly about "Chris and Spencer." Since their decision to do their book five months ago, she and I had never discussed it. I wondered whether there would be residue over my reaction. Did she feel the same "line in the sand" emotion that Spencer did about "my problem"? I expected her to show absolute loyalty to Spencer, and I half-expected her to lay into me.

Slowly and carefully I told Nancy that I longed for her support as Spencer and I moved forward. I said I needed to know that she could work under my leadership. I braced myself for her answer.

"Chris, I have no desire to cause unnecessary stress to you and Spencer. Whatever role you guys come up with for me is fine."

What surprised me as much as the words was the softness in Nancy's eyes, voice, and manner. There was something of a different Nancy in front of me now, with less of a hard edge. And she said more. We talked at length about Spencer and this new role for him.

"Actually, Chris, I'm concerned for Spencer. I'm really not sure how well this new bottom-line role will fit him."

I couldn't remember Nancy ever voicing something like this to me. It wasn't that old loyalty thing I had come to expect.

I had only an inkling of it at the time, and it would be years before I realized it fully, but Nancy and I had something profound in common that day. Like me, she had started looking outside of Antioch for further sources of spiritual renewal, especially in friendship with a native white Mississippi friend named Lisa Ware. Nancy was visiting Lisa every week, going out to Lisa's house by a lake, resting on her porch, pouring out her soul. I didn't know how deeply Nancy was on her own journey. What Clive and John were doing for me, people like Lisa were doing for Nancy. But something about the life of Antioch prevented us from knowing this about each other.

After lunch I felt like another big stone had been budged, making possible a fresh start for Nancy and me, and putting my relationship with Spencer on the verge of a major breakthrough.

I had put a long proposal in Spencer's box the previous day, laying out my thinking with him as the bottom-line CEO, and me the COO and

Training Center director. I told him that I was not just ready to concede, I was ready for a fundamental change, and that I could be content with a new, lesser role, something that seemed to me like a nightmare just two weeks before. I had laid out my fears, too: that our partnership would diminish in his eyes, that Antioch would cheer for him but not me. "But let me be clear," I had written at the end. "Someday I want it to be known that Chris served Spencer to be all that God desired. That Chris tamed his demons."

By the time I walked into Spencer's office I suspected a miracle was in the making.

Within minutes my "miracle" was mush. Spencer and I were in a brutal shouting match, pounding each other with verbal blows that hurt as much as any we'd ever thrown.

It started with Spencer dismissing my proposal. "This doesn't go nearly far enough," he snapped. "I think you should take the Training Center, and I take the rest. We don't need a COO. The executive director should run the organization under my leadership, not through you. And I think Nancy should do it."

Were we on candid camera? Was this some kind of a bad joke, trying to see how I would react? I couldn't believe that he was saying that I'd no longer be directly involved in the day-to-day running of a ministry I'd cofounded.

"You know, Spencer, one of the hardest things about you is that I can swing and miss twice, then smack a hit—and all you want to talk about is my two strikes. And that is so discouraging.

"I have struggled to accommodate your needs," I muttered through my teeth. "I've also tried to make it work for me, because if it ain't win-win, it won't work. I'm open to radical changes, but only if I think you're committed to partnership. Now I wonder.

"You're not the only one who's been stifled in this relationship. I thought we'd each make sacrifices for the sake of coleadership. Why should your desires for growth take precedence over mine? You assume if I just get over this jealousy thing, everything will be okay. For me wanting more room to grow is 'selfish ambition.' For you, somehow, it's fulfilling a legacy." I said those last three words with all the sarcasm I could muster.

He delivered his lowest blow ever. "I don't think you realize how high maintenance you are, Chris. How much work and pain it is to endure in this partnership with you."

"Partnership?" I shouted. "You don't really care about this relationship. All you care about is meeting your own needs!"

"That ain't true! You think I'm supposed to adjust my life around what you want! You're the one who don't really care about me or this relationship. I'm sick of tryin' to take more responsibility and it just makin' you feel bad. I need to be free of that."

We rained verbal blow after verbal blow for two hours. The fight continued for more hours the next day, the next, and the next. When he pushed Nancy being the executive director, working under him and running the daily operations, I said that could eventually squeeze me out. When I tried to bring up how he couldn't be objective about his and Nancy's relationship, Spencer refused to even discuss it, as if it was none of my business. At one point, hearing me go on and on, he snapped, "You know, Chris, I've finally come to realize that your sin is just as bad as mine." After nearly eight years of "constantly submitting" and all of my struggles, Spencer seemed completely fed up.

It was tense and awkward around the Antioch dinner table each night. Afterward Spencer and I left for our separate houses, to lick our wounds.

Back at it the next day neither of us budged, and we continued to batter each other with more stinging blows.

I crawled into bed that last night feeling an intense dislike for Spencer. And how could he not be sick of me? I was spent, ready to gasp, *"No mas,"* and throw in the towel. I didn't think I could go another round in this fight. I fell asleep with an agonized, hopeless foreboding, what I imagined spouses feel when they look at a failing marriage and wonder how it was once so wonderful, because now it was headed over a cliff toward divorce.

In the middle of the night, with Donna sound asleep next to me, something inexplicable began to happen.

Around 2:00 A.M. I woke up. No, I was awakened. It was as if some spirit had entered the room, coming to wrestle with me. My insides began to clench and twist over all the arguments of the previous five days. Sweat began to soak my body. The room and its darkness was caving in on me, suffocating me with panic and fear. The wrestling went on for an hour and another hour. I was being worn down, all my defenses eaten away, sucked out of me.

After two hours, very suddenly, the wrestling stopped. The room seemed quiet again.

A peace began to rush over me, a calm clarity as perfect as a clear, moonlit winter night in north country, when all your senses are alive, when the snow glows and crunches under your feet, and you hear and see your deep breaths, and air and sky have sharpness, and you look up and see stars splattered across the heavens, every one visible, it seems, in its proper place.

No circumstance in my life had changed. But with utter calm, I knew exactly what I was to do.

In the morning, when I told Donna what happened, her eyebrows lifted in wonder.

"I can't help but think of Jacob wrestling with an angel," she said slowly. "What is it you've decided to say to Spencer?" I could see how hard the last few days had been on her.

I told her what I was planning to say, and her eyes widened in amazement again.

After breakfast Donna and I headed over to the Duplex for a scheduled Antioch time of prayer. It just so happened that, this particular morning, the only members who could meet were Spencer, Nancy, Donna, and me—the ones most aware of our deepening crisis.

We decided to go ahead and pray. With just the four of us, alone, there was no pretending now. The others began to pray, with words that were hesitant, unworthy, vulnerable. Why would God listen to a mess like us?

I felt a sudden swelling urge to open up my Bible to Paul's Letter to the Romans, chapter eight. I began to read out loud, my voice shaking. " 'Now hope that is seen is not hope. For who hopes for what he sees? But if we hope for what we do not see, we wait for it with patience.' "

A great brokenness overcame me. " 'Likewise, the Spirit helps us in our weakness; for we do not know how to pray as we ought'—we do not know," I repeated—'but the Spirit himself intercedes for us with sighs too deep for words.' "

Tears began to flow down my face. Spencer's head was down, his face trembling with emotion. No circumstance had changed in our relationship. But the words of two millennia ago seemed to leap off the page and cut to our hearts.

A conviction, an anger took hold of my voice. " 'What then shall we say to this?' " I read, my voice rising, indignant against all that sought to destroy us. " 'If God is for us, who is against us?' Who?" I demanded, daring the enemy to show itself. 'He who did not spare his own Son but gave him up for us all, will he not also give us all things with him?' "

Nancy and Donna were crying too. Conflicts like this were so hard on them, they who carried so much of our pain but did not go through our give-and-take, even though we somehow expected them to ride it out with us.

"'Who shall separate us from the love of Christ?'" I demanded. *"Who?"* My voice broke with sobs, defying anything or anyone to answer me. "'Shall tribulation, or distress, or persecution, or famine, or nakedness, or peril, or sword?'

"No," I cried. "'In all these things'—*in all these things,"* I repeated, "'we are more than conquerors through Him who loved us.' Who loved us! Who loved us! 'For I am sure that neither death, nor life, nor angels, nor principalities, nor things present, nor things to come, nor powers, nor height, nor death, nor anything else in all creation will be able to separate us from the love of God in Christ Jesus our Lord.'"

After a long silence, I opened my eyes.

In a gentle, determined voice, I told Spencer I was ready to meet again. We slipped into his and Nancy's new family room, next to their bedroom. Donna and Nancy had looks on their faces like, "Please, guys. Please make this right."

Spencer sat down in his favorite armchair. I took the couch. I wasted no words.

Without anger or accusation, I calmly told Spencer what he had said that deeply hurt me. Then I put that behind me and told him what I was ready to do. I told him I was ready to accept his proposal, without reservation, with full support, convinced that it was the best possible direction for us to move. And I meant it and believed it, deep inside.

Spencer's spirit had changed, too. He didn't rehearse my hurtful statements to him over the last few days. He was subdued and apologetic. "You reckon you can really get yourself into this new role, Chris?"

I nodded, almost not believing what I was doing.

"I've been thinking more and more about how to be successful," he said, "bein' president. I really believe I can do it."

The more we talked, the more excited both of us sounded about the future.

Raw wounds and all, I felt one with him. And no circumstance had changed.

Two days later, in an upbeat office meeting full of laughter and teasing, Spencer and I presented the new leadership structure to the staff. Spencer would be the president of Reconcilers Fellowship; Nancy would run the operations under him; and I would develop the Training Center.

If someone had told me two months before that it would all turn out like this, I wouldn't have believed it. How I would feel Nancy's full support in spite of my frequent lack of support for her. How Spencer, and not I, would aggressively push our partnership to a new place of growth. How I would be cheering for Spencer like in the old days, content for him to increase and me to decrease, submitting to him without expecting anything in return. I was completely at peace, and I could not explain how I got that way. I could only testify, as old black folk liked to say, "God may not come when you want him. But He's always right on time."

A few days later Spencer put a copy of his latest "Reconciliation Wednesday" column in my box. It told the story of our struggle. "Most white men have not had very much practice submitting to anyone," he wrote. "Chris, however, is an exception. In fact, he once summed up our relationship as 'constantly submitting.' Sometimes we have to get away from each other just so we don't have to submit." I chuckled. Finally, I could laugh about all this.

"For Chris and me, our relationship has been put through another critical test, and it passed. And in the process, my respect and admiration for this white man has deepened. In seeking direction for the next phase of our ministry, we came to the proverbial fork in the road. And as Yogi Berra advised, we took it, together."

A month later, still basking in the newfound peace, Donna and I drove our family's red minivan to Atlanta with Phil and Tressa for a much-anticipated getaway to the Summer Olympics, which cost next to nothing because we stayed with friends. Like a climactic reconciliation rite, the long weekend renewed our bonds of affection, sealing the slow healing that had been taking place since their departure from Antioch ten years before. "I laughed more in those three days than I have the past three years," said Donna later.

It had taken us a long time to learn that Antioch's small circle alone could not provide the diversity of friendships that made for a well-balanced life. Barely aware of it, Donna and I were granting ourselves permission to free ourselves from Antioch's intensity. I was learning to lessen my expectations for Spencer and me, to free myself to be with others as I freed him to do so, not to make Spencer the focus for my well-being. I needed friendships that came hard, but I also needed friendships that came easy, which was what we had with Phil and Tressa again.

In September Donna's and my weary souls gained more refreshment. We went with my family on a trip to Korea to mark the thirtieth anniversary of our first arrival there in 1966. Donna's Aunt Nan and Uncle Jim in California graciously took our kids for a full three weeks, and soon Donna and I, Mom and Dad (who helped pay our way), Liz, and my brother Mark were reunited in Seoul. (To our sorrow, Rick couldn't get away.)

Toward the end of our trip, in a village called Haeinsa, maybe my favorite place on the planet, I climbed the mountain behind our inn, alone. At the summit I peered down through gnarled pine trees and across craggy cliffs to see the tiny speck of a Buddhist temple, heard the distant thumping of its drums, looked upon the mountain ranges stacked like earthen dominoes across the land of my youth, and said to myself, *If somehow I die right now, right here, I die happy. Just spread my ashes over these mountains.* I felt a great peace had descended in my life.

❖

In November Spencer and I took a stage before two thousand people in Pittsburgh for one of our most important talks ever—a keynote address at the annual CCDA conference. Our aim was to share lessons we'd learned since the publication of *More Than Equals* and to introduce a new level of truthfulness to the reconciliation debate. An injection of hope was needed too: *Time* and *Newsweek* magazines had both run articles pronouncing the death of integration.

I opened by sketching some signs of racial progress across the United States the past year. "Racial truces are being signed. Promises made. Tearful confessions spoken, forgiveness granted, and peace pipes passed. But the question we must ask ourselves tonight is this: Will reconciliation die? Or will it multiply?"

I ran though a quick historical litany of underestimating the power of racism, ending with the civil rights movement. "Dr. King's great missionary movement to the white church was largely rejected," I shouted. "White evangelicals, especially, slapped his hand away. And we carry that baggage tonight.

"The last four years have brought some of the most potent symbols of our racial divide: the Rodney King verdict and Los Angeles riots, the OJ murder trial, the Million Man March, and two best-sellers that told big fat lies—*The End of Racism,* and *The Bell Curve,* which promotes a theory of inherent black inferiority.

"Now we have another unprecedented opportunity to be faithful. But will reconciliation die—or will it multiply?"

I told a story from a recent trip to Birmingham, Alabama, about a plain-speaking white friend who had gone to an interracial gathering. He said blacks and whites were sweet-talking, smiling, being nice. But he knew of racial tensions in the city, and he was tired of all this pretending. So he decided to say something.

"So my friend stood up and said to this group, 'It seems to me like, whenever blacks and whites get together, it's like there's this big . . . pile . . . of . . . poop in the middle of the room.'" I gave the word its full, nasty effect, as hoots of laughter broke out in the auditorium.

"'The poop—it's right there in front of us. And everybody sees it. Everybody smells it. And you know what? We all pretend like it's not there.'"

More laughter, as hundreds of heads nodded across the room.

"And my friend said, 'Well, seems to me like if we're gonna get anywhere on this race thing, we gotta deal with this poop first. I say let's get us some shovels and start scoopin'.'

"Y'all, my friend got it exactly right. The challenge tonight . . . is to become poop-scoopers for Jesus."

After the applause and laughter died down, Spencer began naming the unsettling stuff in the middle of the room, starting with black racialism. "I'm tired of us settin' up no-win situations, where white folks fear bein' honest for fear of gettin' jumped on for makin' a mistake or usin' the wrong language. Where if whites don't invite us to the meeting, they're racist—and if they do invite us, they're paternalistic, and we're a token.

"In our better moods, we say we don't have anything against white people. But let one white person do somethin' to offend us, and we get mad with all the white people on the face of the earth." Black folks knowingly nodded their heads again.

"We don't want reconciliation any more than white folks do. Yeah, we want discrimination ended, the laws changed, the playing field leveled. And then? All of you white folks can get out of our face!"

Next I took on the white integration mentality. "Everybody being together without everybody being empowered is just another form of white domination. Is your organization integrating minorities into power—or out of it? The question isn't 'How do I integrate my church?' It's 'How do we join in—as servants—with the faithful mission that's already happening among Christians of color?'"

As Spencer started in on interracial marriage a black sistah near the front teased, "Now you messin', Spencer!"

I told the story of Spencer's and my summer struggle, and with each grueling detail of my experience of it, I heard Spencer grunt softly, as if to say, "I had no idea."

After an hour and a half it was up to Spencer to conclude. He went through a staccato litany of challenges for stepping forward, ending each one with the line "Reconcilers don't die" and getting the crowd to yell back, "We multiply!"

The next morning Spencer and I left the conference early, flew back to Jackson, dusted off rarely used suits and ties, and headed downtown with a gang of family and friends. Belhaven College was giving its Distinguished Service to Mankind Award, presented only once before in its history, to two alumni whose journey together was far rawer than anybody could have ever suspected.

"What the rest of us think, these guys say out loud," said Belhaven's new president, Roger Parrott, as he introduced us. Our remarks were brief, filled with emotion, done side by side. Spencer and I were still on our feet, moving toward the new plateau.

# 34

# SPENCER'S BOMBSHELL

*I*t was late January 1997, 6:00 A.M., and I was relishing the quiet of the Big House downstairs, eager to read my morning newspaper in solitude.

Suddenly I heard pounding on the locked side door. "Chris! Chris! Are you awake?"

I sighed. This was no emergency. It was JP, and no doubt my new neighbor had been up since before dawn, pacing, praying, planning, and yearning to tell someone—anyone!—about his latest brainstorm.

Since they had moved into the Corner House late in the fall, JP and Mrs. Perkins had been all we expected, exploding with both blessing and challenge. At our New Year's Eve party, they had danced down the Soul Train line to laughter and cheers, and joined the crowd doing the new Macarena dance craze. JP wasn't happy if he wasn't buying and renovating property, and the Foundation had bought another house two doors from the Duplex and revved up a youth program. Talia was romping around our room every night to the latest Good News Club songs she'd learned from "Grandma Perkins," and I'd see Christopher, packing a load in his diapers, carrying bricks and toting a hammer for "Grandpa" next door. In my new responsibility as Training Center director, I pulled JP into our planning, and at times he seemed frustrated with my reminders about developing our campus in ways that didn't overwhelm Antioch's community life. Spencer met with him regularly, trying to ensure his father's vast visions didn't overtake our slower pace. We thought we'd had intensity before, but with JP's energy next door, our six-ring circus could easily multiply to thirty-six.

Freeing up Spencer to lead last summer and the new peace we'd found seemed to be ratcheting our work up to a whole new level.

Spencer was reaching out to high-powered whites through letters and friendship, speaking frankly about race and responsibility, and seeking to tie them into financial partnership with RF. We brought in a new staff

member, Jason Dewey, an athletic young white man from Wisconsin with
a familiar tale: he'd left his junior year in college to come work with us.
Jason quickly became like an invaluable right arm for Spencer and me.
We set our sights on three Jackson-based events to widen our work locally
and nationally—a conference for interracial teams called "Yokefellows
Against the Odds," a gathering of Mississippi leaders, and a national conference on higher education and race. And Spencer and I had finally begun
our second book, building on lessons learned since *More Than Equals*.
Every now and then, Spencer and Nancy labored away on their interracial
marriage book, too.

In all my labors with Spencer—dare I say it?—I sensed a refreshing joy
again, a joy I hadn't felt since those old Study Center days, but now with
him as the lone chief at the top. It was actually possible for me to get a
good feeling, seeing glory and credit go to Spencer. From my midnight
epiphany, I had not looked back.

A frigid February evening found us on Harvard University's campus, sitting in a pew in Memorial Church with our eyes closed, not believing
what we were hearing. The worship service ending the reconciliation conference we had led was supposed to be over at 9:00 P.M., but a spontaneous time of confession had broken out among the 150 students.
America's best and brightest were admitting what racial jerks they were.

"I know the feelings I've held on to were wrong," a young black
woman said, sobbing. "The bitterness—not just against whites, but
against the black people who I asked to come but didn't show up."

A young white woman stood up. "I wanted to see this conference fail,"
she admitted, "so I could say we tried reconciliation, and it didn't work."
For nearly two hours the racial pretending that so often passed for pro-
gressiveness was blasted away.

Two weeks later we traded the nation's oldest private university for its
oldest public one, the University of North Carolina at Chapel Hill. It was
a party night, which lowered our expectations for attendance. We were
escorted through a gauntlet of fraternity house porches, where guys sat
on old couches downing vodka from the bottle. "It looks like the 'hood,"
Spencer said. But we walked into an astounding sight: eight hundred students sitting on the floor of a small gym, awaiting our talk, with two hundred more listening on closed-circuit television.

Spencer and I saw a deep hunger among these youth for faith that mattered, that did not ignore the deepest ills and most unsolvable problems,

that met the need with a costly life. February's travels had sent another clear message that the fields of reconciliation were ripe for harvest. But our increasing financial woes said, Slow down.

Over five years with *Urban Family* and now RF, we'd never had enough money. By March we were at the brink of disaster again: bills of $22,000, pennies in our bank account, creditors breathing down our necks.

The buck stopped with Spencer now. It was up to him to lead RF out of this fix. But I didn't see him naming it as a crisis or initiating plans, and in memos and private meetings I spurred him on like in the old days, exhorting him to be more aggressive. He'd declared himself ready for this and was failing, I thought, but I was definitely not going to be the one to say it. And he couldn't point to me anymore and say I was holding him back.

Antioch was in no better shape financially. Spencer, Nancy, and I had been paid half-salary four times and twice nothing at all. Joanie was just getting her Community Law Office up and running in the fourplex. Only Lue and Donna had reliable incomes. On a Wednesday morning in March, with downcast spirits, we sat in the living room of the Duplex, praying. It was the closest we'd ever come to a Pentecostal deliverance service, and desperation drove us to it.

At one point Lue's voice trembled with emotion. She told us she was seeing an image from the Book of Daniel, of an angel being sent to help but being detained by demons. "It was Daniel's prayer that got the angel through," said Lue. "It is by our prayers that God will send help."

Spencer's prayer melted my heart, the brokenness in his voice, the soft tone of his plea, the agonizing I heard behind its simplicity. "God, it seems selfish to think about myself in the midst of all this," he muttered. "I need a breakthrough in what you're callin' me to do. To be. I guess I'm askin' for a miracle, really."

He left much unsaid. But what I heard was the firstborn child wrestling with legacy and inheritance, with the intense expectations he had put on himself and that he felt from others, and a yearning to be free, to find God's destiny for himself alone.

We left that living room, somehow, with hope renewed and stamina to hang in there, awaiting divine breakthroughs, but with no more money in our hands.

---

In early April Jason led the way in decorating the Big House in black and white for a th'ow down for the sixty "Yokefellows Against the Odds" participants. Thirty interracial twosomes came from eleven states, each

bonded in friendship and common mission: pastors, community developers, people working in prisons and health care. For three days we dissected
challenges of race and reconciliation.

Afterward Spencer and I followed through on our pledge to devote
more energy to the state he affectionately called home, the place I considered myself a born-again citizen of, what I'd once considered America's
heart of racial darkness. After all our travels and hearing sordid little-
known stories of segregation in both law and practice from Iowa to California to suburban Chicago, I knew a lot of conflicted history besides
Mississippi's.

Still, two facts remained: Mississippi had an awful, violent past to come
to terms with, and our work and our lives had remained remarkably isolated from Mississippi whites. But a number of local firsts were transpiring.

In Jackson the first African American mayor presided in a city hall built
by slave labor; black judges were ruling on lawsuits between feuding
whites; and Byron De La Beckwith—the man who murdered NAACP
leader Medgar Evers in Jackson in 1963 and boasted that no Mississippi
jury would ever convict a white man of killing a black man—sat in the
city jail, sent there by a racially mixed jury thirty years after the crime.

Over at Belhaven College JP became the first African American commencement speaker, preaching reconciliation to a packed auditorium.

In recent months a miniwave of white Mississippi natives had joined
our church. Donna and I were becoming friends with one couple, two
lawyers named Kelly and Angela Simpkins.

Spencer was also building a new relationship. He was meeting regularly—and fishing, of course—with Stuart Irby, a prominent Jackson businessman and philanthropist, chairman of Belhaven's board, another son
of a locally famous father. Spencer called Stuart his first white Mississippi
friend, and it was, he said, a significant turning point, given his self-
confessed suspicion of white Southern accents.

On top of all this, Spencer and I began planning our first Mississippi-
only conference, meeting regularly with a team of influential local leaders. Besides Voice of Calvary people like Phil Reed and Phil Eide (who
now directed a downtown community development nonprofit organization), the outspoken group included the white associate director of Mission Mississippi (the interracial Christian network), an up-and-coming
black pastor named Ronnie Crudup, a black *Clarion-Ledger* editor named
Eric Stringfellow, and a red-headed journalist named Joe Maxwell.

With characteristic flair, in his proud Mis-sippi accent (clipping off the
middle), Joe coined a brilliant name for the December event. "Listen, y'all,
I got it! I got it! We're talkin' about gathering fifty of Jackson's movers

and shakers, right? From politics, churches, education, business, the media, right? All Christians? All under fifty years old? Half black, half white, right?" Heads nod. "OK, then. Let's call it 'Fifty under Fifty, 50/50'!"

I knew it wasn't Joe's first slam dunk as a wordsmith. Cecil was my first white Mississippi friend, and Joe had become my second.

Joe was a devout Southerner, both proud of it and deeply conflicted about it. "Y'all Northerners," he'd say, "y'all think you got race all figured out, and 99 percent of you haven't known a black person your whole life."

What attracted me to an in-your-face guy like Joe?

His truth seeking, for one thing. Over our many lunches, in stark contrast to Cecil's trailer-park roots, I learned of Joe's impeccable Mis-sippi pedigree, his father a distinguished businessman, his diploma from white folks' beloved Ole Miss (the University of Mississippi), where Joe became known as the fraternity president who helped elect the first black man to the renowned cheerleading squad. He married his Ole Miss sweetheart, whose father was mayor of the town that dubbed itself "The Catfish Capital of the World."

Up north, pursuing his master's degree in journalism, students had asked him questions with all seriousness, like "Hey, Joe, when did you start wearing shoes?" and "Have you ever seen a lynching?"

Then there was the time JP spoke at his campus. "I bristled, Chris, hearing John tell all his violent 'Mississippi stories.' I felt ashamed and embarrassed, and I went up to him afterwards." First he and JP had shared their love of Mississippi, like the piney woods and driving a truck down a dirt road in the summer with the windows rolled down.

"'But John,'" I told him, 'when you talk about all that violence you experienced, don't you realize that's the lasting image you leave these folks of the state we both love?'

"I'll never forget how John looked at me, Chris. He was quiet for a second. Then he said, 'Joe, being a black man from Mississippi is my cross to bear for the rest of my life. And being a white man from Mississippi is yours.'

"Oh, man. That cut me to the heart."

Joe followed where truth led him, to uncomfortable places, probably alienating one family member for good when he invited black students from a local high school over to his house. I admired him. I'd never had to consider betraying my family when it came to race.

By midsummer, plans for "Fifty under Fifty, 50/50" were firming up; we mailed out *Reconcilers* with "Is Reconciliation Too Cheap?" blaring from its cover; and eleven college-aged volunteers were on our campus for eight weeks. Gloria tore herself away from her "babies," as she called the Antioch kids, and she and Kortney headed to Pasadena for a few months, where she would teach at the new school the ministry there was starting. It was a well-deserved break, but it wasn't easy for any of us.

Meanwhile financial troubles continued, squeezing Antioch with the pressure. While I remained silent about what I saw as Spencer's poor presidential performance, he was making a valiant effort on the communal level. After one Antioch meeting in early July, when stress boiled over and tempers flared, including my own, he ripped off a memo, exhorting us to pray more, listing the endless pressures everybody was facing, and calling for attitude adjustments. "Attitude is everything, y'all. Let's not grind out the rest of the summer."

Grinding it out. That summed up very well how I was feeling about Antioch these days. I was finding myself less and less happy in community, and Donna was too.

A couple of weeks later Spencer and I donned our cheap department store suits and headed to the top floor of a tall downtown building to make a sales pitch in the stately dining room of the prestigious University Club.

We always felt a bit like bumpkins in fancy settings. Fortunately my shoe covered the hole at the toe of one of my fine K-Mart socks. I wondered whether I was the only one in the room who didn't groom the growing jungle of hair on my thirty-seven-year old ears and whether everyone else would notice the lapse. Would Spencer order a fine steak and ask the waiter, "Y'all got any ketchup?"

Judging by history, getting our two well-groomed lunch partners into a joint venture on race seemed like a long shot.

Dr. Joe Lee was the president of Jackson's Tougaloo College, a historically black school. Hundreds of Tougaloo students had risked their lives during the civil rights movement (including assisting in JP's Mendenhall efforts), and Tougaloo was a movement icon.

But the fourth person at the table, our friend Roger Parrott, was president of Belhaven College, an institution that was anything but a historical friend of Tougaloo or of racial justice.

Belhaven's roots were Scottish, Presbyterian, and lily white, and in 1954 one president emeritus wrote a pamphlet called "A Christian View on Segregation," which was published by the infamous white Citizens' Council. Until the late 1970s the school's sports teams were called the Clansmen (from Scotland, and not spelled with a K, at least). There was no end to jokes between Spencer and me, given the fact that he had been a Clansman when he played on Belhaven's basketball team. Yet Parrott was the latest in a string of presidents establishing a very different history as the Belhaven Blazers. Nearly 20 percent of the student body was African American. There was also the award they'd given Spencer and me, our several invitations to speak on campus, and JP's commencement address.

Over a buffet tended by black waiters dressed like butlers Spencer and I launched into our vision for Tougaloo and Belhaven to cohost an unusual national gathering. "Your two schools are symbolic of Jackson's racial past," I said intelligently as I chewed the elegant food. "But you also represent the hope of progress and the promise of the future.

"Imagine several hundred national college leaders—presidents, administrators, faculty, campus ministers—converging on your two historic campuses, coming to deal honestly with racial reconciliation. We open the first night with African drums coming down one aisle, beating the harmonies of one heritage. A moment later Scottish bagpipers come down the other aisle, droning the music of another heritage."

Maybe the musical combination was a stretch, but Lee and Parrott nodded politely. Parrott we knew well. It was our first meeting with Lee. We didn't know what he would make of us.

The answer came a couple of weeks later, when both presidents threw their support behind what we had billed as the "College, Ethnicity, and Reconciliation" conference. Another Mississippi first was in the making: the first public event in history cosponsored by these two colleges. Spencer and I were pumped.

But by summer's end, as I saw it, RF as a whole was drowning in disorganization and debt, with no plan from Spencer to free us from it. In early August, when our family headed west for vacation, I was relieved.

The same week Spencer and his family headed north to his beloved getaway, the place in rural Pennsylvania owned by Nancy's sister, Esther, and brother-in-law, Louie. Spencer simply called it "the cabin," and he and Nancy took their kids there almost every summer. In spite of Nancy's frowns, Spencer often hauled a cooler full of fresh worms up in their van.

At the cabin, unknown to me, Spencer was once again wrestling privately with another tumultuous decision about our relationship.

✤

Maybe Spencer came to peace with his decision in the clarity of separation from Robinson Street's chaos and all the demanding voices there. Or maybe it was by the stillness of the cabin's pond, doing what he loved best, pulling bluegill after bluegill out from their beds. Or maybe it was in evening conversations alone with Nancy in the Jacuzzi at her sister's house, in the security of his soul mate's unconditional love. Or maybe it was just watching the geese flying northward, finding their way to their true home.

After we both returned from our vacations Spencer asked if we could meet over breakfast.

As we settled into the booth he took a long look at me. Then he told me he believed he was failing as the leader of RF. He said he didn't think his personality and gifts fit the responsibility, and that this was hurting the ministry. Then, just as I had somehow found peace to submit to him a year ago, Spencer somehow found the peace to submit to me.

"Chris, I've been thinking. Maybe you need to be president," he said.

Hearing those shocking words, the last thing on my mind was "I told you so" or "Finally, my chance at glory."

I felt agony for Spencer. His voice dripped with failure, like he had let everybody down. I felt I was witnessing the slow death of a certain image of achievement that Spencer had been grasping for his whole adult life. But I also felt relief. A decisive change was needed, and it could come only from inside Spencer. The only way for him to find his true destiny was for a false one to die.

We hashed through what our new direction and roles might look like.

"What about me being white?" I said.

"I've thought about that, of course," said Spencer. "I think we're way beyond bein' trapped in a politically correct bubble. When true racial reconciliation is happenin', eventually we free each other to use the gifts we've been given. I think this move could make a powerful statement."

Spencer had prayed for a breakthrough in what he was to do and be. It took enormous courage for him to carry out his decision. But if this was the miracle he had prayed for in March, it was surely not the miracle he'd hoped for. We were on another road we'd never traveled before, with no idea where it led.

I told Spencer I would begin to ponder his proposal, already sensing this would be no easy decision.

# 35

# THE UNBEARABLE
# CONTRADICTION

*J*t was still August 1997, a week after Spencer's bombshell, and
he and I were enjoying a couple of our most peaceful days ever,
at a cabin high in the Smoky Mountains, with clouds literally drift-
ing into the front porch as we hammered away on our RF laptops. We
had come here to write our new book and were soon greeted by a perky,
wandering little dog I named Lookout, after he alerted us about a black
bear lounging by the house. The bear's lazy eyes had turned toward us,
as if to say, "What are you lookin' at, stupids? Ain't you never seen a
bear before?"

That night Spencer grilled steaks while I cooked up pork and beans,
corn, rice, and gravy. We talked a lot, but not about the great changes
ahead. Privately I was thinking constantly about being president, using
my typical deliberate and systematic decision-making style.

By the end of August Spencer was getting antsy. We met in his office,
and he asked me if I'd made up my mind yet. When I told him I hadn't
and that I was planning to take my time, he blew up.

"Well, I'll just continue being president, then," he snapped at one point.

"My decision-making style isn't your style, Spencer. You need to give
me room to be me, man! And don't try to manipulate me!"

*Oh, Lord, please, not another fifteen-rounder*, I thought, as he shot
back, and I shot back, and he shot back. At one point, neck bulging, I
must have said something really snooty. Because Spencer was jumping out
of his chair, slamming it back against the wall, and taking a step toward
me like George Foreman going after puny prey. My eyes widened.

"I'll knock you out, boy!" he screamed at me. Spencer was so mad, I
thought he actually might bop me upside the head. I had no idea what
possessed us.

That afternoon, feeling like steam was still rising from my head, I found
an unexpected note from Spencer in my box.

"I'm sorry," he wrote, "for all the mean stuff I said this morning." I was not believing this. A straight-up apology? From Spencer?

"I think you are right about most of the stuff," he said. *Wow*, I thought, *imagine one of us backing down this quickly.* "I won't speak of me leading RF again. I'm tired, humiliated, and I feel worthless, but I think I can find my way through. I can only go up from here. I'm ready to throw myself into the things that excite and motivate me. Take your time. When you make a decision, we'll talk again. Thanks for bearing with me—I think."

I marveled at this turn of events. In a matter of hours Spencer went from predator to this pledge of patience, and my hard heart melted with agony for him again.

On the Antioch front, though, I was feeling more and more hopeless, and I wasn't the only one. Simmering for many months, our little fellowship's discouragement was coming to a boil, brought on by what I saw as a mixture of intense financial pressures, weariness with the multiplying six-ring circus, unresolved relational difficulties, and inertia toward the "ungrowth" in our midst. We were failing to break through to the new plateau of serving each other that John and Judy had pointed us to. Too much was left unsaid between us or said with too much of an edge to it. I found myself going off on somebody in almost every Wednesday meeting.

At an early September Antioch meeting Spencer quoted familiar words from the King James Bible, words about what had always been our most precious commodity: "'Where there is no vision, the people perish.'" Then, with his classic eloquence, Spencer launched into a passionate pep talk. Maybe he stumbled as the organization man. But this brother had wondrous skills.

"Over eleven years ago, we had a vision, y'all. We made a covenant with God and with each other to take a step of faith together. A step that said we could be better followers of Christ together than we could be alone. And that this new organism was not only for us, but that we would allow God to use us—a bunch of no accounts—to bless others."

*All true, my friend,* I thought. *And it has all come to pass.*

"God has surely blessed hundreds of people through us. And much like the people of Israel, we have experienced glimpses of glory, and we have also wandered in the wilderness.

"But there's one sure thing about wanderin' and losin' sight of your purpose. You start to dwell on yourselves and your individual families. To compare who's gettin' what, tryin' to figure out if our lives are good enough in community. Lettin' the way you feel about someone's personality affect your love for them. Focusin' on the negative qualities of each other instead of the positive, and lettin' your immediate circumstances block your—our—vision.

"Well, all that is a black hole with an endless bottom. Because community is not worth it without a vision."

Right there Spencer nailed it, and he kept hammering.

"Where there is no vision, the people have no reason to sacrifice. No reason not to think only of themselves." He peered around the room, as if challenging us to a gut check.

"Once upon a time, we heard God say there was a unique plan for us. That we could be special forces. Marines. A special order. All of us know that God hasn't changed his mind. We've just floundered and are unable to hear God's voice over our own voices."

But then Spencer began to lose me. I started hearing too much self-satisfaction, too much unwillingness to name the depth of our crisis.

"I'm not one who thinks we're failing. Even when we're bad, because of the commitments we have made to each other, I believe God still uses us. We need to continue to dream together. Dream of what we can be. What kind of impact we can make on the world. What legacy we leave for our children. How we can be sure that this vision that God gave us does not die with us."

The further Spencer went, the more I realized how little I needed this pep talk. I didn't need a mere attitude adjustment. "Impact" on others, or relevance in their eyes, didn't motivate me anymore. Our so-called radical living together had become just a pretentious veneer to me, covering up all the ways Antioch had shriveled up inside.

Spencer came to his conclusion. "Now I'll admit my ego is tied up in this too. But I believe God allows for that. I wanna be part of somethin' significant. Somethin' unique. I wanna inspire others to not be afraid to make a radical commitment like we did."

---

They were masterful words.

But that very afternoon I was downtown at the city library, alone in a study carrel, coming to the dreadful realization of just how far apart Spencer and I had become in how we saw life at Antioch. I had come to decide yes or no on the president role, and I was swamped with emotion trying to discern between the legitimate and illegitimate voices that had always clamored to claim me.

I thought of how the ten years since teaming up at the Study Center had brought Spencer and me so very far. When RF threw our little rocks into the water, the ripples spread far beyond our size and resources.

The truth was that even with big issues to iron out, I knew I could be effective as president. Over these many years the Voice of Calvary community—most of all Spencer and Antioch—had made me capable of leading, and I knew that I would not be alone. I believed I had the right stuff, that I could find joy and peace in doing it, and that my family could still thrive. Donna and I had talked a lot about that. I also believed that Spencer could find a vital new role—writing more, being editor of *Reconcilers,* growing in public influence in ways apart from me, and chairing a reorganized board. All the puzzle pieces for a prosperous new season of partnership were falling into place, and nobody had planned it out. It had only been made possible because Spencer and I had been honed into truer servants.

If only I could have stopped right there and taken my decision to Spencer. It would have seemed a great victory. But I was not allowed to. I was taken painfully deeper. And I saw a great contradiction in my life.

To stay at RF as president for the long haul meant living at Antioch for many more years. I finally allowed myself to see just how unbearable that thought had become. Our public work was life-giving. But all I was doing at Antioch was gutting it out, and that was true for Donna too.

As I forced myself to examine Antioch alone, I saw a swamp of stagnation, no longer a place where Donna and I were growing or helping the others to grow. We had become mired in accommodating each other's weaknesses. More and more I had come to look outside of Antioch for vitality and friendship—to the Franciscans, to John and Judy, Phil and Tressa, Joe Maxwell, and others. It had been so long since I bared my soul to my comrades within Antioch. So much seemed off limits, things Antioch couldn't talk about without igniting huge arguments. I held great affection for everyone at Antioch, and we'd had an amazing journey together. But it had run its course. I didn't just want us to be used to impact others, I wanted joy and peace and growth inside of our life.

Most of all, perhaps, I was just plain weary. Life together wasn't giving me strength, only draining it away. I could no longer continue to live with such excitement and hope in one sphere, while discouragement and hopelessness reigned in the other. I no longer saw enough worth staying for.

Immediately I thought, *But Donna and I can't possibly leave.* I feared even thinking the thought. *Why?* I asked myself. *Why do I fear it so much?*

I knew why, and I let it all sink in.

I so feared leaving, because from the Reconciliation Meetings, to Phil and Tressa, to Harold and Betsy, leaving was always desertion; it was always divorce.

Because I couldn't bear the thought of lost friendship with those with whom I had shared so much blood, sweat, and tears.

Because there was no choice of letting Antioch go and keeping RF. Spencer would never stand for it. To leave meant surrendering a future of incredible opportunity and letting down literally tens of thousands of people who looked to us. It meant giving up influence and a national platform and our little piece of fame. I could not bear that thought either.

Most of all, leaving meant giving up Spencer, breaking the yoke, which felt like giving up everything that my life stood for, everything that gave my life significance. So much was at stake in our friendship staying together.

Suddenly, overwhelmed by fear, caught between the impossibility of staying and the impossibility of leaving, I had a keen sense of a gentle voice speaking within me. The voice said something that broke me, that I could never have come up with myself, given who I was.

The voice said: "Chris. My child. If you stay? I love you. And if you leave? I still love you. You go loved—either way."

Maybe that voice had been trying to get to me in so many ways over the past several years, but only now, in an impossible fix, did I really hear and understand it.

I had never heard such permission before. To be loved? Walking away from more radical commitment? To be loved? Committing the ultimate Voice of Calvary betrayal—desertion? To be loved? In not trying harder or doing more? In surrendering impact and relevance? That morning Spencer had talked about being called to something significant. Unique. Counting for something. I was so tied up in being all of that. But the gentle voice I heard was strong enough to let it all go. Being so completely beloved made the unimaginable imaginable.

Now only this voice mattered to me. I felt a freedom not only to choose but a willingness to force the choice, to risk everything, put myself on the altar, and see if I would be given back to Spencer and Antioch and the work or be taken from them.

And right there in that library stall I put my face down on the wood tabletop and let the sobs come, my shoulders heaving up and down, until snot ran down my face.

After the hardest cry of my life, before I made my way to the bathroom, I tried to pull myself together. I feared seeing somebody I knew.

But red-eyed, slimy mess that I was, I felt freedom and conviction and courage to go on, to own the truth, and to walk into it.

That night, as Donna and I talked, my new freedom seemed to loosen up her own conflicted desires, things she hadn't expressed or verbalized to me. "It's very scary, Chris, hearing you say it might be OK to leave. I've entertained that, as a fantasy, I guess. Being free of so many stresses. But to think of it as an actual possibility? I feel so fearful."

Fear. That was always a big problem for Donna. And entertaining the idea of not living at Antioch somehow felt deliciously sinful. We were clear that Antioch was no cult. Still, we had always felt it was the most authentic way of living out our faith. Now we talked of longings that once seemed disloyal even to think, much less form on our lips. For the first time we actually imagined what we might do if we left. But Donna brought it to an end.

"We need to stop, Chris. There's still so much good here."

That night we agreed we would not move any further without giving Antioch a chance to respond, to show us how wrongheaded we were, to see if others felt as we did, or to see that our differences were irreconcilable. We knew we could no longer go on without baring our souls. For how could we become one in heart and mind with our closest comrades if they didn't know what was in our hearts and on our minds?

Over the next week I continued to test these thoughts in prayer, and with Clive and John by phone and e-mail, all the while wondering whose voice I was hearing.

Just as the horror of where this could lead was making me doubt myself, a long, unexpected letter arrived from my father.

I had called Mom and Dad a couple of days after Spencer proposed that I become president and described the whole situation. They had close ties to Antioch, with many visits over the years and two months of living with us in 1993. Dad was not one to give unsolicited advice and usually hedged even when asked for it. But he had been thinking and praying, he said, and in a way he had never done before, he laid out what he saw.

During their last Antioch visit, in the summer, he said he had sensed more strain, less enthusiasm, and a heaviness that he'd never experienced before. "What I observed," he wrote, "was a group of wonderful people who seemed to be just plain tired out, at times almost overwhelmed."

He told of a stress measurement instrument he once saw which assigned points to a variety of stress-inducing factors. "I think of all the pressures all of you are under—the economic, the high expectations others place upon you, the work you do as individuals, the ministry itself, your openness to others, the responsibilities you carry for the interns, the new dynamic brought by John and Vera Mae's presence next door, the commitments to one another as community members, and the primary commitments you have to spouses and children. In addition are work pressures, whether those at RF or those differently employed. Then I think of all the property you own and are responsible for and the long-range plans for the Training Center."

I was getting exhausted myself, reading Dad's list.

"Added to this mix is the fact that you have no 'getaway' place and are all members of the same congregation, so you share what is happening there as well. Even in the best of circumstances, this tangle of issues, commitments, and responsibilities would place you at the top of the stress chart."

Then Dad drew an image, a parable for me of exactly what Antioch had become. Once, as a chaplain at a chemical dependency unit, he told me, more and more was being expected of the staff, and they enjoyed being together less and less. They settled for a "keep the peace" level of sharing and honesty, their spirit of enthusiasm driven out by frustration, resentment, and feelings of "we'll do it, but only because we have to." To address the demoralization, the staff went out on an all-day ropes course. They were given a bucket filled with water, said to hold the cure for drug addiction and alcoholism. Their assignment was to get the bucket over an obstacle course, spilling as little as possible, and to get the whole group across the course as well. In the end they got the bucket—the cure—across, but they lost a third of the group along the way. Did they succeed or fail?

"Of course, we failed," wrote Dad. "We could have gotten everyone across, with the bucket too. But we got so caught up in preserving the great cure that we did not show concern and care for one another along the way." They realized it was a mirror for what was happening in their work together, and in that mirror I saw Antioch too.

Without knowing all that was roiling inside of me, Dad said something else that nailed me to the wall.

"When a person begins to think that he or she is indispensable to an organization, it is very dangerous, for if the group cannot exist without that person, what does it say about the others? But if God wants a thing done, God will find a way to do it, for He is the One and Only Indispensable."

Those words unmasked a power that gripped my life. To think there was an absolute necessity of Antioch or RF staying together was creating an idol of my partnership with Spencer, an idol of our indispensability. I realized how much my significance was wrapped up with Spencer and our work. I had never thought of it this way before.

Dad told of his sorrow when the chemical dependency unit eventually closed its doors. "One of the most difficult decisions to make is when to close or transform a group," he wrote, "when its purpose has been fulfilled, when those who are a part of it no longer have the will, the vision, the desire, or the resources to keep it going. This is especially difficult when the group has been successful, is known, and has generated expectations for others.

"In a sense, doing this is like the first step of Alcoholics Anonymous—'We admitted we were powerless over alcohol, that our lives had become unmanageable.' We get into a situation that seems to have no good way out, and all we can do is surrender, yield, and let God work it out—which God usually does in a manner we never would have thought of."

It was what I needed to do, to be willing to believe that even if Spencer and I separated, something better would be revealed. I was so thankful my father didn't hide his thoughts from me.

When Donna read the letter tears formed in her eyes. "I can't believe how well this describes how we feel," she said.

On my calendar I sketched the words *D-Day* onto October 1, three weeks away. It would give me plenty of time to write a letter to Antioch, spilling our guts and probably precipitating a crisis, just as Spencer and I were on the verge of our two biggest events ever—"Fifty under Fifty, 50/50" and "College, Ethnicity, and Reconciliation."

The closer October 1 came, the heavier the burden of speaking truthfully became. Donna might have backed away, if not for me, and I was close to backing out myself. Yet I kept receiving courage to go forward.

Over breakfast downtown with Joe I bared my soul, sparing him all the worst details. He listened patiently, and when I finished, he pulled out a piece of paper and drew a heart on it, with an arrow through it. "That's your heart," he said. Inside the heart, Joe wrote the words, "Can I reveal myself and my concerns and have them received with compassion?

"You need to find that out, Chris. If Antioch listens, there still might be hope. If they scorn you for revealing your heart, it's probably time to go. But you must reveal your heart."

---

Wednesday morning, October 1, finally came. In a few minutes, six weeks after Spencer's bombshell, Antioch would hear what Donna and I were hiding in our hearts.

We were overcome by dread. Whatever happened next, our relationship with Antioch was never going to be the same. Even though I felt at peace with Spencer, we were about to force a showdown between his view of Antioch and ours. It might launch the biggest battle he and I had ever had.

Before we went down to the meeting Donna and I faced each other, held hands, and said a final prayer.

We asked for our hearts to be revealed. That we would be received with compassion, not condemnation. That we be given strength to endure, whether strength to stay or strength to go. And we prayed that God would have the final word.

"I love you," she said after we opened our eyes.

"I love you too." We wiped the tears from our faces, embraced, and headed over to the Duplex, as if striding toward doomsday.

Gloria was still in Pasadena. Everyone else was assembled in the living room: Spencer and Nancy, Lue, Joanie and Ron. I took a seat next to Donna, my heart pounding. We had asked for time at this meeting, and I pulled out the long letter I'd written. It was from me, but it spoke for her too.

As much as I felt Spencer was going to despise it, we believed we had to speak of just Chris and Donna, to own where we and we alone were at. To avoid examining our life in the grayness of the group, but to do so in the stark clarity of whether or not we could renew our own vows to life together.

"Donna and I have some things to tell all of you this morning," I said, and I began to read the most important words I'd ever written in my life.

I felt my voice coming forth as a plea, from my heart, with all its angst. I revealed everything that had emerged since Spencer's proposal—my hurt for him, my relief, RF on the exciting threshold of a new era, and my readiness to accept the challenge of being RF's president.

"But I can no longer continue to live with joy and excitement in one sphere," I confessed, "while discouragement and hopelessness reign in the other—within Antioch." I described my weariness, how I was going on less hope than ever before, of Dad's letter and insights, and of letting go.

Conviction rose within me and in my voice. "I no longer believe in gutting out the Christian life, in just trying harder. Yes, we persevere. But ultimately it is God who has to change us through supplying grace and strength even in our weakness. In the past I have received grace and peace and strength to endure. Now, however, I feel little will or strength to go to the next level.

"I don't need a pep talk about why Christian community is important," I said, sure Spencer would read this, rightly, as a critique of his recent challenge. "I believe deeply in the biblical vision that inspires Antioch. But ultimately it is not community itself that matters, only that we are together growing toward holiness. It's not like I'm constantly unhappy or angry with any of you or don't enjoy our relationships. It's the group dynamics I struggle with, the patterns that have developed over time."

I told how Donna and I had drastically lowered our expectations for Antioch over recent years. "I am much more one who enables weakness than one who empowers. After eleven years, you still pay the price if you dare to bring up some things about me, or I about you, or you with anybody else. What does that say about us, if we feel like we'll get jumped on if we reveal our hearts and minds?"

I was so wrapped up in what I was reading, I didn't look up to gauge how anyone was responding. But what I would confess next had never been discussed within Antioch. There was no taking back the distance it might put between us.

"I have never felt comfortable that within our circle there seems to be no good way to go. The only Antioch category for someone leaving is negative. But if someone doesn't feel free to leave, then they are not staying freely. If going is only negative, then Antioch itself can become an obstacle to hearing God's voice. God may call some in Antioch to go someday. Not all of us have geographic or family ties here. That is not what keeps me here. Maybe some of you can't imagine ever leaving Jackson. But my upbringing put the world in my heart, and I want you to share in that part of my heart too."

I laid out the options Donna and I saw.

Maybe we would all see the quagmire in which we were mired and reach as one for a way out.

Maybe Donna and I would see that we were wrong. "Perhaps our vision is clouded by too much weariness and tears. I'm not saying the Rices have been done wrong or that nobody cares about us. If we stand in the way, then God will have to eventually change us or give us peace. Or maybe eventually we'll have to go. We're not dying to leave community. But we're dying."

Maybe, I said, Donna and I were being nudged toward a new chapter, a new mission outside of Mississippi. Saying this, I knew, was asking for it.

"Some of you may already be thinking that our going is now inevitable. I can only say you must believe that is not the case." I told them how we feared being written off, how our lack of trust in Antioch disturbed me.

There were no greener pastures, I said—nowhere. "Just the thought of going is agonizing. But for the first time, I don't feel trapped here. I don't assume I am indispensable to Reconcilers Fellowship or to Antioch."

I came to my conclusion. "Donna's and my pain started small," I said,

> As the pain increased, we've been too proud or scared to have it fully examined. We've gutted it out alone instead. And we have failed and hurt Antioch because we were not honest with you. Now it's gotten worse, not better. The only thing we know to do is take the risk of bringing it into the open.
>
> Each of us has expressed pain. Midlife crises. Feelings of worthlessness. Of never gaining ground. Of stagnation. Maybe it's only a minor back problem. But maybe there's a hidden tumor within Antioch that will only get worse and worse—one that requires radical, risky surgery.
>
> I beg you to look at what I've said, not the weakness of who said it. I don't assume Donna and I are the only ones frustrated or hurting, or that we're right about everything. There are so many good things about life at Antioch. But our soul-searching has caused us to look deeply. This is what we found.

I put down the letter and braced myself for judgment day.

# 36

# GRACE DEBTORS

_____

*J*oanie was the first to speak. "Chris," she said, with wonder, "that letter could have come from me."

I thought, *Are you kidding me?*

Nancy followed quickly, with another stunner. "Several times while you were reading? I felt like standing up and applauding." It meant so much to me, coming from Nancy.

Ron jumped in too. "That letter came to me like a New Testament epistle," he said. "Like a prophetic word to us."

How did Donna and I misread everyone so badly? Why did we wait so long to see what others had in their hearts for our concerns?

Lue was quiet. I was used to her taking time to respond.

Spencer, however, hadn't said anything yet. Was he taking this as a diss of his pep talk?

Finally he muttered his response. "Are y'all committed to stayin'?"

"I can't answer that, Spencer."

"It's a simple question. If y'all are thinkin' of leavin', there's no point in discussion. The only way we can work this out is if you're stayin'."

"I don't see it that way. What Donna and I sense is that we need to put everything on the altar and see what's given back to us."

"That's a buncha crap. Why is it always white folks who got to give some kinda ultimatum?"

This was beyond belief. His headline read: "Yokefellow and Wife Unmasked as Racists." To me it was the kind of knee-jerk reaction Spencer railed against all over the country. This is the best he could come up with? Throwing the race card? After sixteen years in west Jackson for me, twenty for his dear old friend, Donna? It hurt, deeply. Spencer had never, ever directly accused me—or Donna—of such a thing.

"We aren't making an ultimatum, Spencer. But we can't mandate what our next step is, beyond Antioch dealing with some stuff."

Spencer kept pressing us. The more we refused to say we were staying, the more my letter was sounding like a rejection of Antioch, a way to justify our impending departure. Which is exactly what I felt more and more like doing, watching Spencer go after us. I felt like it was turning the others against us. But I wasn't going to say we were staying. I had been freed from that. And now, no matter how loyalties kicked in and Spencer's commanding presence turned things, I knew others—including Nancy—shared at least some of our concerns.

I wasn't backing down. Neither was Spencer.

Once again we were in an impossible fix. And once again Antioch decided to dial 911 to San Francisco.

This time I made the call. "John, I'm pretty fed up," I said. "Donna and I are close to leaving. I don't think I can deal with Spencer anymore. I'm just flat-out weary."

John said they'd be in Jackson in two weeks. I didn't bother saying he and Judy would be overseeing my divorce from Spencer.

It was such a relief, being away from Spencer the next week. I had been accepted into a small leadership development program held in the North Carolina mountains, run by a former colleague of Billy Graham's named Leighton Ford. With a space to reflect, I saw how little I desired to move forward with Antioch, after Spencer's reaction. On the third day I received an inspiration for what to do next.

I stood with several others at the base of a ninety-foot sheer cliff, scanning the unfriendly rock face we were each supposed to climb. *No way,* I thought.

To conquer the challenge, our instructor said each of us would have to play three different roles. We would each climb, harnessed to a rope that was secured to the top and to a pulley below. The key to our climb was teammates—two belayers and a watcher.

"*Belay* is a French term," said the instructor. "It means 'to hold fast.' Each climber will be belayed by two people gripping the rope at the pulley below. They've got to keep it tight, in case the climber slips or falls. But they must also loosen it, when the climber needs slack to go up.

"Now the belayers are under the cliff, so they can't see you climb. A watcher is also needed, to listen to the climber's calls for tightening and loosening and give orders to the belayers. The watcher also scans the rock face and gives the climber advice about routes to take. Remember this:

The success of your climb and your life is literally in the hands of your belayers and your watcher. You must work as a team—or else," he chuckled.

I discovered exactly what he meant.

As I went up, I hit a snag. My watcher said the only way forward was to order a tight grip and swing across the rock to a toehold I couldn't see. My only choice was to trust her. I gave the order, waited for my watcher's command, let go of the rock, and swung into thin air, heart pounding. Below me my belayers held tight, and my foot reached the new toehold. I scrambled to the top. But the greater joy was embracing my team back at the bottom, those to whom I had entrusted my life.

That night I saw Antioch at the bottom of an impossible rock face. I had no idea where the climb with John and Judy would end up. The last thing I wanted to do now was put my life in Antioch's hands. I mean, swinging into thin air, trusting Spencer to keep my line tight? And why should I belay for Spencer? He didn't deserve it. I detested the idea that what awaited me at the top was more of the same life at Antioch. I didn't think there was a land up there worth reaching, worth ten more years in community. I didn't see how it could possibly be flowing with milk and honey, and not be just another stagnant wasteland. I couldn't imagine rejoicing with Antioch at the top of anything anymore. Yet I believed that I must give myself to this climb, reaching neither for Antioch's survival, nor the inevitability of leaving, but only the way of growth, wherever it took Donna and me over the next few decisive days and weeks.

I had been given another parable, I felt. But I hadn't been given the punch line.

✤

John and Judy always spent their first couple days with Antioch with their ears to the ground. This time they called a meeting the first morning, a Friday. I couldn't imagine how they could possibly know what to say without knowing the details. I wished I could tell them about Spencer's ridiculous reaction to Donna and me.

John had a talk prepared for us, peppered with *I don't knoooow*s, meaning there was something very important he thought we didn't know.

He said there was nothing sacred about sharing houses and money, that the form of how Antioch lived was negotiable. I liked that.

He also said there were some nonnegotiables that did matter. First, God's love in action for us mattered. Second, it mattered that Christians lived lives that constantly reminded each other of God's love for us. These were familiar themes that had had an enormous influence on me. But so far, I wasn't hearing a way out of our mess.

Then John used a phrase he'd never used before. "The way you grow into God's love isn't by making demands of each other," he said. "You do it by giving each other grace."

*Grace.* It was John's new pet word. In fact, it was all John wanted to talk about—grace, grace, grace. But this time he wasn't talking about God's undeserved love for us. He was talking about our undeserved love for each other—when it didn't seem fair, or reasonable, when others were being complete jerks.

"Giving each other grace is looking at people through God's eyes. It's internalizing God's love so much that we can get into the bones of others that God loves them—by serving, valuing, and caring for them. The Bible doesn't talk about Jesus' warm feelings for his disciples. It's mostly about how he served them—a bunch of failures, doubters, and traitors. God wants us to use our lives to help each other understand who God is."

The next day Judy took the point, playing the same broken record on "giving each other grace." After the meeting John told me that he and Judy wanted to see Spencer and me privately.

We gathered in my office, and John got straight to the point. "The relationship between the two of you is the key to moving Antioch forward. We want you to talk to each other about what's blocking your relationship. And we want you to do it in a spirit of forgiveness."

We tried. We failed.

The more Spencer and I talked, the madder I got. All the ways we'd each given in, all the grievances I thought I'd forgiven, or been forgiven of, were spilling over. We were like bloated bottom-feeding fish, spewing all kinds of ugly, nasty garbage we pulled up from the mud of our past. It was scary what I reached for, trying to win an unwinnable argument. Grinding Spencer's face in it. Acting like forgiveness was only temporary, until it became necessary to revive old resentments for my own purposes again. All I wanted to do was win.

After two hours even John and Judy looked exasperated. Hope was slipping away.

Spencer finally interrupted a long silence. "I think the only way of movin' forward is to forgive and make a new beginning."

*Yeah, right,* I thought. *Why should I?* It wasn't fair. Spencer didn't deserve to be forgiven. He had failed Joe's test. I revealed my heart, and he didn't show an ounce of compassion. He had even thrown the race card, showing what a total jerk he was. And now this long list of grievances.

And why should he forgive me? I had been snootier than ever. If John and Judy hadn't been there, this time Spencer might have tossed me through the window.

It was time to face the humiliation of calling off "Fifty under Fifty, 50/50," and "College, Ethnicity, and Reconciliation." I was going to have a hard time explaining this to Belhaven and Tougaloo, and all the national partners who had rallied behind us. But my powers to persevere were depleted, and I saw no way forward. It was our darkest moment.

The next morning, on Sunday, I asked John to go out to breakfast with me. As I left my bedroom I muttered a prayer. *God, somehow I will trust you to speak through John right now. I have reached a dead-end. I have no hope that life at Antioch will ever change. I am ready to give it all up— everything.*

John patiently listened for two hours. With his permission to leave, I would have been ready to make the decision in a heartbeat.

"I don't knoooow, Chris," he finally said. "This isn't a word from God, and I'm not telling you what to do." He paused. "But maybe you need to stick it out at Antioch. Simply as a step of obedience. And pray that God gives you the grace and strength and joy after taking that step."

An hour later I stood with the choir during the worship service, singing songs that had carried me through the years, watching Arthur dispense grace with his ever-faithful smile, letting the Spirit lead. I didn't feel self-sufficient any more, like my first days here sixteen years before. So many weeks, worship had become a three-hour scream for help for me too. I was so messed up, so undeserving, so powerless.

But as we sang, I received the words as a promise, a promise that began to reshape my heart and reorder my thoughts, even as I sang.

"You who need mending, stop by the Potter's house, You who are broken, stop by the Potter's house, The Potter wants to put you back together again."

I knew I had my answer. This would be just like you, God, to do the unexpected. To have me climb and give Antioch back to me. To use Antioch and that jerk Spencer to put me back together again. No, I did not like this answer very much. It was beyond reasonable. But I knew it was right. And that I would be given grace to endure. When I talked with Donna after church she, too, had felt a strength to go on, to stay in community and believe that a way would be worked out of no way.

John and Judy were leaving the next day. In the afternoon all of Antioch met with them for the last time. Spencer said he had something to say.

His voice cracked, he paused. Then he spoke monumental words. Words I didn't think he was capable of. Words that I believed came from his heart. "I want Chris and Donna to be happy. If that means them leavin', then I want to help them do that and to be excited about that."

Now I knew what giving grace looked like, and I felt its transforming power.

I said I had something to say too. I told everyone that I was ready to commit my life to Antioch's next chapter, as a step of obedience.

Spencer found the grace to allow me to leave. I found the grace to allow myself to stay.

As we all shared our reflections from the past few days, Spencer said something that captured my imagination. "How are we gonna begin creatin' this new culture of grace, y'all?"

A culture of grace. No, community alone wasn't worth it without a vision. But this sounded like a vision worth sacrificing for. A culture of grace seemed like a beautiful land, one that did, indeed, flow with milk and honey.

To create a culture that did for each other what Spencer had just done for me, by freeing me to stay or leave? Not demanding more or working so hard to change each other, but somehow giving God room to do it? Not slugging every disagreement out until dawn, but making new beginnings? Not telling the truth mostly in terms of "what's wrong with you," but the truth of how much God loves you? Yes, this was territory worth growing into.

As I watched and listened to Spencer, there was a new joy about him. Something profound was going on inside of him. In all of us.

John had some final instructions.

> Grace is really the central Christian idea. Yet Christians aren't known for our deep sense of being loved by a God of grace, nor for that love overflowing from us onto those around us. What we're more likely to overflow is disapproval.
>
> People get pretty panicky at the idea of "just accepting one another." "Doesn't that mean you'll just lose control of them?" Probably. "Won't they just take advantage of you?" Pretty often, in fact. "You mean you're just going to let people sin?" As if you can do anything else!
>
> The truth is, we can't stand the idea of not fixing each other. But insofar as we can fix people at all, we can do it only by forgiving them,

and giving them grace, and leaving them to our loving Father. Grace assumes sin. When we ask you to accept each other, we aren't asking you to ignore hurts between you. People of grace speak the truth. But in an atmosphere of grace, truth seems less offensive and more important. It's no big deal to tell each other how you're sinning. If you talk about people's failures as matter-of-factly as you talk about the weather, they'll hear your love and not your judgment.

You see, people grow when they're watered and given sunshine. Not when they're hacked at and beaten to death.

John left us with a mission, a simple mantra for moving forward. "All Judy and I are asking you to do is this: Care for each other, forgive each other—and keep washing the dishes."

That day John taught me what is enough. It is enough to get the love of God into your bones and to live as if you are forgiven. It is enough to care for each other, to forgive each other, and to wash the dishes. The rest of life, he taught me, was details. And maybe the reason why I had so much trouble confessing all these years, with facing the truth about myself, was because I hadn't gotten the most central things into my bones.

Antioch had begun our greatest cross-cultural journey ever, into the culture of grace.

---

After John and Judy left I marveled at how they had led us, as much by restraint as action. They ignored our endless lists and lifted our vision to a breakthrough in moral imagination, a whole new way of seeing each other, a way that readied me to strap on the harness and look to Antioch as my watchers and belayers.

When Donna and I had left our bedroom that fateful day to bare our souls we knew our relationships with Antioch would never be the same. We were right, of course, but far differently than we expected. Could Antioch, and Spencer, hear the cry of our hearts and still embrace us? The answer was yes, they could.

John and Judy had given us much work to do. Numerical growth, they said, had become important for Antioch now. Openness to new people would bring fresh energy and vision. "But don't just add more Perkinses," John had warned. "Inbreeding gets tricky." Also Antioch needed to get as much energy as RF was getting. This growth was hard work, said Judy, something like Joanie going to law school. Part of the work was Antioch getting more intentional leadership, someone to check in on how people were doing, and to reflect on Scripture with a heart toward pastoring the group toward growth.

We agreed that Spencer should take on this Antioch pastor role, giving him a crucial new niche as I took over RF's leadership and replaced Spencer as president. Donna was appointed to be "the keeper of the flame," helping to see that members followed through on growing in grace, asking each person how she could help keep the flame of God's love alive in their life. One further decision was made: Hereafter Antioch would celebrate October 18 as Grace Day, to remember the breaking in of a new vision for life together, even for life itself.

It was like a new love was being birthed for each other. Lue wrote me a note that meant so much, thanking me for my courage, for forcing Antioch to face some hard truths about ourselves. "I really believe it may be the catalyst to compel us to start actively looking for the answers we need," she said. Over and over again in our meetings during the next several weeks we talked about being back in kindergarten, learning a whole new set of skills, even a new language, after so many demanding years together.

At Thanksgiving before we dug into the feast, Spencer spoke of how each of us owed God a debt of gratitude for grace given to us. He said each person's name at the table, recounting how far that person had come over the past year. "Y'all," he said, "God has been faithful to us. And that's why we're goin' to sing the most beloved song in history."

He turned to his eleven-year-old son. "Johnathan, do you know who wrote 'Amazing Grace'?"

"John Newton."

"That's right. Do you know what he did for a livin'?"

"He was captain of a slave ship."

"Yup. But nobody knows for sure where the music came from. Some think the melody is based on the 'slave scale,' notes that Newton once heard rising from the bowels of his boat. Isn't that an awesome thought? These words, comin' from a redeemed slave ship captain? That music, comin' from slaves, chained together under his feet? God's love and grace are the only things that have the power to redeem a terrible situation like that. And it is the only thing that can reach down and save wretches like us."

We sang "Amazing Grace," and it really was a sweet, sweet sound.

When John and Judy visited again in early December to give us a boost forward, Judy asked us to do something. "Think about yourself in the light of God's amazing love. In that light, what would be a new name you think God might give you?"

It was an emotional time, telling each other our new names and why we chose them.

Lue, Wise Mother. Ron, Beloved Son. Nancy, Full of Grace. I could testify to seeing that in her already, in the softer person she was becoming.

Donna, One without Fear. Donna had always named fear as one of her biggest weaknesses. And after losing your parents and brother, when the worst has happened to you, why shouldn't you fear the worst happening again and again? But she had stepped with me into the unknown, baring our souls and risking loss.

Nearly thirty years before, Joanie had run out of JP's hospital room screaming, "I hate white people! I hate them! I will never forgive them!"

"My name is Forgiver," she said now. "It's what I want most."

The name I chose was Empowerer. I wanted to find my deepest joy in helping others be all they could be, content for credit to go to others and to God.

When Spencer's turn came, he choked up, then spoke in a halting voice. God, he said, was calling him downward. "Do you know what *Spencer* means, y'all? It means 'steward,' 'servant.' That's my new name. That's what I want to live into."

It was Spencer's idea for all of us to sing the hymn "Come, Thou Fount of Every Blessing." When we came to the words

> Oh to grace how great a debtor,
> daily I'm constrained to be;
> Let Thy goodness, like a fetter,
> bind my wandering heart to Thee

I watched tears stream down Spencer's face. It was as if he was seeing who he was and was to be—truthfully, with no condemnation—internalizing God's unconditional love for the first time in his life, taking him places that were changing his understanding of who he was.

The following week we held "Fifty under Fifty, 50/50" in Jackson, meeting at the Mississippi Sports Hall of Fame. "Blacks complain, whites don't talk, nothin' changes," one of our black members had said in a planning team meeting. But those boundaries were broken.

Fifty of Jackson's movers and shakers came together for two full days. We'd fought to keep the event off-the-record, barring the media. We didn't want to score public relations points; we wanted honest conversation. Former Mississippi Governor William Winter spoke the first night, saying that in all his travels on President Clinton's National Initiative on Race, he'd never heard of anything like "Fifty under Fifty."

We put the poop right on the table. Spencer talked about what blacks really think about whites, and John Geary, Mission Mississippi's white associate director, spoke about what whites really thought about blacks. In one transcendent moment of brokenness tears flowed from pastors and CEOs, from politicians and upwardly mobile professionals. These high-powered people had no idea what they had gotten themselves into.

"Fifty under Fifty" was everything we hoped for. But for me the climax of those two days by far was something that happened only a few minutes into the program, at dinner the first night.

Joanie was sitting across from me. Spencer and I had been quietly working away at her for a couple of months, trying to persuade her to come. These were difficult events for Joanie, inspiring painful memories. She didn't see why anyone would want to dredge up all the stuff from the past. It was better to keep it stuffed inside and keep your distance. White folks were just gonna play around anyhow. But Joanie always deserved far more credit than she gave herself.

I saw her scribble a note. She passed it to me with a smile, and I opened it.

"My depositions tomorrow were canceled. Praise the Lord! I wouldn't want to miss this. I'm so excited! And I feel I can be open, and that I might be able to finally forgive."

There was a final P.S. "Maybe I'm losing it . . . due to my excitement. Of course, it could be the Holy Spirit (smile)."

No, Antioch had never met a force quite like this before, the culture of grace.

## PART SIX

# *Separation*

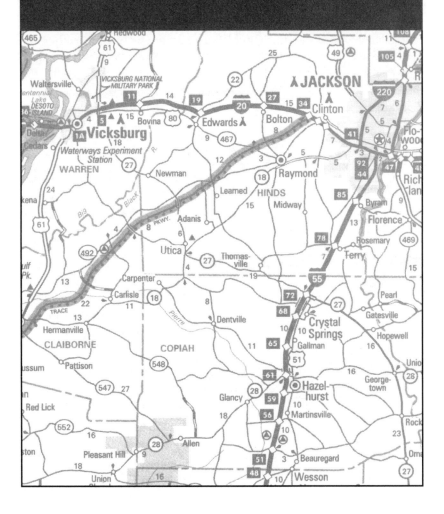

# 37

# BLUE LEG

---

As 1998 began it seemed as if grace was sweeping in and turning all our lives upside down.

Spencer and I were giving each other more roaming space as we led in our different spheres. As I took on the role of president of RF, he split his time between Antioch and RF, doing more writing and editing the magazine and working with Donna on forwarding the "culture of grace."

"I feel like a land-bound duck that just stumbled on a huge pond," he told me. "And ya know, I'm enjoyin' bein' who I am, instead of wishin' I was somebody else." But it was hard, he said, giving up his old ideals.

Grace was also shaking up Spencer's racial thinking. He gave me an article he was writing, pressing a question that faced Antioch and had huge racial implications as well: How do we create a culture of grace, in a way that holds people accountable, and encourages responsibility in growing? What did it mean for African Americans to offer grace to white Americans who mostly wanted cheap grace—with no repentance or proof of a change of heart? The title of Spencer's article was "Playing the Grace Card."

We were all wrestling with giving more grace. It looked like finances were going to force painful job changes. And I could see other showdowns coming up too, as the power of grace and the varieties of stagnation in our lives came head to head.

Nobody faced more pain than Gloria, back from Pasadena with Kortney. She was diagnosed with cancer and about to begin chemotherapy. She was scared, Kortney was scared, all of us were.

Then another reminder of weakness hit. At age forty-three Spencer seemed to be in greater shape than ever. He was taking high-powered walks with Nancy to counter his diabetes and playing on the church basketball team, still hitting three-pointers with his trademark high-arching jump shot. But playing merely "for fun" (as in, not to win), was not a concept. After all, two of his teammates—including choir director Arthur—were Mendenhall buddies from their old high school championship team.

During a game in mid-January, Spencer anticipated an opponent's pass, turned, and lunged to steal the ball (not even coming close to intercepting, he confessed later). He fell to the floor in agony, his Achilles tendon blown. After the operation, wearing a new blue cast, he got tough news: He might never play another game. For him basketball was up in the sacred with bluegill beds. I watched him one dark afternoon struggling and grimacing in a downpour, trying to get across the yard, his crutches sinking into the mud.

The morning of RF's biggest conference ever, a Thursday in late January, Spencer and I sat in Joanie's office. Two days from now we were slated to give the closing message at Belhaven. This was our last huddle. His crutch rested against a wall. His cast stretched toward me on the hardwood floor. Talia called it "Uncle Spencer's blue leg." It was, for me, a symbol of weakness and limitation at a time when his life seemed to be dominated by the theme, even as he was finding new freedom.

Spencer sighed. "This has been one of the most difficult weeks of my life." He talked about the humbling lesson of relying more on Nancy and others. I knew he'd also had a long talk with his parents recently about his changing role. He had just appeared on a national radio show with JP that reached millions of listeners, and his public voice was growing. But at the very same time, at the prime of his life, Spencer was giving up a public role he had coveted for a less glamorous one—the move downward to Antioch's pastor—work done mostly out of the limelight.

Somehow we got to laughing, joking about the idea of sabotaging the hotel-bound participants with an ordered-in soul food lunch—greasy, sauce-smothered E&L rib tips and sugar-packed peach cobbler. "I can see three hundred type A personalities," I said, "suddenly moving very slowly and getting very, very sleepy." Spencer told me he had "new stuff" prepared for our speech from the article he was writing. Leaders who influenced tens of thousands of college students were converging on Jackson, and we were prepared to push them beyond Reconciliation 101.

"I can't wait to give this message, Chris."

⚜

That night, at a downtown Jackson hotel, we kicked off "College, Ethnicity, and Reconciliation." All the people we'd hoped for were there— college presidents, deans, faculty, parachurch ministry leaders, and staff. In the three hundred participants, over fifty different colleges and universities were represented, many in large numbers. As I stood at the podium and challenged them to make racial justice and healing a major focus for their campuses over the next twenty years, I thought, *It's really happening. Here are Spencer and I again, way over our heads with our meager resources, and all these people are looking to us for leadership.* I felt very grateful.

Not long into the conference a participant pulled me aside and told me something strange. When she had stepped on the plane to come to Jackson, she had felt an oppressive force overwhelm her, so overbearing that she almost got off and stayed home.

"I have to tell you, Chris. It was as if something was trying to keep me from coming. But I realized all the more that I needed to be here. Much is at stake this weekend. I believe something powerful is going to happen."

I didn't give much thought to it at the moment.

At the second night of the conference on Tougaloo's historic campus, Presidents Joe Lee and Roger Parrott even indulged my little dream: dashiki-clad drummers played African beats at Tougaloo. Tomorrow night at Belhaven, bagpipers would open the final evening. I saw Spencer hobbling around on his crutches. Twenty-four hours from now we would give the closing message. We had titled it, "Committing for the Long Haul."

The next morning, on Saturday, before the first session started, I was told that several dozen conference participants from an organization called InterVarsity Christian Fellowship had met late the night before. One of their staff had stood up and warned his colleagues that racial reconciliation was not a bandwagon to jump on, that it was a costly calling into a realm of intense spiritual warfare. He had recited a litany of reconciliation leaders in their network who had died early deaths, including Lem Tucker.

A couple of hours later I stood near a ballroom door, taking photographs as someone reported on a meeting of biracial participants. Johnathan had joined them. Spencer and Nancy sat near me, looking on proudly as the speaker complimented eleven-year-old Johnathan on his input to the group.

Suddenly I heard a terrifying scream that ripped my heart. The desperate voice was Nancy's. "Something's wrong with Spencer! Help! Something's wrong with Spencer!"

I saw Spencer's head slumped back in his chair. His body was completely still. His mouth was wide open. His eyes looked lifelessly toward the ceiling.

The rest was a blur.

People crowding around the door.

Me, sprinting down the hallway, sobbing, my chest heaving, racing down the escalator to the front desk to call for an ambulance.

Running back up and seeing JP walking slowly toward me down the hallway, holding his stomach, and muttering and groaning. "He's gone, he's gone, my son is gone."

I had no idea what was happening. But I grabbed JP's shoulders with both hands. "He's not gone, John! He is not gone! That is not going to happen!" His empty eyes stared back at me. Someone came up behind JP and put an arm around him, and I ran back into the ballroom.

I saw the hundreds of people, their eyes closed, lips moving silently, many on their knees, many of their hands stretched toward Spencer. Jason, our indispensable assistant, was on one knee, calmly whispering into his ear.

Spencer's body shuddered.

Oh, God, he was alive. He was rising! Spencer sat up. He vomited. He quietly answered the paramedics' questions as a stretcher was rolled in. They wheeled him down the elevator to the front of the hotel. Nancy went in the ambulance. I jumped into a car with Johnathan and followed them to the hospital.

The emergency room doctor was puzzled. He said it several times. Most of us assumed it was a diabetic coma, but the doctors didn't have a clear explanation for the collapse, the nausea, and the loss of breath. They decided to keep Spencer under watch for a few hours. All that mattered to us was that Spencer seemed to be OK. Relieved, I headed back to the conference.

That afternoon we bussed everybody over to Belhaven for the final night's session. I was scrambling, trying to figure out how to handle the evening program without Spencer speaking.

I got a surprise phone call from Spencer. It was the first time we'd talked since his collapse. He was breathing heavily, but he was upbeat and funny, very funny. "Let's speak tonight," he said. "Let's do it."

"Are you sure?"

"Yeah, I am. But I'm gonna be so embarrassed. I've gotta face three hundred people who watched me throw up this morning—four times."

I laughed. I was so happy Spencer was alive. So happy we could tell the story of being found by grace.

---

✤

---

Spencer arrived right when the program started. I saw him when the bag-piper was walking slowly down the aisle, belting out "Amazing Grace." When the time came for our message, Spencer hobbled down front. Everyone jumped up in a thundering standing ovation. The cheers of those who had begged for Spencer's life to be saved that morning sent tingles down my spine.

Spencer took a seat on a stool to the left of the podium, to save strength. I stood to the right. I felt secure, at peace—and joyful.

I felt a little nervous about him. Spencer was still breathing heavily, as if he'd just finished a mile run. He spoke slowly, pausing often to catch his breath.

"This mornin' . . . I guess I didn't get quite enough attention by just havin' a cast and walkin' around on crutches," he said, and the auditorium exploded into laughter. My friend seemed secure, at peace—and joyful.

That night Spencer and I called for a new vision: a commitment to radical grace between the races. Our emotions were tender, our spirits bold.

"Are we willing to give ourselves to the long haul of reconciliation?" I cried. "Are you willing to give ten years to changing your institution?"

I joked about wishing that reconciliation was as easy as paying reparations. "I'd love to pay my five grand and be rid of Spencer," I said, and laughter broke across the audience.

"I am more and more convinced that reconciliation is really not about the church healing the race problem." Puzzled faces peered back at me. "Reconciliation is about how we as the church will be healed by dealing with race."

As Spencer and I went back and forth that night, I loved his "new stuff." He had never spoken any of this before. The more he understood his belovedness, the more he seemed willing to go places he had never gone before, to risk everything.

Part of him, he admitted, was "screaming with fear" to bring up something that had been conspicuously absent in the racial dialogue. He spoke at length of the time-tested ways that blacks emotionally dealt with whites, keeping them at a distance. He said he knew that the revelation of such secrets in mixed company "bordered on treason."

"But many of us African Americans are gettin' tired of the tiptoein' that takes place in so many racial gatherings. For us it's time to move into deeper waters."

At one point he spoke of our relationship, on the verge of divorce last fall. "Neither of us was prepared," said Spencer, "for the overwhelming simplicity, the complete absurdity, and the illogical genius of God's amazing grace."

He spoke of John and Judy and what he thought of at the time as their ramblings about grace. "Yeah, yeah, I knew all about grace. I could quote John 3:16 when I was knee high to a duck.

"But over all my decades of evangelical teaching, I never understood until now that God intended for grace to be a way of life for his followers. Maybe I'm the only one who missed it. But judgin' by the way that we all get along, I don't think so."

He seemed winded again, and he paused for breath. "At our relationship's weakest moment, Chris and I saw that we could either hold on to our grievances and demand that all of our hurts be redressed or we could follow God's example, give each other grace, and trust God for the lack. We chose grace."

It was time, he said, to take away the race card and replace it with the grace card.

There was complete silence in the room, as if Spencer's words were under sober examination. No way was everybody buying this. Spencer had discussed his article with several African Americans in our church. They knew he was right, they said, but their immediate reactions had ranged from anger, to grudging acceptance, to warning him he would be misunderstood. But Spencer plowed forward.

"The more I have come to know this quality in God, the more endearing God's becoming to me, which makes me want to demonstrate this quality to others all the more."

In the way Spencer spoke of God, I heard a fresh intimacy and affection.

"Grace is not about bein' fair. We wouldn't demand fairness from God— at least I know I wouldn't. What's so amazin' about grace is that God forgives us and embraces us with open arms, even though we don't deserve it! And because we are grateful for what God did for us, we allow God to do the same to others through us."

But a radical commitment to grace didn't mean surrendering a radical commitment to justice. "We must continue to speak and act on behalf of those who are oppressed. But my willingness to forgive oppressors is not dependent on how they respond. Bein' able to extend grace and to forgive people sets *us* free. What I'm learnin' about grace lifts a weight from my shoulders, which is nothin' short of invigorating. When we can forgive and embrace those who refuse to listen to God's command to do justice, it allows them to hear God's judgment without feelin' a personal judgment from us. Which, in the end, gives our message more integrity. Bein' able to give grace while preachin' justice will make our witness even more effective. And the world will take notice."

Practicing grace had devastating consequences. The old would not simply roll over and die for the new. But surely it was devastation for good—a hurricane of transformation, an earthquake of healing, a flood of new growth.

❖

The next morning, Sunday, the conference ended with the Voice of Calvary Church choir bursting out in a gospel version of Handel's *Hallelujah Chorus.*

I wasn't singing with them. I was by Spencer's side, at the front of the audience, him propped on his crutches, the two of us grinning ear to ear and jubilantly clapping to the music. I was worried about him; he was still breathing so heavily. Yet I was full of happiness. The conference had been a resounding success, pushing RF to a new level of authority and influence.

From here Spencer and I could reach a mighty long way—living into our new names, enjoying friendship, creating a new culture, touching the world. Who knew? Maybe he would be back on that basketball court again, and I'd dust off my sneakers and join him. The new was breaking in, the old was passing away.

But the power of both was greater than either of us could ever foresee.

# 38

# TEARS WITHOUT END

<hr>

How do you prepare for a break so sudden, so abrupt, so shattering that you mark life as "before" and "after," as if you have been spun into a different world and never moved?

Tuesday after the conference I took the three RF staff out to lunch, to celebrate. Hellen from Kenya, our do-it-all unsung hero. Jason Dewey, our right arm. Sarah Heneghan, a volunteer from Boston. She had been so moved by Spencer's and my message, embracing me as I stepped from the Belhaven podium. Our spirits were high.

Then, driving back to the office, about five blocks from Antioch, someone waved us down from a car in the other lane. It was Lisa Averill, another volunteer.

"Spencer's at Methodist Hospital." Lisa looked in my eyes like she wanted to burst out crying. "Chris, you need to go. Immediately."

Jason was at the wheel. I was in the passenger seat. As we sped to the hospital, I had no idea what was happening with Spencer. But I felt an anger come over me. I shook my fists and started shouting prayers. Ten minutes later we pulled up to the emergency room entrance.

I jumped out of the car and strode quickly through the door, brushing past a couple of church members. No one said a word to me. Someone pointed me to the hallway where Spencer's room was. I pushed open the door.

There he is, I thought. Oh, thank God. There he is.

Spencer was lying on a hospital stretcher. A semicircle of family members stood quietly around him, facing me. JP, his hands lying gently on Spencer's forehead. Mrs. Perkins, gazing down at her son. Joanie.

I stepped toward the stretcher, looking down at Spencer. His eyes were closed.

"What's his status?" I asked.

Joanie turned suddenly and looked at me. "His status?" She paused, realizing I didn't know.

"Chris," she said softly, "Spencer's gone."

Gone. Gone? "No, no, no . . ." I fell to the floor, moaning, sobbing, wailing.

A security guard rushed into the room.

"I need someone I know," I cried, pushing him away. Out of nowhere Phil Reed and Ron came beside me, their arms tight, their bodies close, holding me up. Suddenly, Nancy was there too. I reached for her, and we fell into each other's arms.

Thirty minutes before, around one in the afternoon, a week after his forty-fourth birthday, Spencer had died of a sudden, massive heart attack at home, sitting in his favorite chair. He was gone.

"Before" was over. "After" began.

Dozens of people were gathering back on Robinson Street, circling the houses and property, dazed and confused. Donna and I had to try to explain what happened to our children.

In the hours immediately after Spencer's death I filled every space with busyness, with responsibility, afraid to look into the void. There were guests to look after. A public to inform. A funeral to plan. Words to get through without breaking down. A despairing communal family to rally. An organization in crisis to be guided.

There was the grief of the Perkins family to soothe—JP and Mrs. Perkins, Joanie, Spencer's other brothers and sisters, and Lue and Jon. There were Kortney and Gloria, still coming to grips with her cancer. Most of all, there were Johnathan, Jubilee, April Joy, and Nancy, who looked so lost. I felt such a tenderness for her. I needed to be strong, to do whatever I could for her.

What would I have done without friends? Joe Maxwell appeared at the office that first night to rescue me. "Let me handle all the press stuff, Chris. Just give it to me. Trust me."

The morning after, I woke early and drifted over to JP's house. I knocked and walked in. I found him sitting in his bed, awake. I sat next to him and started sobbing. He held me. "Oh, Chris, what do we do now? You lost your yokefellow. I lost my son."

What I did was let a rush of responsibility-fueled adrenaline carry me through that time, leading up to the funeral.

The three-hour service on Saturday packed over five hundred souls into the church. We sang "Amazing Grace," of course, and "Come, Thou Fount of Every Blessing," the song that brought Spencer to tears.

Mrs. Perkins stood up and led the congregation in singing, "My Lord knows the way through the wilderness. All I have to do is follow."

JP made a passionate call to action.

I spoke too. I wanted everyone to know the path Spencer was on. At the height of his powers. At the depth of his powers. That after forty-four years of life, he felt like he had been called back to kindergarten. That that was where he finished the race. That he and I had persevered to the end, together.

"I stand before you as a witness, that reconciliation is possible."

Afterward, in the church parking lot, someone I had not seen for a long, long time approached me. It was Harold Roper. It had been eight years since he and Betsy had left Antioch. No words were necessary. We simply embraced, pulled back and looked into each other's moist eyes, and embraced again.

The week after the funeral Johnathan said he was doing better than he thought he would. It was good to see Nancy surrounded by her five sisters and brother who had come together from Pennsylvania and were spending the week with her, while her parents were staying for an entire month.

The day he died I had put a picture of Spencer on my desk. It soothed me, seeing his face constantly, right there. I didn't know the human body was capable of so many tears.

The suddenness of his departure, the rush of visitors, the service—all of it had kept my adrenaline rushing. But a few days after the funeral I hit empty.

It was night, and Donna and I were alone in our bedroom. I was putting clothes away in my closet. Earlier I had talked to my mother on the phone.

"What did you and Grandma talk about?"

"It wasn't anything really," I said. "Just caught her up on stuff I've been thinking about."

"Like what?"

"I'd rather not talk about it now. I'm tired."

"Chris, if I'm going to be any help to you, I need to know what's going on inside of you."

"I said I don't want to talk about it now."

"But, Chris, you . . ." She barely got it out. It could have been any-thing. One final stress to break the dam.

"I don't give a flip about what you need to hear!" I was screaming, at an embarrassing level, at my biggest supporter in the world. "I can't take it any more! I can't handle one more thing! I can't handle feeling respon-sible for anyone else! I can't handle it!"

I started pounding the wall. I picked up clothes and threw them. I whipped my arm across my bureau, and things crashed to the ground. It took an awful lot to get Donna steamed, and I'd crossed the line.

"Chris, stop it! Stop it! You're just thinking about yourself! Stop it!"

Right she was, but it was irrelevant. Something in me had completely snapped.

"I don't care, I can't take it anymore," I screamed. "I *cannot* take it! I *cannot!*" A point that had been well made by now. I crumpled onto the floor next to our couch, hunched over in a pile of tears and sobs.

Donna had her own pain to bear. She was also part of this devastated community. Spencer was her friend too, for more years than me. A pure ineradicable bond had connected them. But a heap of human something was groveling and wailing on the floor of her bedroom, and now it had two pillows over its head.

Donna set fairness aside, got down on the floor, and just held the whole sobbing mess, enveloping me with grace. This boy was actin' a fool, and the fool had come to the end of his powers.

It was painful to own this profound loss. A friend had summed it up pretty well: "Chris, you've lost three limbs: one part yokefellow and friend, one part vocation, and the last part community."

I began trying to let go, to not act as if this was all my problem to solve. It looked to me like God was in a fix, that God had some mighty big problems to face, between Nancy and the kids, Antioch's gaping hole, and RF. I was tired of messing around. Of pretending like anyone but God could make things right. Shouldn't we challenge God to show up? To reach us at the end of our powers?

On Sunday I debated skipping church. I couldn't bear the thought of hearing "How are you doing?" twenty more times. A sermon seemed like forty-five unbearable minutes listing ten more things I needed to do to be truly committed. I went anyway, and I immediately regretted it. I felt suf-focated. I had to get out of Jackson, to get fresh air in my lungs. I had to get back to northeast Mississippi, to the Dwelling Place.

A couple of days later I was set to go. Jason and Sarah stood with me at the office, praying before I departed. Suddenly a voice shouted upstairs.

"Jason! Jason!"

It was JP. He had been pressing me for plans and decisions about RF's future. Doubling his speed was his way of working out grief.

As JP's steps came up the stairs, I sneaked out the back door to my car. Urgency was a voice I had to get away from.

# 39

# THE DWELLING PLACE

*I* brought no music, no work, no books except my Bible. I wanted a showdown at the Dwelling Place, a showdown between God and me, with no distractions.

Looking up at the vast black sky the first night, I felt an overwhelming intimacy with it, as if I was connected to eternity for the first time. Spencer was there, I was here to carry on. I could not bear the thought.

The tears I shed there both wore me out and cleansed me. Maybe part of it was guilt, that somehow all the hurt and struggle I caused Spencer put an awful stress upon his heart. Only now did I understand how much I loved him. It was so hard living with him, and now it was so hard living without him.

Why, God? What sense does it make, at the prime of life? At the crest of this new plateau of grace? Why leave three young children without Daddy to tuck them in, to teach them the songs of his childhood? Why a soul mate cut off from her beloved? Why this loss of a voice that defied the devious circumstances of race, that ascended to rare transcendence? Why him and not me? I felt the world needed Spencer more than me, and I didn't know who I was apart from him. What future was there without him?

I cried out to the sky. "God, I have lost my yokefellow. The yoke is broken. I don't know how to go on."

I began to sense a response, in Jesus' words from Matthew, and what I heard, I held on to tightly.

"Yes, you have lost Spencer. What you invested in Spencer, now invest in me. I am your yokefellow now. 'Take my yoke upon you, and learn from me; for I am gentle and lowly in heart, and you will find rest for your souls. For my yoke is easy and my burden is light.'"

A great weight lifted from me. I heard that there was a friend who would never leave me, who I would sense more closely than ever, who would give rest to my tormented soul. As much as confusion and fear, there was clarity.

The next morning I heard more words coming to me through Scripture, confirmed in the whispers of the wind in the pine trees, in the emerald-green Mississippi grass bending and shining around me. I sensed reassurance that God's word had gone out through Spencer and me, that it would accomplish what God desired. For the first time it struck me that the psalmist did not say, "Be busy, and know that I am God," but "Be still." Know that I am God—not you.

I soaked up all the memories. I burst out laughing to the cows across the fence, remembering being in Norfolk right after the book's release, Spencer and I stuffing that big poster under the table.

Sister Clare and Sister Maggie, in their polyester pants from a bygone era, were a great help to me. Clare was the visionary—thin, bright-eyed, on the move. Maggie was the cook—older, plump, and matter-of-fact, lavishing me with homemade bread and jam. In praying with me and serving me, they embodied the life of a woman who began to take hold of my imagination—Mary of Bethany, friend of Jesus.

I read of her sister Martha's two house parties, with Jesus guest of honor at both. While Martha slaved away, Mary took a pound of costly perfume and anointed the feet of Jesus, wiping them with her hair. That act represented one year of a common laborer's salary, dumped on one who taught his disciples to feed the hungry and clothe the naked.

They were indignant with this waste. But Jesus sided with Mary. "Why do you trouble this woman? For she has done a beautiful thing to me." Busy and pragmatic action I held in high esteem. But beauty?

At another party Mary sat listening at Jesus' feet while Martha slaved away in the kitchen again. When Martha protested, Jesus said, "Martha, Martha, you are anxious and troubled about many things; one thing is needful. Mary has chosen the good portion, which will not be taken away from her."

Such extravagant devotion seemed so irrelevant, even scandalous, in a world of pressing need and injustice. It had never occurred to me to look to Mary as a role model before. Her measure of time and transformation was so different from mine. I was so much Martha, taking myself so seriously ever since I parachuted into Mississippi many years ago. It took a crisis in my life to see it.

I found such inexplicable mystery in Spencer's sudden departure and the days before it.

I remembered the woman who had almost gotten off the plane. The leader's warning about the cost of reconciliation the night before Spencer's collapse. Spencer, looking so lifeless, and the cries of hundreds praying. There clearly seemed to be some connection between his collapse and his death three days later—but I didn't know how to explain it. Some believed his life was literally extended before our eyes, so he could deliver a final wake-up call in halting, panting, gasping words. An African American told me how, at first, he had dismissed Spencer's Belhaven message. "Now I, and many others, are taking it very seriously."

The words of Paul in Romans echoed to me: "How unsearchable are [God's] judgments and how inscrutable his ways! . . . 'For who has known the mind of the Lord, or who has been his counselor?'" There was so much I could not know or understand.

But what was emerging with great clarity was that I could not just move on from such an experience. I knew some would say, "Now is the time to push forward, Chris, to mobilize the masses in memory of Spencer's witness, to launch major initiatives."

It might be the right answer for them, but I knew that wasn't the answer for me. My world had changed. It was already changing even before Spencer's death. For a couple of years now, it had been sinking into my stubborn, die-hard, task-oriented head that Chris Rice was not indispensable to anything. Reconciliation was not Spencer's or my idea, it was God's.

In the words of Isaiah I heard a command to be open to a new thing. "Remember not the former things, nor consider the things of old. Behold, I am doing a new thing; how it springs forth, do you not perceive it?"

I heard it was a time to grieve. Blessed were they that mourned, for they would be comforted. Grieving was not automatic. Space had to be created for it.

I heard it was a time for prayer, not activism. What was prayer but a letting go of control, a seeming waste of time that could be better spent dictating events and influencing people directly?

I heard it was time to slow down, to wait. Waiting was not passive. It was putting all of my senses on full alert to listen to the interruption, to let it reorder my life.

I heard it was a time to stay close to Donna and the children, to care for Antioch, to surround Nancy and her children with love and support.

I heard that all the energy and time I had invested in Spencer I was to now invest in prayer, solitude, and listening. As much as I so desperately wanted him to be back, I didn't want to lose this clarity either.

After two days Donna drove up to join me for two more. We talked some about the future, shaping the alternatives for moving from "why?" to "what next?" But mostly we cried, prayed, and remembered.

❖

Back in Jackson, every day triggered snapshots of what I was doing with Spencer that same day a year before, releasing more tears. Strange new routines of slowing down came over me.

Every Tuesday, the day of Spencer's departure, the RF staff fasted from food and gathered to pray during lunch, often joined by others from the church.

I took Johnathan fishing at one of his father's favorite fishing holes, the one where Spencer had mostly taught me the craft.

Every Friday—during work hours!—I drove down the Natchez Trace to a state park, to hike and reflect. Whenever I rushed back into busyness—trying to push out a special *Reconcilers* issue on Spencer or organize the next conference—something would slap me over the head with a two-by-four, slowing me down again.

In early March Antioch had a meeting with a grief counselor, a woman named Cille Norman who also worked at Belhaven College. Cille's meeting with us brought to the surface our deeply shared pain, especially recounting the day Spencer died and how we each experienced it. Strangely, every one of us had had some particularly special moment with him in the days leading up to his death. All the more I felt caught up in a divine mystery. It was all too big to not allow our lives to be interrupted and changed.

Two weeks later I was at the Dwelling Place again. I'd already taken more spiritual retreats in the last six weeks than in the previous seventeen years.

---

✠

---

In late March John and Judy made their first visit since the funeral. After two weeks, on their last day, they had a final meeting with Antioch.

"To be honest," said John, "much has been disheartening, talking to you about the future of Antioch." He recited a list of reasons, including finances and areas of "ungrowth."

Then he spoke words I found extremely freeing. "Judy and I don't have a sense of whether you should continue or not. It will be much better if this isn't a group decision. Each of you needs to decide what you're going to do and give each other the freedom and grace to choose. Staying because of habit or because it's easier, or putting pressure on someone to stay, is a real bad way to move forward.

"Help each other clarify what each of you really believes, not what 'the group' believes," he advised. He outlined two choices: We could make a fresh start with those who wanted to continue, or we could disband grace-fully. "It's mostly a matter of not hating someone who decides to leave or disagrees with you."

John acknowledged that Antioch's leadership had depended on Spencer in an unusual way. If we decided to make a fresh start, he and Judy were open to coming for a substantial period of time. "Or if any of you want to come to San Francisco and pursue membership with us, we would love that."

He made a final challenge: The basic issue wasn't continuing as a com-munity or not, it was taking care of each other. "You can care for each other outside of living together, although in a different way," said John. "Remember: Keep caring for each other, forgiving each other, and wash-ing the dishes."

After the meeting John and Judy asked me to meet privately with them and Nancy.

I was immediately nervous. With the new tenderness I felt toward Nancy, the last thing I wanted was any strain with her or to add to her pain.

"Nancy really wants to be fully reconciled with you, Chris," said John. "But there are some things she thinks the two of you need to discuss for that to happen."

Nancy spoke. "You and Spencer went through so much, Chris. I find some of the hurt lingering for me."

I understood. With all the fights Spencer and I had had, rarely were Nancy and Donna ever part of the making up. Were they supposed to somehow just ride the roller coaster without complaint? To adjust to con-flict, readjust to peace, and back and forth again and again? If anyone had a legitimate ax to grind with me, it was Nancy.

I so wanted to be at peace with her too. "Nancy, anything you can imagine about how I felt or what I did to Spencer? I'm sure it's not only true, it was probably worse. Far worse."

Silence followed.

And Nancy gave the grace to leave it at that. To not go back over every detail until dawn. Rubbing it all in my face was surely what I deserved. Instead, she declared forgiveness. We sealed our peace in an emotional prayer, led by John and Judy.

⚓

That same day, after John and Judy left, I drove over to Belhaven to meet with Cille, who had become a trusted counselor. She began to prod me about my future plans, and I methodically laid out the many options.

"Chris, forget about all the details. What idea of the future most fills your heart with joy?"

Thinking of the future that way seemed so reckless, so irresponsible. I couldn't have answered truthfully without the beautiful permission John had granted me just a few hours before—to think not of the group but of what was in my own heart, and Donna's, and of us being released to choose. All my time alone over the past weeks, I realized, had given me the answer.

I told Cille that what most filled my heart with joy was to learn how to be Mary. To disengage from the entanglement of responsibility and expectations. To cut RF loose. To high-five Antioch and twelve incredible years, declare victory, and move on from Mississippi.

"Donna and I have been such busy doers for nearly two decades each," I said. "We have a rare opportunity to slow down, process, and get re-energized for the long haul."

I told Cille how the predictability of staying bothered me, how it smacked too much of my indispensability and control. The pressures of responsibility and management—I didn't have it in me now. And long before Spencer died Donna and I had identified a weariness in our lives, now magnified tenfold. In all my years at Voice of Calvary I couldn't remember hearing a single sermon about the Sabbath, and it certainly hadn't been on my agenda. Donna and I thirsted for refreshment and rest, and I yearned to grow intellectually and theologically.

My gut told me that the interruption brought by Spencer's death was too big to go on with the normal and usual, too big not to allow this detour to become a new highway. Deep inside, I said, I yearned for a "new thing."

"Then that's what you should do. Leave Jackson. This year."

But Cille didn't have a clue about how impossible leaving was.

"How can we move on from Mississippi? Leaving people we love so much, who love us."

"But if it's the right direction, there's something better waiting for you. You just can't see it yet, Chris."

"There are too many details that can't possibly come together for us to go." I ticked them off: Antioch's debt, seven houses to dispose of (the four on Robinson Street, plus Valley Street, Donna's, and mine from pre-Antioch days), untangling ourselves from community and RF. So many communities had ended up enemies. There was letting down all the people who looked to RF for leadership. And on and on and on. "I've got a headache, Cille, just thinking about it all."

"But they're just that, Chris—details. All that will be taken care of. They're God's problem. Your responsibility is to focus on the big picture."

Leaving Mississippi was crazy and foolish, leaving the known for the unknown. But as I drove back to west Jackson, with absolute clarity, I knew it was right. Moving on had "Trust Me" written all over it. And minutes later, by the time I got home, I had the faith it could happen.

That night Donna and I talked about leaving Mississippi. Unknown to me, she had been thinking the same thing, and she was warming up to the idea.

But over the next several days, as Easter approached, the cost of such a decision set in, putting me constantly on the verge of tears.

The pain climaxed on Easter Sunday. Watching Donna in her element, so happy, leading sharing time. Hearing Phil Reed, whose preaching had moved me countless times, who I had laughed with, fought with, and made up with in endless elder meetings. The choir singing "Jesus Is Alive," with Arthur's clear, strong tenor leading the way. It was hard to imagine resurrection. All I felt was the bleakness of being gone.

I sat next to Gloria and Lue, watching Talia running back and forth between pews in the new dress Gloria had bought her and thinking of how much our daughter treasured her sleepovers with Aunt Lue, sleeping in her bed, getting all kinds of candy and attention. I pictured our Easter dinner with Antioch, our children running through the grass under the watchful eyes of friends who loved them. Mississippi was their birthplace. It was where Donna and I met and courted and kissed for the first time. This was home.

Sunday evening we savored wine and laughs over a relaxed dinner with Phil and Tressa. As we drove home my doubts about leaving were building.

When we climbed into bed Donna was in a deep funk. Just before we fell to sleep she turned toward me. There was an uncharacteristic hardness on her face and in her voice.

"So. Am I just supposed to leave all my friends? Who's to say that we can ever build a life like this anywhere else? Or find a church with like-minded people like this? Are we just gonna yank the children out of their life here?"

Every one of Donna's fears pierced my heart. *Did I get it all wrong?* I thought. *Can we really leave this place? It is too good to leave.* All night, I tossed and turned.

The next afternoon I drove to the Dwelling Place slowly, the only way you could drive Phil Eide's aging Volkswagen bus that I had borrowed as a second vehicle. I tugged on a cigar and sucked in the beauty of Mississippi.

Clare and Maggie warmly greeted me, and I poured out my heart to them.

"What you sense in prayer and solitude," said Clare, "that's where the Lord will speak. Hold on to that. Remember that the Father loves your children much more than you. If God calls you to move on, God will take care of them."

Clare smiled. "Fear isn't from God, Chris. It's predictable for fear to set in after deciding the right course."

That night, under an overcast darkness, I stretched my arms to the heavens and sensed reassurance. It was not my task to persuade Donna. It was God's problem, not mine. I entrusted my children to God's hands. And if it was God's will, God would confirm this decision.

The next morning I opened my devotional book to a new chapter. It was titled "Growth." I didn't choose it. It was what came next, what was given to me.

The first day's Scripture reading was Paul's words in Philippians: "This one thing I do." *One thing*, I thought. "Forgetting what lies behind and straining forward to what lies ahead."

The day's reading selection, from the black theologian Howard Thurman, exploded off the page: "It is a wonderful thing that inherent in the life process are limitations, so that though new things start growing old things also stop growing. I am always reminded that the experience which may be mine at a particular moment may be an experience in which things are stopping. Or it may be an experience in which things are just beginning. It is important that I know which process is taking place."

The day's prayer sent shivers down my spine. "God's desire to move us on to spiritual maturity is a stronger desire than we believe."

After reading those words I found myself sobbing once again. It was time to be moved on, I believed. Our growth was coming to an end here and beginning somewhere else. We didn't need to know where. It was simply time to take a step of unreasonable, extravagant devotion. It was the one thing needful.

So many people had affirmed that I could carry RF forward and had exhorted me to do so. But my calling had been to relationship to Spencer, not to an organization. The source of my passion was our friendship, and I had no desire to move RF forward now. I was ready to let it all take its course without me. Important stuff. Relevant stuff. Needful stuff.

I felt very lonely. Coming to unity with Spencer had always given me the confidence to make tough, bold decisions. Some would view me as a traitor. I had peace, but I wasn't moving anywhere if Donna wasn't equally convinced, on her own terms.

A couple of days after I returned, on our eleventh wedding anniversary, Donna gave me a letter she had written while I was away, having no idea what I was thinking.

Leaving, she said, played to all her worst fears and anxieties. Her list of positives and negatives was about even. But in her heart, she knew what we were to do. "I haven't verbalized this to you because I haven't been able to," she wrote. "It's too overwhelming, and putting words to it feels like I've sealed our fate."

God, she believed, was leading us to move from Jackson. It wasn't about going to a more exciting or better life.

> I believe God is calling me to trust as never before—to take a huge, terrifying step into the unknown and believe that God will meet me there. To trust God with my well-being, my family, my happiness, my fulfillment, my purpose, my marriage.
>
> But I say all this in great fear and trembling. And I can revert into a sulky, resentful bundle of fear as quickly as the words leave my mouth.
>
> I know there are many agonizing days ahead. Joy and contentment also. But now I trust God will be there, not only on the other side, but beneath each trembling footstep.

Donna was living into her new name, One without Fear. We were both convinced, for different reasons, and ready to plunge ahead together, hand in hand.

We began the painful process of sharing our decision with others. When Donna and I met with the church elders about it, Phil Reed didn't say a word. Afterward he sent me a letter.

"I don't want you to think I am disinterested or don't care about you. I spent most of the time with a lump in my throat, at the verge of tears. I just didn't feel I could speak without breaking down." Phil could have given us a long speech about selling out. Instead, he simply told me how much he was going to miss us.

Meanwhile, after working through her decision with Spencer's family and her own, Nancy had announced that she and the kids were moving to Pennsylvania in August, to be near her siblings and parents.

No one at Antioch had the vision to continue community. It was heartbreaking, talking about dissolving and doing it in a way that looked out for each other.

After lengthy discussions with Antioch and local and national leaders, we made the decision to dissolve RF.

I was at peace. People were so passionate about starting organizations. Why were so few willing to end them? I saw so many more allies on the frontlines now. In Jackson there was a new generation of white leaders like Roger Parrott, Stuart Irby, and Joe Maxwell, and African Americans like Rev. Ronnie Crudup and Eric Stringfellow. There were budding national networks called Healing the Heart of America and the Call to Renewal. CCDA was still exploding with growth, and Spencer and I had witnessed a new generation of reconcilers springing up from Harvard to Tougaloo.

A letter from a friend at the January conference was an enormous help to me in letting go.

"I thought how good it was to be in a large audience with my mentors at the helm," he wrote.

> Your book was the catalyst which propelled me on a journey from which there is no return.
>
> But I had a thought that I should not put my faith and trust in the two of you, but keep it in God. . . . I confess that with you and Spencer continuing to speak and write, a tangible hope and guidance were present. And now it seems I am back to seeing in a glass darkly.
>
> Thanks be to God who gave us you and Spencer, as yokefellows. And thanks to both of you for working through the difficulties of such a "marriage." We are all better for this. Thank you for teaching us about Jesus, in word and deed. May you continue to do so.

The witness and experiences Spencer and I were given were surely not meant to die. Wherever our family went I expected to be enlarged through this move. Somehow, even with Spencer's death, I believed that the idea of reconciliation itself would be enlarged. The old was passing, the new and unknown was coming.

# 40

# RIDING AWAY ON A HARLEY

---

$\mathscr{I}$ treasured a clipped newspaper article that hung next to my desk. A photo showed Chicago Bulls coach Phil Jackson driving away from work for the last time, after six NBA titles. He sat on a black and red Harley Davidson motorcycle, adorned with the team logo and his players' signatures. "His office bare, his memories full," it said, "he wore the contented smile of a man secure in the knowledge he's leaving at the right time."

Over the past few weeks I had often pictured myself carefree on that Harley, departing Mississippi for the last time.

But I would be no easy rider. If Donna and I had gotten mired in the details, we would have never decided to go. Pulling up roots, bringing closure to Antioch and RF, and leaving loved ones behind often felt more like a nightmare of refugees shuffling on a train to Siberia.

Yet peace and clarity carried us forward. I was happy to see how our decisiveness created a vacuum that others were stepping into. JP finally had my decision, and now he could make his plans. He said he wanted to push the Training Center vision forward on the property, and we started negotiating the Foundation's purchase of the Big House, the Small House, and the land. With JP and Mrs. Perkins already living in the Corner House and a church family interested in the Duplex, Robinson Street would still be dedicated to a higher vision.

We planned to leave in early October and to be in Boston by January, with me attending divinity school and our family being near Mom and Dad in Vermont. I believed my activist experiences would be strengthened by a period of study, reflection, and writing.

But John Alexander counseled us against rushing into busyness too quickly. "I don't knooooow," he said. "You and Donna probably need to think more about Sabbath than a next vocational step." John's idea grew on us, to cease from work for three months, to seek refreshment and get to know our children before moving to a new city. We put the word out to our friends around the country, seeking a place of rest.

In early August Antioch closed our joint checking account. Two weeks later we gathered at the church to say good-bye to Nancy, Johnathan, Jubilee, and April.

Before we shared Holy Communion, I said a few words. "For Jesus' disciples, right after he died, their last supper with him must have seemed a sad ending to the life they had shared. But as Jesus broke bread and poured wine, a new story was also beginning, though they couldn't see it yet. Because resurrection was coming.

"We too are sad tonight. But by sharing the Lord's Supper with Nancy, we mark an end and also a beginning. God's story among us is not finished. There are joyful chapters behind. And God has promised joyful chapters ahead—for Nancy and the kids, for all of us."

Donna had coined a new phrase that she and I kept telling each other: "Selling seven houses? It's just a detail." But the week after Nancy and the kids left, as I thought of Benjamin and "A-po" together no more and all the separations to come, as I thought of the pain ahead, of who got what from the houses, and of dividing up money, as I took care of yet another detail like cleaning out the overstuffed attic of the Big House, I felt overwhelmed and depressed.

There I was, working alone on this property that once swarmed with life, dumpsters turning into wheelbarrows, all of us framing up the second story of our palace together, the paradise that would hold our vision for the Sermon's new kind of kingdom. Why did it take so much time to build something and so little to tear it down? I felt like I was dismantling a dream.

That night Donna was a great help to me. "Remember, Chris. All that really matters is friendship and peace with God."

To dismantle community without dismantling our relationships could only be done the way we had built this place—patiently, with care. And as far as peace with God was concerned, if leaving Mississippi was right, it wasn't based on the seen but on the unseen.

---

✤

---

In mid-September I made a trip alone, a rite of passage to say good-bye to many of Mississippi's gifts to me.

I drove the Natchez Trace one last time, windows rolled down, sucking in the end of the long Mississippi summer. I plunged into a warm lake at a favorite camping spot, swimming far out until I found cool water. At the Dwelling Place, Clare and Maggie prayed over me, anointing me with oil, blessing me for the next chapter of my life. Donna and I had been changed forever by Mississippi, and we would take this land with us, wherever life went from here. The fact that one left home and family didn't change the fact that it was still home and family.

The final three weeks were as painful as I'd imagined. I hurt for Lue and Gloria, the two Antioch members who were single, their parents gone, raising Kortney and Jon on their own. Here we were, leaving Gloria behind with her cancer to deal with. I wondered about the older Antioch children, all the confusion and emotions they must be feeling. I couldn't stand the thought of tearing three-year-old Christopher and best friend Varah, Joanie and Ron's daughter, apart.

But what could have easily been another divorce situation was not. In spite of the pain of disbanding, Antioch had been able to give much grace to one another—to dismantle community without dismantling our friendships. There had been an anxiousness about dividing up Antioch's goods, but people were able to get some of their favorite things, and there were no fights over anything.

Agreeing on money could have been awful too. But we crossed the biggest practical barrier to closure, selling the property to the Foundation. All of Antioch's debts and all of everyone's medical bills were paid off. We divided the rest of the money equally between the five families, giving each enough to make a solid new beginning. (Financial matters had been settled long ago with Phil and Tressa and Harold and Betsy in the weeks after each couple had left.) Through all the days of scrimping to get by, of going without stipends, as difficult as times got, that was what we always had—enough.

Nancy was surrounded by her siblings and parents in Pennsylvania.

I was so happy to see Lue and Gloria caring for each other, looking for a house in the neighborhood to move into together with Kortney and Jon.

RF turned over the office to the Foundation, and Ron and Joanie moved into the top floor. They hoped to eventually buy the building and make it their home and Joanie's law office.

JP and Mrs. Perkins were going to tend the Robinson Street vision into a new chapter of ministry for the Foundation, and Jason was staying on to help.

RF was closing down with all debts paid and no money in the account. We had just enough to finish. It was what Spencer and I always had too, just enough.

Forty people gathered on the side porch for RF's farewell th'ow down. I took Spencer's place, manning the barbecue grill. Jason plastered up what we called the wall: old *Urban Family* covers, photos, mementos. After a time of sharing I had the last words. The members of Antioch, I said, were the true heroes of our national work. I gave each of them gifts inscribed with the words, "You lived the dream, and it touched the world."

Our last Sunday morning at church was bittersweet. In the afternoon the congregation held a farewell meal for us. Afterward I asked Phil Reed, "So who are you going to fight with now, Phil?" We both laughed. It was good, we agreed, having friends who love you enough to fight with you. Friends who you rely on so much, they become like a part of your own body.

❖

Our final morning in Mississippi was Monday, October 5, 1998.

How strange life seemed. Once we thought we would live with Phil and Tressa at Antioch forever, all of us growing old on Robinson Street. Then came their painful departure, when I couldn't imagine ever being friends again. And then peace renewed. We had stayed at their house these last few days, experiencing the joy of living together again. Now we would be separated once more. From Mississippi I would take the hope that people can grow and change, that descriptions of pain or joy at any one moment are only snapshots, that only history really counts.

Donna and I drove the kids over to Robinson Street. I ran a couple of last errands, and Donna took Benjamin, Talia, and Christopher into the Big House. Room by room, they said good-bye, talking about the riches that room had offered them in people and memories.

I returned. We held hands together in the living room, next to the stairs Johnathan once said he'd climbed a "zillion" times, next to the bare dinner slab that had burst with so much life, the one Donna and I built with our own hands. Near Spencer's old seat at the end each of us said a final thanksgiving to God for the years this house had given us.

We went next door to see JP and Mrs. Perkins, and they walked back over to the Big House with us.

Seventeen years after stepping into west Jackson I turned our overloaded red minivan out of the gravel driveway for the last time. Behind us, sitting on the front steps were Spencer's parents, whose witness had brought us to Mississippi, whose son was a wondrous gift to me. And we left the place that gave us the greatest joys possible on this earth.

I wasn't on a Harley. Still, it was like I imagined. My hands were shaking; my eyes were wet; and I was headed into the unknown, in the right direction at the right time, hating every moment.

# 41

# SABBATH

---

*Blessed are they . . . who have set their hearts on pilgrimage.*
Psalm 84:5

My computer registered a major marker of our momentous life changes; it featured a new file called Crab Recipes.

Donna, the kids, and I had captured two dozen of the little monsters off a boat in a sunny bay on the Oregon coast. When we pulled up the crab traps the kids had squealed at the sight of a surfacing swarm of claws, pincers, and antennae. Donna and I finished "picking" the last bunch by the cabin's fire, with few cares other than finding a good formula for gumbo.

Fifty hours of driving after leaving Jackson, we had arrived at our sabbatical home in Bandon, a place of rough, crashing sea, grassy and wood-strewn beaches, and four-storied boulders jutting out of the Pacific Ocean. The children had quickly added our hosts to the honored ranks of those they called Grandma and Grandpa. Keith and Donna Young were parents of a good friend in the CCDA network, and their house was behind the cabin that they'd offered to us as a gift for two months. Their Eden-like land burst with nut and apple trees and gardens. A hundred yards away, the Coquille River wound its way into the ocean.

It was just the five of us in an unfamiliar oasis of solitude. Flying a kite on the beach, the whole string zipping out in seconds. Taking long hikes up the forested hill behind our house. Capturing a new pet, a lizardlike "waterdog." Benjamin, now seven, was becoming a bird lover, guided by his mother. Inspired by three-year-old Christopher, the kids put underwear on over sweatpants and transformed into pro wrestlers. One night I followed suit and made a surprise attack. I began days picking berries with four-year-old Talia and ended them in long conversations with Donna cuddled by the fireplace. Our new friends were deer, a pair of bald eagles, diving cormorants, and flocking geese. Every night we read books out loud to the kids. And miracle of miracles, we never even turned on the TV and VCR once.

But it was harder than it would have seemed, living in paradise.

Constantly mixed with rest was a sense of loss. So much of Donna's and my significance and purpose had come from our friendships, our church body, our work. Alone by the beach one day I wondered, *What does it mean, God, to love you here?*

I found an answer. In the face of a world demanding so much to be done we were here to cease and desist, to relinquish control, to tend not to the world but to the One who tends even while we sleep. We were here to proclaim the difference between God and us. We were here, I believed, to worship.

By December we were living two doors from my parents in the small village of Lincoln, Vermont, under the shadow of snow-shrouded Mt. Abraham. Middlebury was just thirty minutes away. At the church down the street, where Dad was associate pastor, the choir sang the African American spiritual "Down by the Riverside." They didn't sing it like home, but Donna and I boo-hooed anyway.

Over the next few weeks we unearthed vast treasures.

*Sabbath candle* joined the children's vocabulary, its lighting every Sunday a reminder to me about being still. There were road trips with my dad, and cross-country skiing with my mom. She and Donna were acting like college girlfriends, having so much fun together. The worn path between the Big House and the Duplex was replaced by the one between my parents' house and ours. I never expected my children to have this gift of being with their grandparents. Added to my knowledge of racism's various breeds were the shapes and colors of red-breasted grosbeaks and Oregon juncos, the kind of bird names I had once laughed at, courting Donna. I was falling in love with her all over again. It was no coincidence, I thought, that this new space had brought these gifts, a second act of fullness following Mississippi.

But this paradise also was not easy for me.

My daily jogs had once passed urban kids yelling "Hey, white honky!" and elderly neighbors smiling from burglar-barred porches. I now jogged where nobody locked their doors, where I saw more moose (one) than black people, and where neighborhood drive-bys were replaced by wild turkey dive-bys. I had no responsibilities save a couple of writing projects and being a good father, husband, and son. How quaint. How unradical.

It was all a bit boring. There were no earthshaking meetings, lives in crisis, conflicts, or national platforms to tend to anymore. The stillness was broken only by Cub Scouts and chickadees. Separated from so much doing, like a fast that squeezes the poisons from the body's pores, my addictions began to ooze out. I was so dependent upon the spectacular, the heroic, the radical.

My self-worth plummeted. Who was I, stripped of my good works, apart from my busyness? Here I was, surrounded by townspeople who worked and loved well in the boondocks, away from the limelight. I had no category for that. I felt out of place, on a foreign soil where everybody looked like us. A depression set in.

It was deeply disturbing, having the yardstick I had always used to measure my significance, even my devotion to God, challenged so much. It was disturbing to be still. The kind of extravagant devotion that Mary exemplified, I saw, could be just as radical as doing justice. It was just as much a discipline, just as much a test of obedience, just as much death to self, just as much an opportunity to grow into joy.

Here were new lessons to learn. I'd come full circle. It was Vermont now, not Mississippi, where I needed to be.

As the end of January 1999 approached, the first anniversary of Spencer's death, I was in a funk. I craved like-minded comrades. I felt inadequate in my writing, which I thought of as my next vocational phase. I went off on Donna one day for no reason. And when you're writing a lofty paragraph that will save the world and almost curse out a precious five-year-old daughter who asks Daddy for a drink, you know you're in a mess. Disengagement's gifts were becoming curses.

On January 26 I woke up feeling sad and emotional. Yesterday, a year before, was the last time I saw Spencer alive. But the only truly bad days, I had learned, were ones where I pushed the grieving away. I went to my father's study, alone, to remember my friend.

I remembered how it was always hard for Spencer to accept who he was, even in God's eyes. But he was far greater than he knew.

I remembered his undeserved embrace of prodigals, from JJ to white folks to me, that Labrador retriever–like stability and devotion, sticking with impossible people.

I thought of how he had kept his vows to his little postage stamp on earth, west Jackson, in sickness and health, through decades long enough to uncover all our masks. He taught me that the measure of a life was not the moment but the long haul.

I thanked God for Spencer's restless truth seeking. For enlarging so many through his gift of language and story. For giving him strength to yoke with me to the end, dragging our plow through sin-thick sod, neither of us easy to love. I terribly missed the holy, muddy ground we shared. The jokes that only he and I laughed at. His hug. His healing words that night—"Chris, I love you like my own brother."

I remembered how our greatest witness was showing up, a black man and white man who cared for one another and stuck it out, that that embodiment was our most important message, even before we stood up to speak. When I left Middlebury for Mississippi, I thought I was giving up the best way to change the world. Maybe instead I had learned what counts the most.

All alone, I fell out laughing, thinking of Bebe. That was the name Antioch gave to a shriveled, abused-looking stray mutt that Spencer took in to everyone else's puzzlement. When Bebe got hit by a car, we all assumed she'd be put to sleep, finding a peaceful end to a life of scorn. But Spencer couldn't bear it. Without our permission, beyond reason, with Antioch in the midst of financial crisis, he spent $300 taking her to the vet, enduring the wrath that followed. But Bebe limped and hobbled her way into our extended family. She was the last outlaw Spencer's affections embraced, his final lesson to me about giving grace.

I believed that God had carried Spencer to the top of a mountain not long before he departed and given him a Moses-like glimpse of an awesome new territory. There Spencer finally saw himself as God saw him— "My beloved son, with whom I am well pleased."

I was very thankful that he'd come down just for a moment to describe the view. What he saw of grace from afar, what he and I had begun to taste in friendship, was still to be possessed. He was indeed far, far greater than he knew.

The next morning, exactly one year after Spencer's death, I woke up with a strength that I had not felt for a long, long time.

Mom and Dad joined us for a special dinner to remember Spencer. I barbecued chicken, and I couldn't wait to tell the bruthahs in Jackson. "Look, Arthur, you ain't barbecued seriously 'til you done it in a snowstorm." Spencer couldn't stand dull colors, and Donna fixed up the table with the brightest she could find. Her banana pudding was off the charts, from scratch, just like Nancy's. Her greens? Well, they couldn't touch Lue's. Still, Gloria, Ron and Joanie, and all the Antioch kids would have felt at home. We put pictures around of Spencer and Antioch, played a tape of the choir, and Donna read a list of all the people who'd stayed at the Big House over the years. The children shared their memories of Spencer. His tummy-blowing. His blue leg. Bringing home his fish, grinning and holding up the biggest one like a trophy.

Later we got an e-mail from Nancy. "Give Chris a hug," she wrote. "We made it one year."

The moon came up over Mt. Abraham that night, as if rising from the wrapping of a gift box, full, round, and bright, bringing clarity to everything around me.

I felt as if a new time was breaking in. As if I had a new body and that I was ready for the next leg of the journey. As if Good Friday had passed, and resurrection had come.

# EPILOGUE

WHEN I WENT BACK to Jackson in February 2002, three and a half years after leaving Mississippi, I realized that every piece of that city still has a claim on me.

Voice of Calvary's deeply embedded traditions continue: At a home Bible study with Phil and Marcia Reed, I joined blacks and whites who shared a meal, teased, discussed Scripture, joined in prayer, and talked about "our neighborhood," as if it was all very normal. Sunday worship was emotional, sitting next to Gloria, who is recovering well from her cancer. Arthur nodded me up to sing with the gospel choir again. I didn't know the first song, but picked it up quickly, found my part, and belted it out, watching Arthur grin the whole time.

JP has Robinson Street bursting with life: land razed for baseball fields and basketball courts; endless houses being renovated; the Big House full of staff, volunteers, and people in crisis surrounding the old dinner slab. I missed seeing Joanie, but Varah's smile was radiant as ever, and I went with Ron to his philosophy class, to see him teach. One night I stayed up late with Phil and Tressa, us talking noise about living on the same street somewhere as families again.

Gloria's son Kortney towers over me now; he graduates from high school this month. With him, Gloria, and Lue at their house (Jon was out visiting Pasadena), they had my sides aching with laughter, with their politically incorrect commentary on neighborhood life ("things are deteriorating a bit," said Lue), and their equally honest assessments of my book.

"Oh, Chris, I had to put that book down!" said Gloria, speaking of my first chapters and how I saw things in my early Mississippi days. "Knowing all it took for us black folk in Jamaa to stand up and speak out? And then seeing how you perceived the Reconciliation Meetings?"

She had called Nancy. "I said, 'Does it get better?' Nancy said, 'It gets better. Keep reading, Glo.' It did get better. After reading it all, I finally understood you, Chris! There's so much I wish I'd known at the time."

Such regrets had come up a few weeks earlier, when I visited Nancy and her and Spencer's kids in Pennsylvania. Discussing the book opened up grace-filled conversations I will never forget. Those last several years in Jackson, I discovered, she was struggling and moving in the same direction as I was, but somehow I didn't know it. We agreed: there was so much Antioch did right, and so much we could have done differently.

I brought Benjamin with me on my visit with Nancy, and we all quickly fell into our distinctive Antioch vocabulary. April and Jubilee whipped me at cards, Johnathan cracked me up with stories of Antioch's mangy mutt, Bebe, and I teared up as I watched Nancy being inducted into membership in a local African American church. Our two families remain woven across the miles by memory, prayer, and abiding concern.

It was John Alexander's fault, really, that Donna and I ended up in Durham in 2000. We had been all set to go to Boston, then John said, "Chris, you need to go to Duke Divinity School. I have friends there who won't mess you up." Donna and I visited Durham and saw a place we have found to be a good space for this new chapter of our lives.

I was counting on having John continue speaking into my life. But on Ash Wednesday 2001, John entered the hospital with leukemia. Six weeks later, at age sixty, he died on Good Friday.

At the memorial service, etched into the side of a simple pine casket built by the members of John's church, were the words, "It is well with my soul." Inside, John's body was wrapped in a quilt the church made out of patches of his clothing—including a piece of John's beloved tie-dyed T-shirt.

Judy said of his last hours, "Not that many people die with so much love around them." It was John, of course, who taught me such love is enough, that the rest of life is details.

*Durham, North Carolina*                                    CHRIS P. RICE
*May 2002*

# ACKNOWLEDGMENTS

My wonderful Jossey-Bass editor, Sheryl Fullerton, has been a constant joy to work with. Her name should be on the cover somewhere. Thanks also to Paul McCarthy, who moved the bar higher and higher.

The idea of this book was birthed in Bandon, Oregon. I will never forget Jeff and Heidi Johnson opening the way for our sabbatical there, and the hospitality of Heidi's parents, Keith and Donna Young.

In Lincoln, Vermont, David and Donna Wood gave us a house, the United Church of Lincoln welcomed us like family, and Carolyn Corts loved our kids beyond the call of duty.

Glenn Loury offered the support of Boston University's Institute for Race and Social Division during my first year of writing, and dozens of friends contributed to our needs during that period.

I am deeply grateful for those who read the manuscript: Phil and Tressa Eide, Gloria Lotts, Lue Shelby, Ron Potter, Phil Reed, and John Perkins. I especially wish to thank Spencer's wife, Nancy, for reading the manuscript, helping me be truthful and accurate, and giving me grace to tell the story as I experienced it. Greg Jones of Duke Divinity School was an immense help in reflecting on my writing.

Mom and Dad, from resurrecting flooded libraries to raising mohair goats, you continue to live life to its fullest; you will always point the way for me.

Last Thanksgiving, when I stayed in Durham to write while my family went to Jackson for the week, my children starting calling this "Daddy's S.B.," as in "Stupid Book." Benjamin, Talia, and Christopher, thank you for keeping my feet on the ground, reminding me that living life is more important than writing about it. I pray that you and all the Antioch children will travel far in the culture of grace.

It's true, I think: wherever she goes, Donna radiates light, and I experience it every day. Without her, I don't know who I'd be.

Above all, I am indebted to the God of grace, for giving me a story to tell, and carrying me along the way.

# THE AUTHOR

CHRIS P. RICE is currently pursuing studies at the Divinity School at Duke University. He is the winner of a Critic's Choice Award from *Christianity Today* magazine for his book, *More Than Equals: Racial Healing for the Sake of the Gospel,* coauthored with Spencer Perkins. He has been a research associate for the Boston University Institute on Race and Social Division and a columnist for *Sojourners* magazine. A writer for *Christianity Today, Discipleship Journal, The Other Side, Re:Generation Quarterly,* and *Urban Family,* he has spoken and taught extensively on the subject of racial reconciliation. Chris lives in North Carolina with his wife, Donna, and their three children.